8/16

Also available from the
8 Keys to Mental Health Series

8 Keys to Mental Health Series
Babette Rothschild, Series Editor

The 8 Keys series of books provides consumers with brief, inexpensive, and high-quality self-help books on a variety of topics in mental health. Each volume is written by an expert in the field, someone who is capable of presenting evidence-based information in a concise and clear way. These books stand out by offering consumers cutting-edge, relevant theory in easily digestible portions, written in an accessible style. The tone is respectful of the reader and the messages are immediately applicable. Filled with exercises and practical strategies, these books empower readers to help themselves.

8 KEYS TO RAISING THE QUIRKY CHILD

MARK BOWERS

FOREWORD BY BABETTE ROTHSCHILD

W. W. Norton & Company
New York • London

I have chosen to alternate masculine and feminine pronouns throughout the book. I hope the book will be equally useful to parents of daughters and parents of sons regardless of pronoun usage in any particular example.

For information about permission to reproduce selections from this book, write to Permissions, W. W. Norton & Company, Inc., 500 Fifth Avenue, New York, NY 10110

For information about special discounts for bulk purchases, please contact W. W. Norton Special Sales at specialsales@wwnorton.com or 800-233-4830

Manufacturing by R. R. Donnelley
Production manager: Christine Critelli

Library of Congress Cataloging-in-Publication Data

Bowers, Mark (Psychologist)
8 keys to raising the quirky child : how to help
a kid who doesn't (quite) fit in / Mark Bowers ;
foreword by Babette Rothschild. — First edition.
pages cm. — (8 keys to mental health series)
Includes bibliographical references and index.
ISBN 978-0-393-70920-9 (pbk.)
1. Parents of autistic children.
2. Parents of exceptional children.
3. Parenting. 4. Child rearing.
I. Title. II. Title: Eight keys to raising the quirky child.
HQ773.8.B675 2015
649'.15—dc23
2015004622

W. W. Norton & Company, Inc.
500 Fifth Avenue, New York, N.Y. 10110
www.wwnorton.com

W. W. Norton & Company Ltd., Castle House
75/76 Wells Street, London W1T 3QT

1 2 3 4 5 6 7 8 9 0

Contents

Acknowledgments

I would like to thank the following people for reasons that I will hold close to my heart:

Kelly Bowers, my everything.
Addy, Charlie, and Emme Bowers, my children.
Deborah Malmud, my editor.
Babette Rothschild, my series editor.
Laura Poole, my copyeditor.
Katie Moyer and all the staff at W. W. Norton & Company.
Tom and Nancy Bowers, my parents.
Mike and Kevin Bowers, my brothers.
Diane and Mark Leyda, my in-laws.
Rick Solomon, my practice partner.
Amy Saalberg and Pat O'Connor, my practice colleagues.
Dave Provorse, my mentor.
Jeff Dolgan, my mentor.
Martin Leichtman, my mentor.
John Spiridigliozzi, my mentor.
The faculty at The University of Kansas-Clinical Child Psychology Department.
The faculty at Washburn University-Clinical Psychology Department.
The faculty at The Children's Hospital, Denver, CO.
Don Sellers, my writing mentor.
My extended family and friends.

Foreword

Foreword by Babette Rothschild, Series Editor

A quirky child is one who stands out from the crowd. He may be the kid who is obsessed with video games, a boy who gets picked on because he is not good at sports, or the track star who is sometimes too aggressive. She might also be one who has trouble reading and gets enraged when assigned a book report, or is a math whiz who can talk of nothing else, or the class clown known for making inappropriate remarks.

What quirky children (and, for that matter, adults) have in common is that they all have deficits in social skills. They stand out because they do not know how to blind in with others. Everyone knows at least one quirky child or adult. We all have one or more in our family, school, congregation, clubs, and neighborhood. It may be a child, parent, cousin, in-law, neighbor, friend, or even oneself. Some families are full of quirky children and adults.

As Mark Bowers reminds us again and again through his thoughtful, warm, and accessible book, quirks in and of themselves are not problems. In fact many of the most meaningful contributions to the progress of the world have been from quirky kids who became quirky adults. Do you have an iPhone, iPod, or Mac computer? Thank the once quirky child and later quirky adult, Steve Jobs. Numerous people who make the films we love to watch and the music that we love to hear were quirky children and many are still quirky adults. Scientists and scholars constitute scads of once quirky children. Recent films such as *The Theory of Everything* and *Imitation Game* feature life stories of quirky children and the contributions they made as adults. Indeed quirkiness can be a wonderful gift. Like every thing else life hands us, it is what one does with the quirkiness and how one learns to manage it that will make all the difference.

Bowers sees human behavior on a continuum. At one end of the spectrum is behavior that would be considered usual, not quirky. At the far other end of the spectrum is behavior that is so extremely dysfunctional that it would fall more into the category of mental illness. In between those two extremes lies a broad area of quirkiness, from just a few or very slight behavioral differences from the norm, to quite different, though not pathological. The majority of people probably fall somewhere in this middle area of the continuum, as most of us have one or more distinguishing eccentricities. And it is on this point that Bowers models how important it is to accept and maximize the advantages of this or that quirk. He sees them as differences rather than defects.

And, truth be told, how far from the norm a quirk falls is often a matter of opinion within a particular culture or context. I am a good example. One of the quirks I am known for in my clinical training programs is my straightforwardness. I cut to the chase, rarely soft-pedaling. In the United States, Denmark, and Australia, this manner of being is usually much appreciated. In Ireland and the United Kingdom, on the other hand, my tendency to straight talk can surprise or even shock a student, causing some a certain amount of distress. In some cultures this quirk is considered common and acceptable, in the others it is unusual and unwelcome. So it can be the same with a child's quirks. In one school or congregation, his particular quirks fit right in; in another school or a scout group, they do not and he does not.

Bottom line, the commonality among quirky children is isolation from their peers. Sometimes isolation may be self-induced, a withdrawal from interactions. At times it is because students and playmates are less than accepting of kids who are not like themselves. But often social isolation is the result of a deficit of skills needed to manage one's quirkiness and still fit in. Bowers, a pediatric psychologist, knows this dilemma very well and his book, *8 Keys to Raising the Quirky Child*, is full of guidance on how to help your quirky child to fit into her peer group despite—and even with—her quirks.

In this book you will learn, among other things, to teach your child how to talk with another child, how to listen, how to engage in activities together, how to deal with frustration when things don't go as expected, how to deal with emotions, and so on. Bowers shows parents how to support their child with peer relationships and age-appropriate self-management strategies without losing sight of the special talents and skills that are also part and parcel of being quirky. The book is packed with discussion of necessary social skills and instruction on how to teach and encourage them in your child—and in yourself, if that is useful.

This is not just a book about raising quirky children, however; it is also a manual on how people, in general, relate to others. Bowers has clear insight into how people engage in and deepen personal relationships. For example, as we get to know someone who will become a friend, we move from general topics of conversation to more personal topics and eventually to private and intimate sharing that we reserve for our closest family members and friends. I found these insights enlightening in thinking of my own relationships. I will admit, albeit slightly sheepishly, that there were a couple of social skills discussions that I found relevant for myself. All of us have quirks to one degree or another, and Bowers nailed a couple of mine. I found his advice most helpful!

Throughout the book, Bowers's writing is positive, well organized, accessible, and warm. He offers digestible doses of neuroscientific theory to back up his opinions. The theory is presented in a smart manner, but never over the heads of the reader. The theory always dovetails with what parents need to know to understand and support their children. His goal is to help quirky children to have the option of more normative behaviors depending on the circumstances, to facilitate more cohesion with their peers. He helps the reader to easily distinguish between behaviors that are usefully or acceptably quirky from those that might indicate the need for some type of professional intervention. And he shows parents how to help their child improve social interactions, their communication with peers and significant adults, and broaden their repertoire of interactive activities.

Parents, caregivers, and teachers of quirky children will find Bowers's insights and guidance a welcome support for guiding their children to more satisfying relationships while realizing their potentials.

8 KEYS TO RAISING
THE QUIRKY CHILD

INTRODUCTION

For the past 15 years, I have worked with children in hospitals, schools, residential treatment centers, outpatient clinics, and private practice as a pediatric psychologist. I began my training in psychology treating children with depression and anxiety before narrowing my clinical interest into the area of neurodevelopmental delays. This area of specialization focuses on conditions that result in the pediatric brain not developing at the rate that is expected for chronological age. Thus, I work with children who experience speech delays, physical/coordination challenges, social skills deficits, behavioral difficulties, and learning or cognitive delays. Most of the children I evaluate and treat have an autism spectrum disorder, learning disability, traumatic brain injury, attention deficit/hyperactivity disorder (ADHD), or are just quirky. I operate a private clinical practice in Michigan along with a developmental and behavioral pediatrician.

Several years ago, I developed a mobile app for Apple devices called Sōsh (pronounced as in "Sōsh-ial"). It was developed to help individuals monitor and improve their social skills in real time and review their findings later for continued growth and development. The Sōsh app is based on a social framework that I developed with the help of my wife and colleague, Dr. Kelly Bowers. Sōsh has been acclaimed by parents, professionals, and schools around the world and is being used in the classrooms of schools across the United States to help students improve their social skills. It is included on the recommended apps lists by special education programs across the United States and has been presented in live demonstrations at numerous educational conferences to thousands of attendees. The Services for Students with Disabilities staff at Massachusetts Institute of Technology (MIT) invited us to present Sōsh at one of their recent conferences. Given the innovation that comes from MIT, hearing their excitement about the technology we created with the app was one of my career highlights thus far. In addition to developing the app for social skills, I also published a book to explain the methodology behind the app, *Sōsh: Improving Social Skills for Children and Adolescents.*

All of my experience gathered while helping quirky children and their families for the past 15 years has culminated in this book. My hope is that the information contained within will calm the hearts and minds of those who worry about a child who doesn't fit in and offer hope to anyone who is seeking strategies to support a quirky child's overall development.

Outliers and What It Means to Be Quirky

In statistical terminology, an *outlier* is a data point that sits alone, away from the center or normative distribution where most other data points fall. My clinical practice and career focuses on these so-called outliers. I find this term to be too clinical, statistical, and harsh. As a result, I began using the word *quirky* to describe this phenomenon.

The word *quirky* means "characterized by peculiar or unexpected traits" or "different from the ordinary in a way that causes curiosity or suspicion." Synonyms for *quirky* include *eccentric, idiosyncratic, unconventional, peculiar,* or *unusual.* To me, *quirky* sounds more user-friendly than *outlier* and is a relatable for most people. Who among us doesn't have at least one or more quirks?

Quirky is not necessarily a bad thing. Individuals in the arts and fashion world, as well as some in the technological world (e.g., Steve Jobs of Apple) are often admired and emulated for their quirks that push the boundaries of what is generally deemed mainstream or conventional. But what if the quirks begin to add up and pull an individual's position further away from the normative group in a way that adversely affects his or her life?

To understand what it means to be quirky, you may want to understand what is means to be "normal." *Normal* means conforming to a standard; usual, typical, or expected. I am opposed to the use of *normal* when differentiating children because it assumes that if you are quirky then you are not "normal." *Normal* implies something about who you are as a person. We may hear others say, "He's not normal" as if it's something ingrained in his personality structure that cannot be fixed. I find this distinction to be offensive, and I'm sure you would agree. Indeed, many of us are considered "normal" but still do quirky things.

As a result, I use the term *normative* to differentiate one person's way of relating to the world from that of a quirky individual. Normative has to do with how an individual relates to his or her surroundings and adapts to situations. Normative is a way of doing something, considered to be the usual, expected, or correct way depending on the context and what is developmentally appropriate. Thus, normative is *what you do* rather than *who you are*.

As stated previously, a person can generally operate within the normative range of functioning and still demonstrate quirky behaviors or otherwise interact with the world in a quirky way. Some individuals, however, demonstrate a frequency and intensity of quirky behaviors, explored later in this book, that pushes them further into the quirky range of relating to the world around them (i.e., outside of what is expected for the context). If the nature and intensity of the person's profile begins to interfere with everyday functioning, then the individual travels further along the continuum into the realm of pathology. Visually represented, this continuum would look like this:

NORMATIVE ↔ QUIRKY ↔ PATHOLOGY

Notice the arrows that point toward and away from each category. This indicates that a person is not a static or unchanging being in all cases. A person can experience anxiety, for example, when facing a feared situation that causes them significant challenges, and as a result they enter into the pathology category by reacting in a manner that is unexpected given the stimulus (e.g., only a small percentage of airline passengers have a panic attack while flying). However, once the stressor is removed, they return to the normative level of functioning (the plane lands and the panic symptoms go away). Indeed, many children will move right to left along this continuum during child and adolescent development, and sometimes throughout their lives, depending on the situations and people they encounter and on how they are able to cope with or navigate those encounters. It should be noted that not all pathology can be reduced to quirky or normative levels of functioning. Schizophrenia, for example, is firmly in the pathology category. Although the symptoms of schizophrenia can be reduced with medication in some cases, individuals diagnosed with schizophrenia will unlikely ever move along the continuum into the normative level of functioning.

Multiple factors need to be considered when differentiating normative from quirky and pathology categories of development, with primary emphasis on what is developmentally appropriate or expected from an individual based on age, context, and a host of other factors. For example, a toddler who runs into the kitchen of the family home with no pants on and giggles may be viewed as "cute," and this situation might result in all adult witnesses laughing (i.e., interpreted as normative due to the child's lack of awareness of social conventions). However, a teenager who engages in the same behavior would cause those who witness the situation extreme discomfort, and this attempt at humor would be cause for concern (i.e., entering into the quirky or possibly pathology category).

When considering your child's profile and attempting to determine whether they are quirky or perhaps even experiencing enough of a challenge to warrant a formal diagnosis (i.e., entering the pathology category of development), it can be useful to consider what is expected for the situation or context, and from those around the child, to fit in and connect well with others. When I begin teaching quirky children how to figure out what is expected behavior (i.e., normative) in any given context or situation, I have them ask themselves the following questions: (1) Where am I? (2) What am I doing? (3)Who am I with? For example, if I answer the questions: (1) in the library, (2) singing loudly, (3) with my classmates, then my behavior is quirky because I am singing in a library, which is a behavior that violates the social code or "hidden curriculum" (to be explored further in Key 4) of expected behavior in the library. If I am: (1) at a concert, (2) singing loudly, (3) with my friends, then my behavior is normative because singing is considered socially acceptable behavior at a concert.

Sometimes it's easier to search for the absence of appropriate and prosocial behavior when investigating a child's developmental profile. Thus, you need to be aware of what types of behaviors or interactions are considered normative to understand what the child should be doing relative to other children. The following are a list of questions regarding generalized characteristics of normative behavior (these questions apply to children who are at least two years old unless otherwise specified):

- Is the child meeting the expected *developmental milestones* for his age? Information about these milestones can be found in Keys 4 and 6 of this book.
- Does the child demonstrate a *natural curiosity* about people and new things?
- If the child is at least six years old, does he or she attempt to make *small talk* with others (both adults and other children)?
- Is the child *approachable* by both adults and children (even if the child has a shy temperament)?
- Does the child explore a *variety of interests* (or a willingness to explore novel activities)?
- Can the child understand/use *humor and laugh* when appropriate?
- If the child is at least five years old, is he or she a *flexible thinker* (i.e., able to see things from the point of view of others or adjust his way of thinking to suit the context)?
- Is the child *adaptable to change* in routines (i.e., not requesting

that others adhere to rigid routines or interactions that result in stress if not followed)?

- If the child is at least five years old, is he able to *regulate* himself behaviorally and emotionally, even when excited or frustrated?
- Is the child's *affect appropriate to the context* of the situation (e.g., smiles or laughs when happy)?
- Does the child demonstrate an *awareness of her surroundings* (e.g., scanning the room to see what others are doing, pointing to objects of interest, remaining close to a caregiver in unfamiliar situations)?
- Does the child use *two-way communication?* The child uses non-verbal gestures (smiling, eye gaze, babbling) prior to language development. The child uses both verbal and nonverbal communication together following language development.

Obviously no child (or adult for that matter) will achieve or even demonstrate all of these normative characteristics all the time. The question becomes, does the child demonstrate enough of these (i.e., at least six) to be able to function adequately in different situations? Furthermore, if the child fails to demonstrate one or more of these characteristics, what is the effect on that child?

If the effect is deviance, distress, dysfunction, or danger, as presented in the Four D's model in the next section, then the child may be entering the abnormal, or what I refer to as pathology category. If this is the case, you will want to investigate further with a professional evaluation, which involves the procedures detailed in Key 7.

To understand the pathology category of functioning, you must understand the concept of abnormality. One definition of *abnormality* considers whether an individual's way of thinking, behaving, or relating to the world is rare or statistically unusual relative to a reference group. If it is, then it may be classified as abnormal and would fall into the pathology category. This definition can be somewhat problematic, though, because abnormality can also be positive, or it could just represent a quirky behavior.

For example, it may be abnormal for a three-year-old to read fluently. Many people are excited if their three-year-old begins to read independently, and it can be a tough sell to convince a parent that this is not necessarily a good thing. It can be a "splinter skill" that is commonly referred to as hyperlexia, which can be an early indicator of autism spectrum disorder.

By itself, a high intellect or reading ability at a young age can be a desirable trait. We must consider the context of that abnormal trait to determine what effect, if any, it is having in other areas of the individual's level of functioning. Thus, a child who reads at a high level early, but who is also socially engaged and interactive and emotionally and behaviorally regulated would be considered to fall within the normative category of functioning. This normative category will be explored, as well as the categories of quirky and pathology, throughout this book.

The Four D's

Before diagnosing a psychological disorder (i.e., determining whether an individual has entered in to the pathology category of functioning), clinicians must study the themes, also known as abnormalities, that comprise psychological disorders. The most prominent themes consistent with psychopathology consist of *deviance, distress, dysfunction, and danger.* These themes are known as the *Four D's,* which help differentiate abnormality from Normative and Quirky levels of functioning.

The Four D's must be considered when defining abnormality. It is important to note that an individual does not need to be experiencing heightened levels of each of these categories to meet criteria for pathology. The Four D's are described in detail as follows.

Deviance refers to specific thoughts, behaviors, and emotions that are unacceptable or not common in society. Cultural factors need to be considered when assessing deviance. Thus, we define an individual's actions as deviant or abnormal when his behavior is deemed unacceptable by the culture he belongs to. For children, the assessment of deviance must consider not only cultural but also developmental variables. Thus, a teenager who colors her hair pink may be viewed as expressing her individual style, but an adult who does this may have a difficult time finding employment in certain occupations.

Distress refers to negative feelings experienced by the individual with the symptoms. He may feel deeply troubled and affected by his symptoms. The expression of these negative feelings varies with age. A child who is preverbal or nonverbal may demonstrate distress with persistent and intense whining, crying, or inconsolable behaviors. Depending on the child's developmental stage or chronological age, he may be fairly oblivious to the negative effects that a particular symptom or cluster of symptoms is having on his everyday functioning and those around him.

Therefore, distress criteria can be met if the adults or peer group who regularly interact with the child are experiencing distress because of that child's profile, even though the child remains oblivious. For example, a preschool child may consider it a funny game or joke when he rips up all of the art projects in the classroom, while the teachers and students feel upset and distressed that their hard work was destroyed. This destructive behavior may require a consequence or punishment such as time out or no treat at the end of the day (because the child ripped the art projects) to cause any distress reaction in the child. However, as you will learn in Key 5, although he may experience stress and frustration about being punished, he may not connect his actions to the stress reactions he invoked among the others in the room.

Dysfunction involves maladaptive behavior that impairs the individual's ability to perform normal daily functions, such as getting ready for school in the morning, functioning adequately in school, or participating in extracurricular activities. Such maladaptive behaviors prevent the individual from living a normal, healthy lifestyle. A child who demonstrates a hyperactive energy level or is otherwise so behaviorally dysregulated that he is not able to slow down enough to get dressed or sit long enough to finish a meal would meet dysfunction criteria.

Danger involves dangerous or violent behavior directed toward oneself or others. Danger in children is usually directed toward others, such as throwing objects, hitting, biting, slapping, and kicking. However, danger can also include a lack of awareness of surroundings, such as running from the car to the entrance of the grocery store without checking for moving cars in the parking lot. As was the case with deviance, distress, and dysfunction, the evaluation of danger needs to be considered based on the child's level of development. A preschool-age child with an expressive language delay or an average toddler who hits others to communicate frustration may not be considered "dangerous," but a high school student who hits his teacher after receiving a bad grade on an exam would be.

Danger toward oneself in childhood or adolescence can also include serious acts of self-harm, such as cutting oneself, biting oneself, banging one's head against objects, and even suicidal behavior. It should be noted that a child could still enter into the pathology category of functioning if he is not demonstrating dangerous behaviors. Indeed, an anxious child is unlikely to be a danger to herself or others, but she may be experiencing enough distress and dysfunction to interfere with her daily functioning and receive a clinical diagnosis of an anxiety disorder.

Is My Child Quirky?

Given that you are reading this book, you probably would like to know whether a child you know falls into the normative category of functioning, is quirky, or whether the child's profile is indicative of something more serious that may warrant a clinical diagnosis. Quirky children overlap with both the normative group and the pathology group in many ways. For instance, quirky children typically possess a number of strengths and talents. However, these positive traits can often be overshadowed by other factors unique to a quirky presentation and, as a result, those who spend time with the child may lose sight of those positive qualities. For example, a boy who is reading fluently in kindergarten can attract positive attention from both the teacher and his peer group. However, if he is disruptive during any activity that does not involve reading, the other individuals in the classroom quickly forget about how well he reads.

When the challenges exceed the positives, the adults who love and care for the child, as well as the peer group who tries to connect with him, often experience stress. If the levels of distress, dysfunction, and deviance become more pronounced, or if danger is involved, then the child needs to be evaluated by a developmental specialist such as a psychologist for their likelihood of functioning within the pathology category. The details of such an evaluation will be described in Key 7.

What it Means to Be Quirky: The STRESSED Model

Over the past decade, I have developed the acronym STRESSED to describe the feeling that quirky children, adults, and peers can experience while interacting with each other and help families and teachers understand what to look for when attempting to fully understand what could be a quirky profile.

The use of the word *stressed* is also designed to indicate that there is a difference between the quirky category of development and meeting criteria for pathology or a formal diagnosis. Quirky children tend to experience some levels of stress in their daily lives as a result of some challenges fitting in and connecting with others. However, if the stress becomes intense enough (to meet criteria for distress as described in the Four D's model) that the child begins to experience significant levels of dysfunction or deviance from the norms at school or in the home, then a clinical evaluation for pathology is indicated. In the event that you have to wait to obtain a clinical evaluation by a developmental specialist. In the meantime, I hope that you find the strategies presented throughout this book, especially in Key 5, to be helpful to begin to address any concerns you may have regarding the Four D's.

The following domains of the STRESSED profile of the quirky

child, to be described fully in Keys 1 and 2, should be considered
if you are questioning whether your child may be quirky:

- S: social challenges
- T: transitional stress
- R: regulatory difficulties
- E: executive dysfunction
- S: sensory sensitivity
- S: smart/social imbalance (high IQ/low EQ)
- E: emotional reactivity
- D: depth seeker/disinterest in imaginative play

If you answered "no" to any of the normative questions presented earlier and *also* answered "no" to the Four D's criteria for
pathology, then you can begin to look at the STRESSED profile
because you may be dealing with a quirky child. Some parents are
interested in addressing emerging concerns in an effort to keep
them from developing into something more significant, whereas
others are already observing significant concerns and seek strategies to help their child achieve the best possible outcomes. Once
you know what you should be looking for, or confirm what you
already have observed, you can follow the strategies described
throughout this book to address the child's development in any
particular areas of interest or concern.

If, in fact, your child is demonstrating a quirky profile, then
you may also wonder how quirky that profile really is. The *quality*
of the child's quirkiness is just as important as the *quantity* of the
quirky characteristics, and both must be considered to determine
where the child measures up relative to the normative distribution of behaviors, interests, and so on. The question of how a
child's quirky profile affects him or her at any given point in development is important to ask and have answered because a child's
profile is never static or unchanging. As a child progresses through
development, a quirky behavior may be more or less acceptable
than had previously been the case. For example, I often work with
children who throw tantrums when they cannot be the line leader

to walk down the hall as a class. The child's emotional reactivity to this scenario is less acceptable and more consistent with deviance and distress of the Four D's model the older the child becomes. A first-grader might not experience as many social or disciplinary ramifications from such an outburst, especially if it only happens once (i.e., low quantity) and does not persist (i.e., mild quality). If a fourth-grader had a similar reaction, however, there is greater cause for concern among adults and peers who witness such an outburst, and the peer group may begin to resent such behavior and avoid or even bully the child.

Quirky versus Pathology

There is overlap in terms of the quirky traits a child may experience, as presented in STRESSED model, and a variety of clinical diagnoses that would result in the child entering the pathology category of development. When the overlap begins to reveal a pattern of symptoms that are specific to a clinical diagnosis, then the possibility of pathology must be considered. Most overlap occurs among quirky children and children on the autism spectrum. Specifics regarding diagnosis will be presented in Key 7. As you will learn there, the primary distinguishing factors between a child with an autism spectrum diagnosis and quirky child are that children on the autism spectrum display most (although not all) of the following:

- Difficulty forming relationships with peers.
- Difficulty demonstrating empathy toward others (usually due to a lack of understanding or being overwhelmed by the feeling states of others, rather than not caring or being concerned about others).
- Inability to understand and participate in give-and-take activities, like sharing toys.
- Challenges reading and responding to social cues.
- Exhibits extreme distress over minor changes in routine.

- Has an overly narrow area of focus when playing or a very restricted range of interests.
- Engages in repetitive or stereotypical behaviors (e.g., spinning wheels on toys, jumping up and down or hand flapping when excited, opening and closing doors repetitively).

As you become more familiar with the characteristics of the quirky child, you will notice overlap among autism spectrum disorder diagnostic criteria and characteristics included in the STRESSED model. Historically, one would look for an expressive and/or receptive language delays and stereotyped or repetitive behaviors (e.g., hand flapping, lining up toys, spinning or rocking), in addition to social challenges (e.g., difficulty with back-and-forth conversation or nonverbal communication, little to no referencing or interest in others socially) when making a clinical diagnosis of an autistim spectrum disorder.

Current diagnostic criteria (DSM-5; American Psychiatric Association, 2013) does not require a language delay to receive an autism spectrum diagnosis. Additionally, the child does not need to experience the stereotyped or repetitive behaviors previously required to meet criteria for the diagnosis. You will notice that expressive and/or receptive language delays, as well as stereotyped or repetitive behaviors, are also not included in the STRESSED model. Thus, we must return to the Four D's to determine the difference between the quirky category of development and the pathology category (e.g., an autism spectrum diagnosis).

To better understand and differentiate quirky versus autism spectrum disorder, a closer examination of the current autism spectrum criteria reveals incorporation of the Four D's of pathology. Language from the DSM-5 (American Psychiatric Association, 2013)—such as "Persistent deficits in social communication and social interaction across multiple contexts," "very restricted range of interests," and "exhibits extreme distress"—highlights the deviance and distress criteria previously explained in the Four D's that result in a pathology classification. Additionally, the diagnostic criteria state, "Symptoms cause clinically significant impairment in social, occupational, or other important areas of current functioning."

An important criterion for autism spectrum disorder was added to the DSM-5. It states, "Symptoms must be present in the early developmental period (but may not become fully manifest until social demands exceed limited capacities, or may be masked by learned strategies in later life)." This is an important consideration when working with a child in the quirky category of development, because it is possible that the child can eventually enter into the pathology category. I frequently evaluate children who seem to be able to "hold it together" for the first few years of elementary school, but inevitably experience challenges beginning in the fourth to fifth grade, intensifying through middle school as the social demands intensify at a fast and furious rate.

Consider the case of John, a second-grade boy who has an IQ in the very superior range of intelligence. He taught himself to read and is an expert on Harry Potter and the *Titanic*. When I greeted John in the lobby of my office, he did not say "Hello," but instead began to quiz me on whether I knew anything about his particular set of interests. He stood very close to me and talked at me in a manner designed to give me information, with little to no consideration of whether I was interested in the topics he was discussing. There were no pauses to assess if I wanted to hear more. John was excited to be passing his knowledge on to me. His parents were very proud of their son. They were frustrated that many adults in John's life were concerned about the quality of his interactions. After all, he was initiating conversations with others and was very friendly and outgoing. Indeed, the quantity of his interactions was good. For the most part, John's peer group tolerated and accepted him. The girls in his class "mothered" him and looked out for him. John was happy.

No clinician has a crystal ball to fully predict the future. However, pediatric psychologists like me are trained to study patterns of behavior and make reasonable predictions regarding how likely a behavior that is presently demonstrated by a child will persist and the degree that this behavior will adversely affect a child's level of functioning if it should persist. My prediction is that John's challenges will intensify as the social demands increase around him with each passing year of school. However, because his symptoms have not yet caused clinically significant impairment in social, academic, or other important areas of current functioning, he remains in the quirky category of development, under my watchful eye during quarterly follow-ups (or sooner if concerns emerge).

Cases like this are difficult to navigate with families because I am not able to assure the family that John is "out of the woods" yet. He may begin to experience difficulties that warrant a clinical diagnosis. In these cases, I recommend that families begin implementing the strategies detailed throughout this book and regularly consult with me to build the child's social skills in an effort to help him keep up with the peer group and not experience the stress of not doing so.

8 Keys to Raising the Quirky Child

This book focuses on the children who demonstrate quirky behaviors, mannerisms, or ways of thinking and relating to the world that may or may not fall within the category of pathology or meet the necessary criteria for a clinical diagnosis, but who have enough of a challenge navigating through the day that they are not necessarily in the normative category of development either. Quirky children often experience enough differences relative to those around them to push them closer to an outlier, in statistical terms, rather than the normative group, but not enough of a difference to enter the pathology category (i.e., not causing enough stress or dysfunction) that would result in a clinical diagnosis.

These differences and difficulties fitting into the normative category of development can intensify with age and as social demands increase, such that trying to keep up with the peer group and fit in becomes increasingly difficult. As a result, you support your child best by continuing to monitor his or her profile and assist him or her accordingly using the strategies outlined in this book and by seeking the guidance of a developmental specialist who is well versed in children with social interactional challenges to help keep levels of distress and function manageable to continue to experience positive outcomes. Regardless of how much support you provide a child, however, there are many cases in which entry into the pathology category is inevitable. There are many diagnoses that are biologically and/or genetically driven and cannot be prevented from occurring (e.g., autism spectrum disorder, bipolar disorder). If this is the case with your child, you will need to come to terms with this and begin to provide your child with the necessary treatments.

This book is not a treatment manual for how to address a child's specific pathology. This book focuses on the *differences* quirky children demonstrate relative to what is considered normative. This book is not about *defects*. Furthermore, this book is not a how-to guide of how to make your child "normal." (I have an issue with the term *normal* more so than most might have with the term *quirky*.) In many ways, trends and advances (technology) in our society are blurring the lines in terms of what is quirky and what is normative. For example, it was once expected that you called your friends to make plans, but now you text them. Many children view online communication with a headset while playing video games a more appealing method of social communication than inviting a friend over to play the same game in person. My hope is that by reading this book, you will be able to promote your child's development so that they can preserve their self–esteem, increase their confidence, and have more success connecting with those around them.

The aim of this book is to give you peace of mind, when possible, that you can support your child according to his or her unique developmental profile. If this book helps you discover that there is something more significant occurring that meets criteria for a clinical diagnosis, then I hope you realize that help is available.

As a developmental specialist, I appreciate and acknowledge

all of the strengths and talents that quirky children possess. I don't want this fact to be lost on the reader. It's a huge part of what makes them quirky, as you will learn in the smart/social imbalance domain of the STRESSED model to be explained in Key 2. Pioneers of industry like Steve Jobs and Henry Ford were often viewed as quirky by those who knew them well. They were smart, and their inventions have changed the world. Despite their immeasurable levels of intelligence and creativity, however, they managed themselves in a way that kept them out of the pathology category and instead somewhere between normative and quirky.

What follows in this book is an explanation of situations and behaviors that may arise and present challenges for a family who believes they have a quirky child. Everyone's experience will be different, and I don't have a crystal ball to tell you for sure that these will be your experiences. However, based on my work with quirky children over the past 15 years, I seek to help you anticipate the most common issues that can arise and provide strategies to help address the major characteristics of a quirky profile.

Even if your child's profile falls somewhere between the normative–quirky categories of the continuum (i.e., mostly normative but a little bit quirky), then the information contained in this book will still serve as a useful guide and reference. Again, this book is not about pathology, so if you have already received a clinical diagnosis for your child or you determine that you will seek out a professional evaluation and most likely receive a diagnosis, then you need to defer to your treatment provider for specific treatment strategies and recommendations relative to your child's unique profile.

In the event that you know a child who experiences any of the STRESSED characteristics, I hope that this book serves as a guide to help you understand the child's experience and provides some practical and effective strategies on how to address these characteristics. An obvious caveat is that I have not met with or evaluated your child, and thus I am describing patterns and responses in general terms. If you remain concerned about your child's specific profile and would like strategies specifically tailored to him or her, then you are strongly encouraged to seek out an evaluation and treatment by a developmental specialist in your area.

My assumption while writing this book is that parents don't need to read a book to remind them how wonderful their child is. I want this book to be available to those who might be curious about their child's unique way of relating to the world around them and who have an interest in strategies to best support that child and ultimately promote the child's overall development.

Many parents seek out my services not to label their child with a diagnosis but to fully understand their child and know how to best respond and parent them on a daily basis. I believe that all parents have a strong desire to understand and connect with their child. When a child is not responding in an expected manner to common parenting approaches, this can create stress and frustration and potentially interrupt and strain the parent–child bond.

For those who are not sure that they need to seek out the help of a professional, perhaps this book is the first attempt at changing the way in which the family approaches the child. Maybe a teacher wants to learn more about a child in their class who is just a little bit different, or an extended family member wants to better understand their niece, nephew, or grandchild better.

Quirky children are amazing. I would not devote my career to working with a group of people that I did not like spending time with. They likely do not realize how much they teach me each time I have an opportunity to spend time with them. Every day I am at work, I hope to return the favor and teach them a thing or two as well. As a parent to another parent, I hope this book provides you with some comfort knowing that there are many children out there who have quirks, too, and there are is an understanding of who your child is and what you can do to be the best possible parent to him or her.

Book Outline

In Keys 1 and 2: Identify Your Child's Quirks, you will learn what to look for in a child's profile to determine whether they fall within the quirky category and what you can begin to do to support a child's unique profile. Key 3: Support Brain Functioning explains the neurology behind quirky behaviors and intense interests that may be displayed by a child. You will also learn about executive functioning and what you can do to support your child's development in this area. Key 4: Optimize Social Skills devotes an entire chapter to understanding social skills development and presents a variety of strategies to improve a child's social functioning. Key 5: Respond Effectively will help you understand how to determine what is triggering a child's behavior and how you can respond effectively. Key 6: Track Your Child's Development provides you with grade-specific developmental milestones that you can review to determine how your child is doing relative to same-age peers and what to expect as your child progresses through school. Key 6 also includes school-specific strategies that can be used if educational accommodations or a school-based behavioral plan are indicated for a child. Key 7: Understand Diagnostic Criteria and Treatment explores various neurodevelopmental diagnoses that can emerge from a quirky profile as well as the specialists who can evaluate a child and some common treatment approaches if your child receives a clinical diagnosis. Key 8: Manage Challenges at Home describes challenging behaviors that commonly occur in the home and strategies to increase comfort for both the quirky child and the family.

NORMATIVE	QUIRKY	PATHOLOGY
Meeting Developmental Milestones	**S:** Social Challenges	Deviance
Curious About New Things/ People	**T:** Transitional Stress	Distress
Comfortable with People	**R:** Regulatory Difficulties	Dysfunction
Approachable (Even when Shy)	**E:** Executive Dysfunction	Danger
Variety of Interests	**S:** Sensory Sensitivity	
Understands/Uses Humor	**S:** Smart/Social Imbalance (High IQ/Low EQ)	
Flexible Thinker	**E:** Emotional Reactivity	
Adaptable to Change	**D:** Depth Seeker/Disinterest in Imaginative Play	
Can Self-Regulate (Emotion and Behavior)		
Affect Appropriate to Context		
Awareness of Surroundings		
Effective Two-Way Communication		

IDENTIFY YOUR CHILD'S QUIRKS: PART I

A quirky child experiences difficulty fitting in and connecting with others due to a variety of reasons explored throughout this chapter, often despite a desire to be able to connect. These children are not loners by any means, although some may find more satisfaction or stress relief when engaged in solitary activities, whereas others may experience rejection or failure when attempting to connect such that time spent alone becomes the preferred option. I often remind parents that being alone does not mean that a child feels lonely. Many individuals, especially those with a more introverted personality, find great joy and comfort in time alone or while engaged in solitary interests. However, the difference between a quirky profile and an introverted one is that when a person with an introverted personality must interact with others, they are usually able to do so effectively.

The introduction of this book introduced the acronym STRESSED to help you begin to understand what characteristics are included in a quirky profile. These domains are:

S: social challenges
T: transitional stress
R: regulatory difficulties

E: executive dysfunction
S: sensory sensitivity
S: smart/social imbalance (high IQ/low EQ)
E: emotional reactivity
D: depth seeker/disinterest in imaginative play

The purpose of this chapter is to describe these quirky characteristics in more detail. You may recall from the introduction that quirky children may or may not experience stress as a result of experiencing some of these characteristics. Age, insight, and self–awareness can influence a child's stress experience. A toddler who grabs a toy out of another child's hand, resulting in that child crying, would probably feel happy that he now has the toy he wanted and not reflect (for long at least) on the emotion the other child experienced. However, a fifth-grader who is teased and bullied by his peers because he cries when he is not allowed to read a book that interests him during a math lesson begins to feel the stress associated with being teased and disconnected from those around him.

Even if the child, regardless of age, fails to experience stress, adults and children around him are likely to do so. If the expression or experience of any quirky characteristic intensifies to a degree that results in significant challenges in one or more areas of the child's daily routine (home, school), the child may be entering the pathology category, which could result in a clinical diagnosis. What follows in this chapter are the quirky characteristics that comprise the STRESSED model. The hope is that you can begin to identify the areas of competence and challenge in a child who may be experiencing some challenges in his or her everyday life. As you read through each of the characteristics, try to keep in mind what is expected for a child who is the same age as the child in question. Spend time observing other children your child's age in various situations. Furthermore, use the information presented throughout this book, especially in Keys 4 and 6, to track your child's development relative to that of normative development.

Social Challenges

The first characteristic of the STRESSED model involves social challenges. A quirky child will often experience difficulty interacting with others and can present as peculiar and awkward in social situations. He may find it challenging to make friends easily, but he may connect well and quickly with other quirky kids. Indeed, when you surround yourself with other people who relate and interact with the world in a similar manner, albeit unknowingly, your profile appears more in the normative category, at least for what is expected among that particular group or people. The challenge is that other quirky kids may not be available in a child's daily environment, and thus the child may begin to experience stress as a result of difficulty fitting in with the available peer group.

Thus, a quirky child spends considerable time trying to figure out how to navigate an increasingly complex social context. The pressure to do so and the skills required to effectively do it increase significantly every year of the child's life, with significant demands on all children during the middle school/junior high school years of development (fifth grade and beyond). If the child is motivated to connect but experiences challenges, he is at risk for social isolation, anxiety, and mood difficulties. The social characteristic of the STRESSED model is so complex that an entire chapter of this book has been dedicated to it (see Key 4: Optimize Social Skills). The remainder of this section reviews some common social challenges that a quirky child may experience, as well as introduces common social communication challenges that may further exacerbate social interaction difficulties.

Parallel/Perimeter Play

One social challenge that a quirky child may experience is that she may not be very interested in interacting with others. Or, if she is interested, she may have experienced challenges while trying to connect and now prefers to avoid the feeling of rejection, embarrassment, or shame. This particular social profile results in more parallel play during the preschool and kindergarten years (although some parallel play, especially during preschool, is still expected), and more "perimeter walking" or solitary play (e.g., playing on the monkey bars or swings during recess while all of the other fifth-grade girls play each other in a game of soccer) during the elementary years.

"Perimeter walking" or "perimeter play," terms that I have coined over the years, are the behaviors that occur among some children who have difficulty with the social context, such as during recess or during a gathering such as a family party, at a park, or while participating in a club like Boy or Girl Scouts. The child may walk or stand away from the action on the perimeter of the scene and perhaps be paying attention to what is happening, but he does not attempt to join in or engage in any of the activities. In some cases, he may be completely immersed in his own world of pretend or fantasy play and remain oblivious to what others are doing around him. Children who observe this type of play may see the child having a sword fight with an imaginary opponent or perhaps talking to himself or to an imaginary playmate. The parallel player, on the other hand, will play near others but does not generally engage or interact with them. Thus, a parallel-playing child may set up cars or train sets alone during free time at preschool or kindergarten, while the other children play pretend school, house, or kitchen with each other.

Take-home point: One of the most effective ways to help a child who remains on the perimeter of the social action is to create programs with peer mentors or adult facilitators so the child can be engaged with others in cooperative and interactive activities. Although setting up such a program may require a little time in the formation stage, they do not typically cost any money to run because they depend on peers as volunteers. Some established peer-to-peer support programs like Peer Assisted Learning Strategies (PALS[1]) or the LINKS Peer to Peer Program[2] are good

---

1. http://kc.vanderbilt.edu/pals/
2. http://www.gvsu.edu/autismcenter/peer-to-peer-support-2-140.htm

places to start to begin to learn how to create one of these at your child's school.

Excitability and the Social Intruder

Another social skills challenge results when a child is overly excited to interact with others and intrudes on the play. This may be a child who invades the personal space of others or attempts to join the play without permission. This could be the result of impulse control challenges, hyperactivity, or anxiety. This intrusive approach could also be caused by sensory seeking, which a developmental challenge that will be explained in the sensory sensitivity domain of the STRESSED model.

Although impulse control difficulties and hyperactivity will inevitably lead to bodily "blurting" or intrusion onto the play or into the personal space of others, anxiety plays a very different role in a child's social approach. Anxiety can result in one of two behavioral approaches by the child: (1) she may avoid social inter-actions or remain quiet and timid, perhaps even unresponsive if others attempt to interact with her; or (2) she may experience a nervous energy burst in the social context that results in an intru-sive or invasive approach, almost as a means of releasing the stress or tension she is experiencing. Regardless of the reason behind a child intruding or impulsively engaging with others, this approach results in social stress for all involved, and this approach generally results in rejection or at least separation from others. Children must be taught to use a calm and regulated approach that involves observing the situation, walking toward the group, and calmly or slowly entering the play or the discussion.

I use rhymes whenever possible to help students easily remem-ber the strategies I teach them during counseling or social groups. I began using the rhyme "observation before participation" to help students remember to approach others slowly to be able to get a sense of what they were doing or discussing. I then often add another rhyme, which is "participation requires negotiation." A quirky child may approach another child or group of children and say or do something that is off topic or disruptive to what had already been going on. The child needs to learn how to effectively negotiate the requirements of the specific social context he is facing and negotiate what will be discussed, played, and so forth if he wants to continue to participate.

Excitability can also create challenges for a child socially. Consider the case of Michael, a fourth-grade boy, who prefers to play alone on the perimeter of the playground each recess period. One day, he is having a virtual light saber battle with an imaginary opponent, and a few of his female classmates walk by and ask him what he's doing. Michael does not answer but instead begins to chase the girls with his "light saber." The girls scream and begin to run, and Michael becomes excited because he sees this as a game. The girls, however, quickly become tired of this chase game and want some time to themselves. Michael is excited by their reactions and does not read the cues that the girls no longer want to be chased. The girls decide to ask the playground monitor for help, and Michael is told to sit against the wall. He is again isolated, and once he completes his punishment, he resumes his virtual battle alone until the next group of unsuspecting peers pass by. Michael's social development does not improve as a result of these previous experiences because he was never provided with any explicit feedback or instruction on what he could have done instead. Strategies to help a child like Michael will be presented in Key 4.

Social Communication Challenges

Children with social interaction challenges often experience difficulty with social language known as pragmatics. *Pragmatics* refers to the ability to change language according to the needs of a listener or situation, as well as the ability to follow rules for conversations and storytelling. Examples of changing language include giving background information to an unfamiliar listener (e.g., "I played Super Mario Brothers last night and I made it to level 4!" versus "I got to level 4 last night!") and speaking differently in a classroom than on a playground. Following rules for conversation requires the speaker to rephrase when misunderstood (which requires interpreting a quizzical or misunderstood reaction), know how close to stand to someone when speaking, and use appropriate facial expressions and eye contact.

It is not unusual for a quirky child to demonstrate pragmatic problems in only a few situations. However, if problems with social language use occur often and seem inappropriate considering the child's age, then a diagnosis such as autism spectrum disorder or social (pragmatic) communication disorder may apply. These diagnoses and recommended treatment approaches are explained further in Key 7. Peers may avoid having conversations with an individual with pragmatic challenges because of the lack of two-way communication that results as well as the discomfort that can accompany conversing with a person who does not modulate verbal/nonverbal communication well or does not change their communication approach to fit the situation they are in.

One-Way Communication

One-way communication involves a sender or speaker transmitting information to a receiver who does not have an opportunity to provide any feedback or ask questions. One example might be going to hear someone give a public speech in which you are not allowed to ask questions. As an audience member, you are there for the purpose of taking in the information as it's presented to you, which is appropriate to the context of that situation. Two-way communication, on the other hand, is interactive and allows for clarification and feedback to keep the communication going and fully understand the message.

Quirky children tend to engage more in one-way communication, which can resemble "show-and-tell" or speaking in monologues that involve giving information to people with little sense of whether the receiver is interested in hearing more. I compare the experience to listening to someone read to you from an owner's manual. The child is providing you with information, often with little consideration as to how interested you actually are. Connection with others suffers when a child continues to use a one-way communication approach as they grow older. As self–awareness and insight develops, she may begin to realize that she is not getting feedback (or the feedback she receives is avoidant) and as a result she begins to gravitate toward more interests that allow her to continue to pursue one-way communication, such as reading a book or watching videos. More information about the show-and-tell style of relating to the world is presented in Key 4.

Jacob, a patient of mine who is in the seventh grade, often picks up where he left off discussing his love of military weapons when he arrives for each session. When I greet him in the lobby of my office, he frequently has a model of a tank or plane in his hand that he immediately shows me and begins to describe. "Look at this Sherman tank!" may be the first words out of his mouth when he sees me. Jacob wants to engage me in a show-and tell interaction. Many adults will humor a child like Jacob and say, "Wow! That's really neat!" This does not help him. Instead, I either wait patiently for him to greet me appropriately (we have been practicing this so he knows what I'm doing), or I say, "Hello, Jacob. How are you today?" and then I work with him on returning the social inquiry.

It is important to remind children like Jacob that what you are doing (activity) or what you are interested in (topic) is never as important as who you are spending time with. This idea has to be drilled into the child's thinking because long after any activity is completed, most of us think about the experience and connection we had with others rather than what it was we did or discussed. Adults do this all the time after they meet someone new that they connect with. Adults will say, "He was really nice" or "She's a lot of fun" or "I like them." I like to think of it as connection before direction. I'm not going to give instruction to someone who I have just met socially about how to play the guitar (one of my passions) when I first meet them. In fact, it may never come up in conversation unless I am asked about it or I find that the person I am speaking with also enjoys the guitar and we establish a connection about this topic. Even then, I want to be sure I learn more about them and their interests, and not just discuss the guitar when I am with them.

Topics, Personal, Private

When I explain the importance of two-way communication to students in my social skills groups, I use a model that divides conversations into three categories: (1) topics, (2) personal, and (3) private. I teach children that topic conversations, such as telling someone everything you know about a particular video game, are often socially acceptable as your primary method of communication until about fourth grade. Beginning around third or fourth grade, children will continue to discuss topics with each other, but they gradually shift their approach to communication to involve more personal discussions. Indeed, they become less interested in what you know a lot about or what you like, and instead become curious about who you are, what you do, and how you relate to or think about the world or specific situations. This personal focus of communication allows others to begin to connect on a deeper, more interpersonal level. Thus, instead of asking others if they play a particular video game, children begin to ask each other what they are doing this weekend. Children begin to wonder more about each other's families, siblings, summer plans, where they live, and so on.

These categories of topics, personal, and private also represent the progression from an acquaintance to a friend. As you move through these levels of conversation, you deepen the intimacy of the connection or relationship. We reserve private discussions or conversation for those people that we trust the most. This may only occur among family members, and there are times in which even family does not know certain private information about you. Best friends as well as romantic interests, partners, or spouses may also be included in private conversations.

Within the context of a typical social exchange, such as meeting a group of new people for the first time, examples of private discussions would include things like religion, sex, and politics. These are often viewed as "off-limits" subjects when meeting people for the first time. Topics of discussion can remain one-way, especially if a quirky child is describing his lifelong passion for a video game and all of the details of that game, while personal and private discussion require two-way communication because they are aimed more at connecting with others rather than transmitting or acquiring information.

What is fascinating when I am modeling the topics, personal, private categories of discussion with children in my social groups is that as they begin to practice personal discussion, they tend to omit feelings from their description of personal experiences. An example of this would be a quirky child who tells the other group members, "I went to Disney World over spring break." A child in the normative category of development, and thus naturally skilled in the area of social communication, would tell the group, "I went to Disney World over spring break. It was amazing! I had *sooo* much fun!" There would be affect and inflection in the statement versus a matter-of-fact report of where you went and what you did.

When I am coaching the parents of my social group members about this phenomenon, I encourage them, along with the students, to include more feelings when engaging in personal discussions. If necessary, prompt the child. In other words, you would say to the quirky child, "You went to Disney World? What was it like? How did you feel when you got there? What was your favorite ride? How fun was it?"

The Development of Two-Way Communication

An inability or apparent disinterest in trying to establish and/or sustain two-way communication can play a large part in a quirky child's social makeup. Two-way communication, verbal and nonverbal, is essential to establishing and maintaining social relationships beginning at birth. Within weeks of a child's birth, an infant's visual acuity is good enough to begin to lock in nonverbally using eye gaze with their caregiver, and this helps facilitate and strengthen the interpersonal bond between caregiver and child. Infants have certain involuntary responses, such as moving their mouth into a smile formation, which leaves adults mesmerized by the idea that the infant is smiling at them and this keeps the adult and infant engaged in this interaction. Thus, the infant in the normative category of development is essentially hard-wired with the innate ability to draw others in, which promotes their overall social and emotional development.

A quirky child may not be properly hard-wired to make the tasks of socially and emotionally relating to them easy for others. Some parents, who have not had much experience with children or an understanding of child development may miss these early milestones of expected interpersonal interactions. If you're not sure what should be occurring, you won't know what is missing. This is especially true if it is your first child because there is no basis for comparison. Perhaps it's not until you are in the developmental specialist's office because your son is not connecting with the other children at school that you realize he was not really connecting with you and relating to you as much as he should have as an infant.

Neuroscientists are investigating the nonverbal interpersonal interaction patterns of infants ages nine months and younger and working to correlate those patterns with later social interactional challenges. There are times when parents may interpret the child's calm demeanor and lack of fussiness as being an "easy" child. Although it is certainly possible that this style of interaction is attributable to the child's temperament, it might also be possible that this child is at risk for developing some interpersonal challenges later. Once we fully understand these risk factors among children as young as infancy, we can begin developing more specialized approaches to improve their social and emotional functioning as early as possible.

Expressive Language Development

Once the developmental window of expressive language commences, parents are more likely to notice and tune in to any delays the child may be experiencing. We expect the child to have early building blocks of expressive speech during infancy in the form of cooing, babbling, and using utterances that many parents describe as gibberish. By around 12 months of age (give or take 3 months) children begin to formulate single-word utterances, usually of a high-value target such as "Mama," "Dada," "up," "more." Boys may fall slightly behind their female counterparts in terms of expressive language development. However, by approximately 18 months of age, we generally expect children to use 50 to 150 words with the possibility of combining some together. We also look for the ability to combine nonverbal gestures and facial expressions with some of these simple expressive language utterances.

For example, the child who references an airplane in the sky but cannot name it verbally should be able to point at it from a distance and then nonverbally reference their caregiver, using eye gaze, to check and see if they noticed the airplane as well. This is a classic nonverbal example of two-way communication in which the child looks up to see the airplane, looks toward the caregiver to see if they saw the airplane, and then looks back up to reference the airplane again and share the experience with the caregiver.

This method of interaction is referred to as *joint attention,* which is a social means of requesting that the world around us (e.g., our parents) pay attention to what we find to be enjoyable or interesting. Joint attention is generally a well-established ability by 18 months of age. It can also be referred to as social referencing, meaning that we are always scanning our environment and trying to share the experiences with those closest to us. Children within the normative category of development want to share that excitement and joy with others, and do so more with words and emotions during personal conversations (explained in the previous section) once they acquire the necessary expressive speech. This is the essence of how we connect with those around us and use shared experiences to do so.

Parents who have concerns about expressive and receptive language delays typically discuss these concerns with their pediatrician or conduct their own research and seek an early childhood evaluation through their local school district. If, by the age of two, the child is not speaking or is failing to demonstrate other essential elements of nonverbal communication, such as eye gaze or gesturing, the school district and/or a private speech therapist may determine that speech therapy is indicated to help promote language acquisition. Speech therapy can help the child begin to develop or promote more expressive and receptive communication, but it remains to be seen whether the child will use this language effectively to draw other people in socially in a two-way or reciprocal fashion. Indeed, the child may go on to use his newly acquired language to only discuss topics that interest him.

If the child is unable to acquire the necessary social, pragmatic, reciprocal communication skills (i.e., follow the rules and give-and-take of communication), then what often results is a child who is most comfortable speaking in monologues or providing detailed scripts or volumes of information on a topic of very high interest to him. Provided that the child has access to other individuals who share that interest, such as elementary-aged children who discuss video games, he can maintain some semblance of interpersonal interaction. However once the discussion shifts away from specific topics or communication of specific facts (i.e., topics), and instead must rely on exchanging ideas, thoughts, feelings, and beliefs (i.e., personal), then this individual may struggle to remain socially connected, especially due to the spontaneous format that is required for success with this style of communication.

The occurrence of talking to people about topics of interest brings us back to the qualitative versus quantitative analysis that is necessary to fully understand a child's profile (normative, quirky, pathology), which was described in the introduction of this book. In the case of an elementary-aged child who talks regularly to others about a topic of interest, the quantity or amount of interaction is good. However, older children must be able to qualitatively connect with others about a variety of topics to be socially successful. A common response that I hear from teachers when I ask how a child is doing during recess is consistent with a quantitative analysis. The teacher tells me, "I think he's doing well during recess. I watched him the other day and he was walking up to lots of different kids and talking to them." What is missing from this observation is the quality of those social overtures and interactions. Why was he walking up to so many different groups of kids? Was it because they were not interested in what he had to say? What was he saying to them? He racked up a strong quantity of social initiations, but the quality may not have been sufficient to sustain the connection or engagement with others.

Idioms, Figures of Speech, Inflection

Quirky children may focus on the literal meaning of the words being spoken and less on the nonverbal messages that accompany expressive language. Complicating this issue, the English language is full of metaphors, idioms, colloquialisms, and figures of speech. The various levels of inflection that speakers use while communicating are incredibly complex. We not only need to listen to the content of what's being spoken when we are having a conversation, we also must try to infer the meaning behind what they are trying to say. As expressive language develops, young children can get their needs met simply by saying, "I want a toy." Adults tend to comply and hand it over, especially if the child is polite about the request. With normative development, all of the nonverbal aspects of communication will be easily interpreted. But what if the child or the parent of a child is not able to pick up on these cues? For example, a child is told, "Take a hike!" by his peer group may respond by remaining still and looking quizzically at the group. Perhaps this child thinks to himself, "Hike? I don't like to go on hikes. Why would they want me to do that?" Or a child is instructed by his coach to cheer on his teammates, but she cheers very loudly and at the wrong times, annoying them instead. After all, she was doing what the coach asked by cheering for her teammates, correct?

A quirky child who does not naturally understand the meanings behind idioms and figures of speech and who struggles with nonverbal communication requires explicit coaching and encouragement. Approaching idioms or figures of speech as you would if you were trying to teach a word definition is indicated if your child struggles to glean meaning behind various figures of speech or idioms. English as a second language (ESL) websites are great places to start because non-native speakers also have to learn idioms by studying them, and this method is effective. My favorite ESL website for idioms is http://www.usingenglish.com, which is full of these commonly used expressions often heard when interacting with others.

Inflection plays a huge part in how verbally presented information is interpreted. Some communication experts argue that only 7 percent of interpreting communication involves the actual words we use. The rest involves how the words are presented. A classic example is the phrase, "I didn't say she stole the money." Read the sentences below and change your inflection on each of the italicized words to change the meaning of the sentence.

- *I* didn't say she stole the money.
- I *didn't* say she stole the money.
- I didn't *say* she stole the money.
- I didn't say *she* stole the money.
- I didn't say she *stole* the money.
- I didn't say she stole the *money*.

The words used in the statement are the same each time, but you can see, for example, that "*I* didn't say she stole the money" implies that someone else must have said it, whereas "I didn't say she stole the *money*" implies that she stole something other than money. Failing to pick up on the inflection or emphasis used in each statement completely changes the way the words are interpreted and can result in challenges responding effectively or accurately during conversations. Quirky children often require explicit instruction in these subtle nuances of language, not only to promote effective social communication but also during reading comprehension. Not being able to infer meaning during dialogue will cause challenges when interpreting stories. Thus, specific exercises in what others are thinking and trying to communicate must involve assistance during conversations, while reading, and even while watching television. If you are concerned about inference, take some time to read, and watch sitcoms or other social situations with the child and discuss what is happening and how you know this to be the case.

Monologuing

Monologuing is a term that I use to describe when a child attempts to speak for lengthy periods of time on a topic of interest. This is often done with little to no consideration of the recipient's interest in or feelings about this information. Children in the normative category of development tend to be more direct when it comes to reacting to a child who monologues. They will walk away or tell the other child they don't like that topic or don't want to talk about it. Adults, who are probably trying to be nice to the child, tend to humor these monologues by nodding, saying "uh huh" and generally tolerating the approach.

I urge any adult to be direct when a child is speaking to them with a monologue approach but do so in a manner that protects the child's self-esteem. Tell the child, "I like talking with you, but I am not interested in that topic." The child, despite this attempt, may persist and continue with the monologue, or they may become frustrated and even say, "Okay, I'm almost done" and try to continue. "Almost done" is a relative term in this scenario that can involve ten or more minutes if you do not intervene. I often compare this monologue style of speaking to playing a game of Ping-Pong in which the child stands on his side of the Ping-Pong table and holds the ball while you wait at the other side of the table with the paddle in your hand. Often, the child is so excited about the topic that they fail (or in some cases are unable) to consider your lack of interest, boredom, or frustration. In essence, they never serve the ball.

Some strategies that I use in my social skills groups may be effective during your everyday attempts to redirect monologuing. I often use humor because I am not trying to hurt feelings, but I often need to be dramatic to make the point because simply asking the child to stop monologuing is usually ineffective. I will playfully walk away, walk over to the wall and pretend to gently hit my head against it, completely turn my back or chair away from the child and flop over in the chair, or open my office door and begin to walk out to send an obvious message that I am bored with the topic. When other students are present, as is the case in my social skills groups, I ask the others to slowly raise their hands into the air as a "boredom meter" to make this cue more explicit. When the arm is fully extended, one has reached the maximum level of boredom with the topic. We may even individually turn our chairs 180 degrees away as we become bored with the topic. When all chairs are turned, the child needs to stop speaking or shift onto another topic.

It should be noted that teaching a child to stop monologuing is only half of the equation. Children need instruction on how to engage others in personal discussions and reciprocal communication such as how to ask others about their interests and experiences, even if those are different from your own. Much like the Ping-Pong game, the game ends unless the ball is hit back and forth, or perhaps it never begins. If one player holds onto the ball, the other player will either want to stop playing or ask the other player to give them a turn.

Another strategy I use in my social groups is to actually play a game of Ping-Pong with the group members while teaching them about the importance of two-way communication. My version of the game is a little different, but this approach can be effective, especially because you don't have to have much coordination or even be good at Ping-Pong to play it. I ask two group members to stand on each side of the table. Player 1 gets to say something and then is instructed to hit the ball. Player 2 can then respond by making a comment about the previous statement or asking a question about it, and then hits the ball. The two-player team that has the most back-and-forth hits wins a prize.

Pedantic Speech: "Precise Is Not Always Nice"

Previously in this chapter, one-way versus two-way communication was discussed. This section addresses the quality of speech and focuses specifically on a formal or pedantic style of speech. A quirky child may use a pedantic style of speaking. Pedantic speakers often come across as if they are talking down to others, as if the listeners are intellectually inferior. In general, though, it is most often characterized as a matter-of-fact, lecturing style of speaking. Pedantic speech is acceptable in certain contexts, such as individuals in the academic world like a college professor or the director of a scientific or military organization. There may also be some leeway in terms of college-age individuals and adults who use this style of speech, often referred to as "intellectuals" or "pseudo-intellectuals." However, children who speak in this fashion do not mesh well with their peer group. Although this style of speaking may be somewhat endearing if the child's parents are highly academically oriented or around adults who may see it as amusing that a child is able to engage on an intellectual level with them, the peer group will perceive this style of speaking as entitled and arrogant and as a result will keep a distance or perhaps bully or tease the child.

When I am working with a quirky child with a more formal or pedantic style of speech, I have to also work closely with her family to be sure that this style is not being reinforced. Pedantic speech is often the result of a high IQ/low EQ profile (to be described in the smart/social imbalance domain of the STRESSED model later), and families that emphasize high IQ may hold this style of speaking in high regard. However, pedantic speakers need to be taught that there is a time and a place for this style of speaking. Indeed, when helping a child with the pragmatics of speech, as previously described, the child is taught that you talk differently to a baby than you do to an adult. You also talk differently in the classroom versus the playground, and you change the way you speak when you are with your elders versus when you are with friends. I ask families to be sure to lighten up the tone at home and not always speak formally to each other. Speech pathologists can help provide exercises to increase the child's awareness of his style and provide strategies that allow him or her to change approach depending on the situation (also described in Key 7).

On a final, important note about pedantic speakers, I coined the phrase "Precise is not always nice," to help students remember the time and a place rule. If your classmate asks you to proofread his English paper, then you need to be precise, and you are granted consent to correct any errors. Pedantic speakers may attempt to correct the grammar of others while they are speaking with each other. This never ends well, for both children and adults. Indeed, children are looking for communication partners when speaking with others, not the editor of a manuscript! No one wants to feel nervous that their speech is going to be corrected when trying to have a conversation. If your child makes others feel this way, it only increases the social distance between him and his potential communication partners. I often have to teach quirky students to correct the error in their mind but not out loud.

Prosody

Prosody refers to the rate, rhythm, volume, and modulation of speech that is required to effectively communicate the meaning behind words. The prosody of words used in speech can change the course of conversation depending on how the words are expressed. Consider the word *no* for example and play with the many ways that you can say this word to effectively change the meaning. For example, a sharp "No" can be said in a manner to be stern and keep someone from doing something or it can be emphasized in a playful manner to egg someone on.

A quirky child may demonstrate voice prosody issues in the form of speaking in a monotone or robotic quality, a higher register, or with a sing-song style of speech as if there is a melody to the way they talk. One of the most common prosody challenges that can make a child stand out is the volume of their speech. Some children speak at a volume that sounds like they are reciting in a robotic manner through a loudspeaker or as if they need to be heard, much like someone would converse in a crowded environment like at a concert. The difference for the quirky child is that they are not at a concert even though they continue to speak with that volume level.

Speech prosody is another marker of the quirky child, and a speech pathologist is often well versed in this area to be able to evaluate and begin to treat this speech pattern to promote the child's social success. Another tool is an app that I developed for Apple devices called Voice Meter, which allows an individual to speak into their phone and measure the volume of their speech and learn to adjust their prosody. Audio recordings made while a child is speaking and then reviewed with the child can also begin to increase his awareness of the manner in which he speaks.

Transitional Stress

Transitional difficulties due to stress or rigidity of thinking (e.g., black-and-white thinking) are the hallmark of the second domain of the STRESSED model. A quirky child can experience rigidity in her thinking that makes shifting from one activity or thought to another challenging. A reasonable degree of stress may be expected in any child, such as a brief protest when being told to stop playing a fun game. Consider recess as an example. Most children are involved in an enjoyable activity with others during recess when the bell rings or the whistle bows to indicate it's time to stop. Most children in the normative category of development successfully down-regulate, which means slow down what they are doing and get in line or otherwise prepare themselves to reintegrate into the academic context. While driving a five-speed car, this process would be similar to down shifting to slow down the speed of the vehicle.

A quirky child may require some additional time to down–

regulate and voice some objection to the transition, perhaps even with whining or stubborn behaviors, but will eventually reintegrate. If a child experiences a full-blown tantrum when asked to make a transition, especially if the tantrum reaction occurs consistently when transitions are made, it can be a sign of something more significant that should be monitored to determine if the child is entering the pathology category of development. Indeed, in this example, the quantity and quality of the child's reaction is outside of the scope of what is expected, especially when the majority of the peer group can transition with little or no emotional or behavioral reactivity.

Transitions are required throughout the day. In school, the child transitions in and out of the school, in and out of the classroom and the desk, and from subject to subject or activity to activity. At home, transitions occur from the moment the child wakes up each morning. Some of the more challenging ones are getting ready to leave for school in the morning, stopping an enjoyable activity or participation in play to do something else like come to dinner, and the bedtime routine.

Most children, especially those age seven and younger, experience some disappointment or express some frustration with transitions, especially those that take place in the home. If your child is having strong emotional or behavioral outbursts such as screaming and crying or is aggressive, oppositional, or defiant during transitions, this would be a cause for concern and begin to fall within the quirky category of development. If these reactions persist and remain equally intense each time a transition needs to take place, you may want to consider whether the distress criteria for pathology is being met. Children in the normative category of development, regardless of age, will often express some disappointment or frustration with having to stop doing something fun, but they generally recover quickly and develop additional coping skills to effectively manage their levels of frustration with each transitional encounter.

Most advice about how to handle difficult transitions involves giving adequate warnings, such as "five minutes left." This may

help some children prepare themselves for the impending disappointment of stopping what they are doing, but it may not be
enough for a quirky child. Threats, intimidation, or raising your
voice will only escalate the situation and possibly give the child
incentive to wage a control battle with you. It would be convenient if you could just give a verbal command for a child to stop
what he is doing and he would comply. Unfortunately this approach
is rarely effective, especially with a quirky child, and this is a time
in which being parent results in some inconvenience. If you want
to avoid the emotion and power struggle, try the following take–
home point.

Take-home point: Go to the child, sit with him, and join him
in what he's doing. If he's playing a video game, for example, sit
next to him and watch what he's doing. Comment on what he's
doing and even ask him some questions about it if possible. Study
the game play for one or two minutes and look for a good time
when he can stop or save his progress. Tell him to finish the current section of play and then inform him he needs to stop and
save his progress.

If it's a television program he is watching before bedtime, for
example, sit and watch with him until there's a commercial or
allow him to transition once the show has ended, provided that it's
within a reasonable time. *Hint:* The closer you are to the child in
terms of physical proximity when you inform him of a transition,
the more likely you are to have a successful transition. Take a
moment to consider the transition from the child's perspective.
Sure, from your perspective you want to get the bedtime routine
completed and have some free time for yourself, but how would
you feel if you were in the middle of your favorite football team's
playoff game, fourth and inches and going for it with the game
tied in the fourth quarter, and you were summoned for dinner?

Finally, be sure to consider what you are allowing your child
to do before a transition will occur and consider limiting or prohibiting access to activities that will be especially challenging to
transition from. It's a lot easier for a child to stop doing homework

or chores and get ready for bed than it is to stop playing a video game, playing a game outside, or watching television!

Regulatory Difficulties

The next characteristic of the STRESSED model of quirky children involves challenges with behavioral regulation. This can include hyperactive or high-energy behaviors (running, jumping on furniture), blurting (interrupting others in conversation or yelling out answers in class without being called on), and personal space invasion (standing too close to others, hugging/kissing/touching others).

Most children in the normative category of development are able to regulate themselves beginning as young as three to four years old. This is the age in which many children begin to attend preschool and they can control their behavior and energy well enough to participate in the activities of the day. Even if they become overly excited, they are usually able to quickly and easily redirect and calm themselves down. Children in the normative category almost instinctively know how to assess their surroundings to see what they should be doing. Thus, if they are expected to sit at their desks and read quietly, they would not want to disrupt this activity for others by behaving disruptively. Furthermore, they contemplate the social ramifications of dysregulated behavior and, especially among elementary school children, monitor and regulate their own actions to blend in with the group so as not to be labeled by peers as a "weird" or "annoying."

For a quirky child, these displays of behavioral dysregulation are often triggered by excitement or during school situations in which there is not as much structure or order, such as field trips, in the lunch room, on the playground, or while lining up/walking down the hallway. In the home, these challenges can take place during rough-and-tumble play, in parking lots during errands, and during the morning or bedtime routine, to name a few examples. If these behavioral challenges are occurring during other times of the day as well, or if they are difficult to interrupt or redirect because of frequency or intensity, then the child may be entering the pathology category of development. Regulatory challenges are often symptoms of several neurodevelopmental diagnoses that will be explored further in Key 7.

Depending on the intensity and frequency of the child's regulatory challenges (and the amount of distress and dysfunction that results), a developmental specialist such as a pediatrician may recommend medication as a means of helping the child regulate himself. Medications such a stimulants (e.g., methylphenidate or amphetamine) are usually reserved for children ages six years and older in the pathology category of development. There are costs and benefits to this approach that should be discussed in detail before making a decision to use medication. If you are opposed to using medication or would prefer to explore nonpharmacological challenges first, then you should consider the following take–home point.

Take-home point: Children with regulatory challenges often have an innate drive to express themselves physically and possess high energy levels. If you know that this is true for your child, then you need to be prepared to channel this energy productively and wear him or her out in the process. Consider a "heavy work diet" that involves engaging your child in physical activities throughout the day to allow him to burn off this additional energy. Examples of heavy work activities include filling a backpack with heavy books and having the child walk around while wearing it, pushing a full shopping cart, sweeping, shoveling snow, and vacuuming. Obviously it helps if the child enjoys the activities that you select. You can perform an Internet search for "heavy work activities" and find additional ideas.

Furthermore, if you find that your approach is to redirect, yell, or punish when your child demonstrates a regulatory challenge, then you will want to review Key 5 to learn more about why these responses are generally ineffective and can make the situation worse and what you can do to produce more desirable outcomes when parenting your child.

Some regulatory challenges become so difficult to manage that the child has a hard time participating appropriately in school, and thus learning suffers. If this is the case, you may need to explore an option of a paraprofessional who can be assigned to work one on one with your child in school to keep him on task and out of trouble. This option will be discussed further in Key 6.

Executive Dysfunction

The first E in STRESSED involves executive functions. The executive functions are a set of processes that all have to do with managing oneself and one's resources to achieve a goal. It is an umbrella term for the neurologically based skills involving mental control and self-regulation. People use executive functions to successfully complete or perform activities. Executive functions include planning, organizing, strategizing, paying attention to and remembering details, and managing time.

A quirky child may have challenges with executive function (executive dysfunction) when she has difficulty planning projects, lacks an awareness of how much time is required to complete a project, or struggles to initiate activities or tasks or generate ideas independently. Children in the normative category, on the other hand, learn executive functions through trial and error. When children in the normative category of development have challenges with a particular executive function, they are generally amenable to additional assistance or are willing to practice improving their executive functioning skills with the help of adult coaching or supervision. These children want to be successful and please the adults with whom they interact on a daily basis, which helps motivate them to improve. They are also able to remain calm and patient with the learning process and view any new ideas and strategies for improvement as helpful to their long-term success.

Executive functions are controlled by the frontal lobe of the brain, located directly behind the forehead. Perhaps one of Mother Nature's cruelest jokes is that the frontal lobe is essentially under construction and not fully developed until we reach our mid-twenties, well beyond the average age of college graduation! Certainly, some people naturally have average to above average executive functioning prior to the completion of frontal lobe development. For anyone who is struggling with executive functioning, awareness of frontal lobe development offers a reference point for the importance of continuing to work on these functions until early adulthood. Thus, you should not panic if your child is having executive functioning difficulties, but you should determine the child's specific executive functioning challenges and provide support as needed. Each executive function is fully explained in Key 3 along with suggestions to support you child in any area that may be creating challenges.

IDENTIFY YOUR CHILD'S QUIRKS, PART II

Sensory Sensitivity

Quirky children tend to exhibit sensory sensitivities in response to certain sound, texture (e.g., food or clothing), temperature, touch, olfactory (smell), and visual reactivity. Examples of temperature sensitivity would be hot and cold temperature sensitivity for climate as well as food temperature. Texture sensitivity can be related to clothing, such as not liking the feeling of tags against one's skin, becoming upset with the toe line on socks, or disliking the feel of blue jeans because they are too tight or rub against one's skin in an uncomfortable way. Touch or tactile sensitivity would result if a child has an aversion to physical contact such as being hugged or if others are standing or seated too closely. Sound sensitivity can occur in the form of wanting to cover one's ears with the sound of singing (e.g., "Happy Birthday" song), toilets flushing, hair or hand dryers, vacuum cleaners, crowd noise, or loud unexpected sounds such as buzzers, sirens, or alarm bells. Visual reactivity can occur in the presence of bright lights or fluorescent lighting.

Many children are identified as having sensory sensitivities early because the child's reactions to various stimuli are easily observable and often pronounced. When these sensitivities cause extreme distress, then the child may have entered into the pathology category of development and may meet criteria for a sensory processing disorder (described in Key 7). Although many children in both the normative and quirky categories of child development will cover their ears when a toilet flushes or when a vacuum cleaner is turned on, or dislike the feeling of tags inside their shirt when they rub against their skin, a child with a pronounced sensory sensitivity will have an extreme reactions to these sensations and often avoids these situations reoccurring at all costs.

Children can exhibit a hyposensitive profile, meaning that they tend to respond best to deep pressure or higher levels of stimulation; or they can exhibit a hypersensitive profile, meaning that small amounts of physical contact or stimulation will cause a response or reaction. Children can also be mixed-reactive, which would be a combination of the hyposensitive and hypersensitive profiles. Additionally, some children are classified as sensory seeking, meaning that they constantly explore their environments to touch, manipulate, or examine objects (e.g., opening doors, turning off lights, putting objects in their mouths, pushing their bodies against objects) and stay moving to do so.

Children can and do exhibit pronounced sensory profiles that exist in the absence of any additional developmental concerns. However, a pronounced and persistent sensory profile often contributes to a quirky developmental profile. Families are encouraged to monitor their child's profile if these sensory sensitivities appear and determine whether there is a consistent and intensive pattern in which the child demonstrates aversion to certain sensory input. This is especially important because many young children, especially during the toddler ages, experience certain sensitivities, such as not liking the feeling of tags on their inside of their shirt or the feeling how a sock's toe seam line feels. Over time, however, most of these sensitivities will become lessened simply by repeated exposures (e.g., continuing to flush toilets in public restrooms and realizing that no harm results) and will not bother the child anymore. Indeed, many times parents or caregivers unknowingly reinforce a child's sensory sensitivity by reacting to a stimulus or situation in a manner that is consistent with the child's intense startled reaction. Children, especially younger children during the toddler years, regularly look to their parents' reactions as a guide for how they should be feeling. If a parent is reacting to a child's sensory sensitivity in a worried or stressed manner, this signals that the fear is legitimate and that experience should be avoided in the future. Parents should attempt to approach stressful sensory situations in a matter-of-fact way with minimal talking or reassurance. Instead of avoiding situations such as flushing a toilet in a public restroom, simply saying, "That's loud" and remaining calm can help the child develop the necessary coping and model that there is no danger or harm, simply a brief, uncomfortable experience.

One or two of these sensory sensitivities may require some simple workarounds such as selection of preferred clothing, but if it begins to significantly affect the child's ability to get through activities of daily living, keeps them from going into certain environments such as shopping malls or bathrooms, or creates significant emotional responses for a sustained period of time, then it would be a good idea to seek a professional evaluation.

Most developmental specialists who work with neurodevelopmental disorders are well versed in these areas, however a licensed occupational therapist (OT) would be the treatment provider of choice to evaluate a child's sensory profile and help him or her address these sensory sensitivities. The role of the OT in a child's treatment will be explained further in Key 7.

Take-home point: If your child's sensory profile is causing enough distress or dysfunction to interfere with their daily functioning, I highly recommend contacting a licensed OT in your area to evaluate your child's sensory profile and recommend intervention or treatment strategies, if indicated. OTs work with children who experience too much or too little stimulation through their senses and have trouble integrating the information they're receiving. As a result, it's difficult, if not impossible, for them to feel comfortable and secure, function effectively, and remain open to learning and socialization.

OTs are often employed by a school district and can also be located in private clinics and hospitals. The OT may recommend follow-up treatment in a clinic, which is often fun for the child and full of toys and play equipment. The OT may provide you with strategies to use at home to help address your child's unique sensory profile. During an OT evaluation, you can expect that the therapist will interact with the child in a playful and fun manner to determine his likes and dislikes as far as sensory input. The OT will also ask you, the parent, a series of questions about the child's daily experiences and will probably ask that you complete some standardized questionnaires to help determine the child's sensory profile relative to the normative group.

Smart/Social Imbalance (High IQ/Low EQ)

Having a child who demonstrates intelligence early in life is exciting to parents. It is true that people can be highly intelligent and also have well-developed social skills. However, a quirky child (and really any child for that matter) who possesses a strong intellectual ability is at a higher risk of sacrificing or forfeiting similarly developed levels of emotional intelligence (i.e., high IQ/low EQ).

The ability to express and control our own emotions is important (to be explored in the emotional reactivity category of the STRESSED model in the next section), but so is our ability to understand, interpret, and respond to the emotions of others. A person's Emotional Intelligence quotient (EQ) refers to the ability to perceive and evaluate emotions and respond accordingly by adjusting one's emotional status. While most developmental specialists believe that emotional intelligence can be learned and strengthened, others claim it is an inborn characteristic (you either have it or you don't). EQ is essential for relationship development, making friends, and socializing. Several assessment measures are available to measure a person's emotional intelligence (e.g., Multifactor Emotional Intelligence Scale; Mayer et al., 2001), but they are not nearly as developed or accepted as providing a reliable measure of EQ as is the case with an IQ test.

Intelligence Quotient or IQ is the measure of a child's intelligence on a standardized assessment that allows an evaluator to compare a child's intellectual ability with that of other children the same age to see where they are functioning. An IQ standard score of 140, for example, would mean that the child is demonstrating intelligence on the assessment that only 1 percent of other children that age also demonstrate. This score would be characterized as "very superior" intelligence.

IQ scores are not necessarily a true measure of intelligence, and it is often argued that intelligence comes in many forms that are not all measured by an IQ test. Indeed, many highly successful people have average intelligence. A quirky child who is smart but lacking socially may win a Science Olympiad or a robotics competition, or be able to design and build amazing structures out of Legos or on the video game Minecraft, but have little interest in interacting with others at school or inviting friends over to play or attend his birthday party.

There may be a time in your child's academic career when EQ challenges, despite average or above average IQ, result in academic performance decline. Indeed, I work with many highly intelligent students in elementary and middle schools who fail to complete their assignments because they don't think the information is important or relevant to their current or future goals. I also see many high IQ/low EQ students refuse to participate in group projects or assignments because they have significant difficulty navigating the social interactions that are required to successfully work with others. This is highly problematic, especially for future career prospects if the child is grows into an adult who is incapable of working alongside or with others.

Regarding the importance of EQ in terms of a child's developmental and life success, Daniel Goleman (2005) wrote a fascinating book called *Emotional Intelligence*. Goleman and his team concluded that IQ only accounts for 20 percent of life success. Whether this percentage is empirically supported remains debatable, but it does raise an important question. Given how many parents value their child's intellect, how important is IQ when it comes to future outcomes? Although I won't be able to resolve that debate within the context of this book, there is an important consideration regarding IQ when it comes to understanding a quirky child.

I use the terms *IQ* and *EQ*, as previously defined, when attempting to fully understand a quirky child's profile. In my experience, quirky children tend to have at least average if not advanced IQ but often forfeit a significant amount of their EQ, especially in comparison to their IQ ability. This creates an imbalance between the smart and social categories of development. You don't need to be the life of the party or the most popular kid in school to be successful in life. However, you do need to have at least some EQ to connect and interact with the world around you.

Goleman (2005) established five areas in which individuals should focus their efforts to promote emotional intelligence. It is interesting to note that these areas often overlap with quirky characteristics of the STRESSED model, meaning that these are all potentially areas in which a quirky child will require direct instruction and assistance in developing.

- **Self-Awareness**: People with high EQ are usually very self-aware. They understand their emotions, and because of this, they don't let their feelings rule them. They're confident because they trust their intuition and don't let their emotions get out of control. They're also willing to take an honest look at themselves. They know their strengths and weaknesses, and they work on these areas so they can perform better. Many people believe that this self-awareness is the most important part of emotional intelligence.

- **Self-Regulation**: This is the ability to control emotions and impulses. People who self-regulate typically don't allow themselves to become too angry or jealous, and they don't make impulsive, careless decisions. They think before they act. Characteristics of self-regulation are thoughtfulness, comfort with change, and the ability to say no in an assertive rather than aggressive manner.

- **Motivation**: People with a high degree of EQ are usually motivated. They're willing to defer immediate results for long-term success. They're highly productive, love a challenge, and are very effective in whatever they do.
- **Empathy**: This is perhaps the second most important element of emotional intelligence. Empathy is the ability to identify with and understand the wants, needs, and viewpoints of those around you. People with empathy are good at recognizing the feelings of others, even when those feelings may not be obvious. As a result, empathetic people are usually excellent at managing relationships, listening, and relating to others.
- **Social Skills**: It's easy to talk to and like people with good social skills, another sign of high EQ. Those with strong social skills are typically team players. Rather than focus on their own success first, they help others develop and shine. They can manage disputes, are excellent communicators, and are masters at building and maintaining relationships.

During Goleman's research, he surveyed employers and asked them what they were noticing in recent job applicants and what they were looking for when hiring employees. His surveys of U.S. employers revealed that more than half the people who work for them lack the motivation to keep learning and improving in their job. Four in ten were not able to work cooperatively with fellow employees; just 19 percent of those applying for entry-level jobs had enough self-discipline in their work habits. Goleman noted that more and more employers are complaining about the lack of social skills in new hires.

In a national survey of what employers are looking for in entry-level workers, specific technical skills are now less important than the underlying ability to learn on the job. After that, employers listed:

- Listening and oral communication
- Adaptability and creative responses to setbacks and obstacles

- Personal management, confidence, motivation to work toward goals, a sense of wanting to develop one's career and take pride in accomplishments
- Group and interpersonal effectiveness, cooperativeness and teamwork, skills at negotiating disagreements
- Effectiveness in the organization, wanting to make a contribution, leadership potential

Of seven desired traits, just one was academic: competence in reading, writing, and math.

In many careers such as business and entertainment, one must possess a high level of "street smarts." There is also a great deal of real-world intelligence that is acquired via experience, such as business negotiation, which cannot be taught by reading a book. If parents choose to have their child's IQ tested and receive news that the child demonstrates superior intelligence, they are often excited. However, this IQ score in and of itself is not necessarily predictive of life success, although it certainly is a nice head start.

It is easy to become excited when your child possesses intellectual talent and interest in learning new facts and information. However, the child must also have the ability to perceive and evaluate emotions and then respond accordingly if he is to be successful in most areas of his life. What you know is important in terms of knowledge, but you must find balance and be able to communicate that knowledge effectively with others while remaining interested in the information you may acquire through relationships.

Some highly intelligent children fall into a category of functioning referred to as "twice exceptional." This means that the child possesses high levels of intelligence and also experiences one or more developmental or learning challenges that can detract from his or her intellectual prowess. For example, a child can be intellectually gifted and also have an autism spectrum disorder or ADHD. Thus, the child is very bright, so you might expect him to thrive in school. However, his ADHD diagnosis results in focus, concentration, and attention challenges as well as hyperactive behaviors that make learning difficult if not impossible at times. Another child may be in the superior range of intelligence but have a reading disorder such as dyslexia. Thus, high levels of intelligence often do not occur "in a vacuum," and the child's overall profile needs to be understood to determine how to best support him through his academic career.

Take-home point: I often caution parents who have children younger than six years old to wait if they are interested in IQ testing until first grade to allow for a more accurate assessment of the child's intelligence. Although IQ testing is available for preschool children, I have observed cases where the results elicited false positives (meaning that the child tested in the higher range only to have their score decline at a later age) or false negatives (meaning that the child tested poorly but later demonstrated strong scores). Regardless of your child's IQ scores, consider the information presented in the preceding section about the importance of EQ and provide your child with the necessary experiences and feedback to promote their EQ development.

Emotional Reactivity

The emotional characteristic of the STRESSED model refers to a quirky child's tendency to react emotionally to a situation in an intense, out-of-proportion manner or in a way that is unexpected for a child given their current age or stage of development. Emotion control challenges can be the result of cognitive rigidity, but it can also be the result of underlying anxiety or other emotional or situational/environmental stress. As defined in the previous section regarding the smart/social imbalance characteristic, a person's EQ refers to his ability to perceive and evaluate emotions and then respond accordingly by adjusting his emotional status. A quirky child may have a low EQ that results in difficulty accurately interpreting or "reading" the emotional context of various situations. Perspective taking often plays a role in strong emotional reactivity such that an individual over- or misinterprets a situation, which leads to an intense emotional reaction. Individuals with low EQ will inevitably experience perspective taking challenges, which result in stress, frustration, and subsequent emotional control difficulties.

Perspective Taking

Perspective taking is considered an important step in the cognitive and emotional development of children. Very young children don't understand that other people have different feelings and experiences from their own. This is why your toddler, who just experienced the same thing as you, will want to tell you what just happened. This is also why your toddler believes he is not visible to others during a game of hide-and-seek when only his eyes or the top half of his body are covered. If he can't see you, then you must not be able to see him.

Quirky children ages six and older may understand the concept of perspective taking but have a difficult time applying it to their everyday interactions. Still others may not fully understand perspective at all. Perspective-taking ability develops over time until it becomes sophisticated in adults.

As children mature, they consider a variety of information when spending time with others. They realize that different people can react differently to the same situation. Children develop the ability to analyze the perspectives of others in a situation from the viewpoint of an objective bystander. By considering the perspectives of others, children learn to negotiate and keep peace with a group during social interactions by understanding how others feel. This process promotes empathy and improves the quality of relationships.

Children with social challenges are sometimes described as lacking empathy. This is usually not the case. Instead, the child is struggling with perspective taking, which makes empathy difficult. If they could understand the perspectives and emotional status of others, they would empathize. Indeed, many quirky children empathize quite well with others, provided that the other person is experiencing a strong, obvious emotion that can be easily understood (sad, angry, happy). It is the more subtle or gray area experiences and less obvious emotions that tend to be missed or misunderstood. Thus, when perspective taking is low, so is empathy, but it does not mean the child lacks empathy.

When interacting with children, adults may end their statements with how the behavior affected others. For example, "You hit me, and that hurt my feelings." For children who have difficulty understanding that others feel and think differently than they do, these statements may carry little weight. The child may understand that it is, in fact, bad to hurt someone's feelings but not understand why that's the case. The why question is a difficult one for the challenged perspective taker to answer. This causes problems not only socially but also academically, especially in the area of reading comprehension. Indeed, many quirky children who begin life as strong readers reach a point in school, usually beginning in second grade, in which they are asked to infer why things happen in stories and why characters in books behave the way they do. Although the quirky child might be able to answer the who, what, and where of the characters, plot, and setting, the why question escapes them; this is another indicator of perspective-taking challenges.

Children within the normative category of development, on the other hand, are constantly seeking explanations for why things happen. When you listen to elementary-age children in the normative category of development talk to each other, they will say things like, "Why did you do that?!" When they are discussing gossip about each other, they will often try to understand from the other's point of view. For example, they may say, "Sally didn't invite me to her party because she's probably mad I was rude to her when we were at Jessica's house."

Often, children with perspective-taking challenges seek to level the playing field following emotional experiences using the eye-for-an-eye mentality. "If you hurt me, then I will hurt you." The child understands that both people are now feeling the same way and can then understand the other child's feelings because those feeling are now the same. Without consideration of how this approach further escalates situations and intensifies emotions, a child may continue to use this ineffective and potentially damaging approach to problem solving.

A quirky child tends to feel justified regarding his social interactional approach based on a black-and-white thinking style. For example, a quirky child in the second grade might correct others students in the classroom who are not following the rules. Children at this age will tattle on each other, but they are beginning to understand that the teacher is responsible for monitoring rule following and correcting other students should be left up to the teacher unless there is some element of danger involved. A quirky child may adhere to the rules so rigidly and correct others so frequently that they miss the perspective of others—that being corrected by a peer is annoying and makes you want to avoid a person who does that to you. If you ask a quirky child about why they corrected the other student, you will often hear the black-and–white reasoning: it was the rule and I was helping her follow it.

Take-home point: We strive to teach our children that two wrongs don't make a right, but this lesson is often lost on a child who struggles with perspective taking. In addition, the child may fail to understand the social effect of his own behavior in the absence of direct feedback from others. Teaching perspective taking to quirky children requires a marathon approach. Unfortunately, the teaching attempts often come after the child has made an error and failed to consider the perspectives of others.

The quirky child will not usually learn from her mistakes in a way that will improve perspective taking considerably in the future. Thus, you need to use a variety of other modalities to talk through perspectives so that they have the necessary information in advance. Perspective-taking exercises can include role-playing, pretend play with action figures while talking out the thought process of the characters, watching sitcoms on TV and discussing the characters' points of view, and reading children's books together while discussing the characters.

As you will learn in Key 4, one of the most effective ways to teach a child abstract concepts such as perspective taking is to expose her to as many different people in as many different situation as possible. As stressful as it may be to expose the child to more opportunities to struggle, it provides the necessary opportunities to coach and provide experiences that are necessary to truly develop their understanding of the emotional experiences of those around them.

Depth Seeking/Disinterest in Imaginative Play

This section deserves its own book to fully address, but what follows is an overview of the key elements of this domain, which consists of two interrelated parts of the STRESSED model: depth seeking and disinterest in imaginative play.

Depth Seeking (versus Breadth Seeking)

Children in the normative category of development are generally intellectually curious about their world and those around them. The majority progress through their development as breadth seekers and continue this throughout their lives. I coined the term *breadth seekers* to describe individuals who like to experiment with a variety of interests and are willing to explore topics that are not always their first choice, for no other reason than just the experience. Breadth seekers exercise their curiosity across a wide variety of interests and people with whom they choose to explore these interests. This is essential to healthy social, emotional, and academic development. Thus, breadth seekers intrinsically follow the most substantive recommendation of all social skills research to date, which is that individuals who want to improve their social skills need to be exposed to as many different people in as many different contexts as possible (White et al., 2007). Children in the normative category of development are breadth seekers by nature.

Breadth seekers protect themselves from anxiety and boredom with novel tasks because they see them as opportunities to explore and learn more about themselves, others, and the task at hand. Breadth seekers will certainly engage in many things that they determine to be too difficult or of little interest to them and eventually move on. However, their intellectual curiosity keeps them hungry for more experiences because you never know what you're missing until you try.

Quirky children, as well as those with significant and persistent enough social challenges that may necessitate a specific diagnosis (e.g., autism spectrum disorder), tend to be *depth seekers*. Generally speaking, depth seekers like to cut their losses and stick with what they know and do best. They protect themselves from discomfort by exploring a highly selective set of interests, or perhaps just one interest at a time before moving on to another one, a process that could take years per interest, and they gather as much knowledge and experience as possible about it. This results in a significant social disconnect because they narrow themselves to interacting with others around a highly selected set of topics or interests.

This tendency to engage in depth seeking is often closely linked to the smart/social imbalance characteristic previously described in the STRESSED model. It's inevitable that you would become smart or an expert of sorts on a particular topic if you spent enough time thinking and learning about it. Thus, depth seekers may become well versed or "smart" in highly selective areas, but they miss the bigger picture (i.e., social and emotional context and information) that is often promoted among breadth seekers by virtue of exploring a variety of interests and interactions with one another.

Take-home point: Additional information about the neurological driving force behind depth seeking is presented in Key 3. You will learn that you are competing with a powerful neurological opponent when it comes to encouraging a quirky child to seek out a breadth of interests. In case you were wondering, there is no pharmacological solution to this challenge. Thus, you must pursue the following two strategies when trying to encourage breadth seeking for your child: (1) containment of the deep interest(s), and (2) engagement of the child with a variety of people, activities, and interests.

Containment of the child's depth-seeking interest does not require elimination of the interest as long as the child can tolerate limits set around it. Containment of video games, for example, would involve limiting the child's access to no more than one hour of video game play on school nights, and no more than two hours on weekends. If the child fails to explore other interests during the time that he is not allowed to play the video game and can only think about when the next time he will play, then you may need to consider complete elimination of the game system or lock it up or remove it from the home for an extended period of time, such as over the winter break or summer months.

Regarding engagement, you may have told a child that he could not engage in his preferred interest such as playing on the computer, and he replied, "I'm bored!" In an effort to help your child alleviate the feeling of boredom, you then rattled off a list of possible alternative activities ("How about you . . .") to which he repeatedly replied, "I don't want to do that!" While a child who is in the normative category of development can often easily find something else to occupy the time and engage his interest (i.e., breadth seeker), a child in the quirky category is struggling to get their thinking to shift away from whatever they would rather be doing to focus on what else they could be doing.

To help the child seek out more breadth seeking, you must engage them in the new activity for long enough that thought about what they would rather be doing dissipates. This can be time consuming, but if you want this to work, you must put in the time. Thus, simply suggesting, "Try this" will result in frustration and will keep the child stuck. You may have to pick the activity and begin doing it in their line of sight so that they can think about what it is you want them to do. You may have to, dare I say, bribe the child initially to do it ("You can stay up an extra 15 minutes past bedtime if you come and work in the garden with me"). Only use such incentives when the child is really stuck or else he will quickly learn that he can refuse an activity that he might otherwise participate in just to get a privilege or a prize. As children enter the elementary school years, especially fourth grade and up, it is strongly encouraged that you make it a household rule for the child sign up for one activity outside of the home during the school year. This not only promotes breadth seeking, especially for a child who is getting older and should not only be at home doing activities with a parent, it also creates opportunities for more social interaction.

Disinterest in Imaginative Play

When I was growing up, I played in the neighborhood from the time I arrived home to the time I had to come in for dinner. I had homework, but I had the time to complete it and still play most of the afternoon. I grew up in a subdivision, and my parents installed a bell outside our back door that they would periodically need to ring to call us in for dinner because we were several houses away, playing in the neighbor's yard. My father installed floodlights over the garage so we could play basketball and other games into the evening and sometimes the night hours. Kick the can or catching fireflies were staples of early evening play activities, and there were lots of kids regularly available to play together.

With so many opportunities available to play with others, why does a child in the quirky category of development not take advantage of them? Quirky children are at a high risk of experiencing social challenges because they are often depth seekers who are more focused on topics rather than the personal, social, emotional experiences of those around them. Solitary activities are often preferred over cooperative or collaborative activities, especially if competition occurs during the activity as is the case during sports or other win-lose games.

Two things exacerbate the risk factors for quirky children. First, a quirky child may attempt to engage others during play, but struggle to do so effectively (i.e., social challenges characteristic from the STRESSED model). They may become easily upset if a rule is broken during a game or if the game is lost (i.e., regulatory difficulties, emotional reactivity). They may try to join play in progress without permission (without asking "Can I play?"), or they may not possess the necessary skill set to be a part of interactive play (e.g., only wanting to play out their own ideas with little regard for other's ideas) (social difficulties, regulatory difficulties). Thus, the quirky child may then retreat to solitary activities where negotiation is unnecessary and comfort remains high (i.e., disinterest in imaginative play).

Second, the quirky child may not find social interactions appealing in the first place. Sometimes observations of the peer group reveal conflicts and negotiations that seem stressful and undesirable. These emotional experiences are often uncomfortable for the child because he struggles to interpret why they are occurring and what to do about it (i.e., perspective-taking challenges inherent due to smart/social imbalance characteristic). While the children who are engaged in such social negotiations and conflicts are building their social muscles (i.e., breadth seeking), the quirky child retreats from the experience of discomfort and plays it safe by engaging in low-stress, solitary activities. These children will quickly report how bored they are in a situation where play is available and their comforting solitary activities such as video games or reading a book are not. Or, if they have to interact, they may attempt to keep the discussion focused on topics of interest, such as providing detailed information about the video games they enjoy playing. If they can't have their first choice of playing the game, at least they can talk about it.

Most kids within the normative category don't just give information or make demands during play. They discuss what they are doing and how they are doing it. They ask for feedback and quickly learn to make requests in a manner that does not irritate their play partner(s). The motivation is to keep the play going. Indeed, these kids use statements such as "How about we set the cars up over here?" rather than demanding, "No, the cars have to go here!"

A child within the quirky category on the other hand, tends to demonstrate rigidity in play while also lacking the necessary perspective taking to realize that their play partner is not happy with the approach. When the play partner leaves the play, the quirky child is left to continue with more solitary play and is often content to do so. Perhaps future play situations are then "guarded" by the quirky child to avoid the discomfort of having to negotiate, such as choosing to perform a task or activity suitable for one person only (reading a book on the playground during recess or using the swings).

What parents need to realize is that play is equally important to a child's future life success as anything gleaned from a textbook in school. Recall the smart/social imbalance characteristic of the STRESSED model and the emotional intelligence work of Daniel Goleman (2005). Knowledge needs to be applied to real-life situations, which will help one develop the skills necessary for career and life success. A quirky child can often tell you what they should do in a social situation if you discuss it with them, but once they have the chance to put this knowledge into action, they may forget or struggle and ultimately fail to achieve success. They simply do not possess the experience base to effectively respond to the situation.

Children within the normative category of development are simply naturals when it comes to social savvy, and the effects of limited play opportunities may not adversely affect them much. Indeed, many children grow up in rural areas or farming communities, where there are limited opportunities to interact with other children, but once they arrive at school they are fully neurologically equipped to play well with the other children or at least learn from their mistakes and try again if things do not go well the first time. They persist and are motivated to get it right and succeed.

For a quirky child, the consequences of limited playtime can be disastrous. They can shut down and dig deeper and deeper into solitary interests until sometimes it's just easier to let them be content rather than deal with the outbursts that result from trying to get them out and about. Before you know it, the child is 18 years old and is experiencing "failure to launch," meaning that you and your child are trapped in the family home together and the idea of sending her out into the high-stakes and challenging world without the necessary skills would be cruel and result in even more stress. Thus, you remain together and the child is now an adult living at home with her parent(s).

Take-home point: When families ask me how to solve this problem, I first cite the cultural issues that are working against them: less free time, more work, and fewer available play partners. Thus, families must maximize the time they have available to engage with others. School breaks can offer a healthy dose of play, provided all of the available play partners are not away at camps or on vacations. If they are, perhaps your child needs to be enrolled in a camp with other children to provide the necessary social opportunities. Without the stress of school and homework, breaks are a rich opportunity to exercise the social muscle. I stress the importance of allowing free time to be just that . . . free. Set up the environment so that free time can be used to choose from active/interactive play (e.g., board games, physical play, pretend play) rather than passive activities (screen time). Siblings can serve as appropriate playmates when the neighborhood is absent of anyone else to play with. Camps, although fairly structured and adult directed, can offer opportunities to exercise the social muscle. Cost may be a factor that limits a family's accessibility to camps, although scholarships may be available.

Some parents may shy away from enrolling a quirky child in a camp because the social context is stressful and the child may act out. This is a major catch-22 for many well-meaning families. They want their child to participate in the social world but struggle to get them involved because of how averse they have become about engaging in such situations. Don't be afraid to explain your child's profile to the camp in advance and see if the staff can pair your child up with a counselor or a supportive peer who can keep them engaged in the activities but allow breaks when needed. Much like a strenuous workout in the gym, quirky kids need to rest periodically and briefly during social interactions to keep going.

A long break from school (summer or holidays), however, does not provide a strong enough dose of social exposure if we want any gains to be sustained. I implore any parent reading this to follow my school year rule: the child must participate in one activity outside of the home with other people. The ideal goal is for the child to experience a sense of accomplishment in something other than a home-based, solitary activity. Parents can check their local community recreation and education centers to find clubs, group, or classes that may be appealing to the child in terms of topics of interest. It may be an easier convince the child if they know they are going to be with a group of kids who also share their love of robotics, role-playing games, or computer programming.

Be persistent and keep looking for opportunities for engagement and connection even when previous attempts were unsuccessful. Remember: children require as many social exposures with as many different people as possible to improve their social functioning. For children with more significant social challenges, arrangements must be made to provide coaching and facilitation during these social exposures so that the child does not self–destruct. Additional strategies and recommendations are provided in Key 4.

Setup versus Play

A quirky child can be highly precise and analytical in his style of thinking (i.e., smart/social imbalance). This tendency shows up early in childhood, typically in the manner in which a child approaches play with toys. Many quirky children have a challenging time engaging in pretend play independently or even with the help of the peer group. As a result, a quirky child might gravitate toward more structured or analytical play, such as building train tracks, completing puzzles, or building with Lego sets. Although these interests and activities are commonly enjoyed by many young children, what is not so common is for children to continue to exclusively pursue these activities in a solitary manner when potential play partners are available.

What is often notable about a quirky child is that he can spend so much time setting up his play that he leaves little time for the play itself. This is in stark contrast to children in the normative category of development who are less inclined to set their play up in a "just so" fashion and would rather hurry up and get to the play no matter how sloppy or imprecise the setup may be. Another challenge for a quirky child who spends time with more structured play or setting up for play is that he often want to do it his way and thus when others try to join in, it can cause stress and frustration that results in rejecting the prosocial overtures of the peer group.

The problem for a quirky child in the setup versus time spent playing scenario is that the peer group is ending their play, which has been going on almost immediately since the play opportunity began, right around the time that the quirky child has finished his elaborate setup. This is one more facet to the quirky child's social profile that makes it highly challenging for them to connect with the peer group at the necessary level to remain connected. The goal when facilitating play among quirky children and their peer group should be to speed up the process of setting up or, if necessary, have the materials already out and ready to go so that you can begin to coach and try to facilitate the interaction as a means of helping the children remain connected with one another.

Take-home points: There are two points to follow to begin to promote imaginative play skills for your child. The first approach is to set up play dates in your home for the child and one peer. Perhaps the greatest obstacle to this approach is finding the ideal play partner for your child. Although the play date approach will be described fully in Key 4, the basics are to invite a play partner for your child to your home, plan a one-hour play date with three to four planned activities, remain a part of the play during the entire visit so you can keep engagement high and help negotiate decision making and problem solving, and end on a high note so that both children end the play session feeling positive about the experience.

The second approach is to use what I have called the five-and-five exercise. This approach is also explained in further detail in Key 4. A brief overview of the method is as follows. To complete this exercise, tell the child you, the parent, want to play with her, but in a special way. For the first five minutes, she is going to have to play a game that is *your* idea. When this time period is up, you will stop and then the child is allowed to play something that is *her* idea. When you are first introducing this, it is helpful to use a timer to properly follow the rules of the exercise and keep the routine as clear as possible. I suggest that the parent go first because it will be easier to stop the parent's play and move onto the child's than if the child had to stop and play something differ-ent. Even if you are having fun during the first five-minute seg-ment of play, you must still stop and move on to the child's portion of play. Some parents choose to keep the items they were using during their play out if they are going to repeat the exercise and would like to go back to their idea.

The Evolution of the Quirky Child

A child in the quirky category of development begins the early years of his life fairly insulated from the demands of the social world. This experience is the same for children in the normative and pathology categories as well. The family home environment provides certain predictability and routine that can buffer the chal-lenges that may be on the horizon once the child is introduced to the social context, which now includes adults and peers who may use different routines, different responses to the child's behavior, and different structure than what the child is typically accustomed to. Many families unknowingly adapt to the child and adjust their home routines to suit the child's particular needs. This is not nec-essarily a negative thing, but the degree to which a child (rather than the adult) can adapt to situations out of their control will, to some a certain extent, determine future outcomes.

Aside from daycare, the preschool period of development for children three and four years old represents a child's first entry into a more structured social and emerging academic context. Preschool should focus primarily on routines and play. I know some academically oriented parents who grow increasingly frustrated that they pay for a preschool and every time they visit the class it seems like all the kids are doing is playing! In their minds, preschool is the era of alphabet, numbers, colors, and shapes. Although all of these core concepts are important, the importance of play cannot be understated in terms of its massive contribution to future social, academic, and emotional development. Play truly is how young children learn to be successful in life.

It is important to understand, from a developmental perspective, that play is the gateway to socialization, and socialization is the key to future academic, interpersonal, and life success. Fast forward 19 years from the first day of preschool and imagine your child is now being considered for a job against another candidate who is just as qualified in terms of grade point average, test scores, and experience. The job interview is just as much a social assessment as it is a competency review. How does the employer decide between these two highly qualified applicants? In most cases, it becomes an interpersonal tiebreaker. Was the applicant able to make small talk, infuse appropriate humor at the correct time, make the interviewer like them and feel comfortable hiring them? Was their demeanor and affect inviting, and did the applicant give the impression of someone the employer would like having around the office? If it's a sales job, can the applicant effectively interact and engage with people? There are plenty of smart people in the world, but social competence is what distinguishes the best applicants from those who are merely qualified. Especially in today's competitive economy, every distinguishing attribute you can put forward gives you an edge or advantage and increases your likelihood of success.

In my clinical practice, I find that many quirky children fly under parental radar until introduced into a consistent, structured social context. We begin offering preschool to children at three years of age for a reason: they're developmentally ready for it. What does preschool readiness look like? A child can enter preschool without the ability to properly hold a crayon or pencil, and without being able to write or even recognize letters of the alphabet. They may be able to count to five or ten, or they may not. They may not know all of the primary colors.

One common criterion for preschool admission, other than age, is toilet training. Many schools don't want to have to change diapers or pull-ups. Other than that, a child is generally deemed ready when they are three or four years old. Many preschool and kindergarten programs throughout the United States and even internationally, however, are beginning to add a social observation day to their admission process to make recommendations on the appropriateness of entry into their program based on how the child relates to others and follows the routine of the classroom.

The reason we wait until the age of three or four years to begin introducing schooling is because children this age possess an important life skill, albeit in its earliest stages of development: tolerance for boredom. This is an important academic, interpersonal, and overall life skill that allows the child to listen and participate in conversations or activities with minimal interference. Observe any circle time meeting in a preschool classroom and you will see motor restlessness, nose picking, inattention, and fidgeting. These behaviors are expected to some degree. When interference behaviors such as blurting, hyperactivity, or intense emotional outbursts extend beyond these expected behaviors, either in terms of quality or intensity, a quirky profile may become more evident in this structured preschool context.

In some cases, a quirky child may not have even made it to the circle time area of the room yet. They may still be engaged in an activity from before, and the difficulty with transitions becomes readily apparent. Some quirky children may feel compelled to complete a task or activity before moving on due to transitional stress. Preschool children in the normative category of development make up the majority of most traditional preschool classes. These children are able to stop what they're doing, even though they may not really want to, and move with the group because that's what they were asked to do. They want to be seen as "good" and make the teacher happy (i.e., perspective taking). This is important to them, even at such a young age!

The preschool-aged child in the normative category sees herself as part of the group and often aims to please the teacher and love to point it out to that teacher (e.g., "I made you a picture" or "I'm listening, Mrs. Smith!"). This emerging perspective taking into the feeling states of others is an early indicator of appropriately developing social cognition and awareness. Thus, the child within the normative category begins to think from the perspective of the teacher and what would make that person happy with them.

The child in the quirky category, on the other hand, may look at the world almost like one would see things with blinders on. If it's not seen from within that vantage point, then it's not considered, thereby reducing awareness and perspective taking. The quirky child seems to be thinking, "Why would I want to go over there and sit with all of them when I'm perfectly content completing the current task or activity?" Perhaps the child fails to notice that the group has shifted on to something else altogether. This child is thinking from her own perspective rather than considering the perspective of the group. The challenge moving fluidly through a schedule and routine (which allows most preschool children to thrive and prepares them for the more structured and academically rigorous environment of elementary school) is often due to difficulties with perspective taking as well as executive dysfunction, especially in the areas of shift or mental flexibility (described in Key 3).

Most children begin preschool with an innate ability to be flexible thinkers, unless of course they want you to buy them a toy and you say "no." They are still toddlers, after all. However, even despite the frustration of being told "no," even very young children, as long as they are within the normative category of development, can regain emotional composure, recover and reset, and move on. One early indicator of shift difficulty (i.e., mental inflexibility) that shows up before entering preschool is a child's ability to get ready for bed and leave the home in the morning. If the child has not participated in daycare or other activities that require attendance at a designated time, families may not yet have a true sense of how well the child does getting ready to be out the door on time in the morning. It's only when this process is a factor that true challenges will be noticeable. If repeated exposures (i.e., at least three months) to the transition of getting out the door in the morning do not result in transitional or shift improvement, then the child is likely experiencing difficulties consistent with the quirky category of development, and potentially the pathology category. Although it's developmentally appropriate for children ages three to six to still require assistance to get dressed, brush their teeth, eat breakfast, and gather their belongings, it would be an indicator of entering the quirky or pathology category if behavioral/routine rigidity or a significant meltdown begins each time this routine presented itself.

Once the child enters the preschool classroom, any challenges transitioning from one activity to another become easily observable. In the event the child has eventually transitioned to the required activity, perhaps with the assistance of an adult, their brain may remain "locked" on the idea of the previous activity, and they may experience stress or anxiety about having made the transition. Thus, the child has behaviorally transitioned and is now seated where she needs to be, but she has yet to mentally transition and engage in the new task or activity because she is still thinking of what she had been doing before. This thinking style can result in emotional and even behavioral outbursts.

The quirky child may also experience the feeling of boredom with the activity, perhaps circle time, and either verbalize this ("I'm bored!") to the group or move their body away from the group by turning away, flopping on the floor, or even moving around or out of the room. Add in any sensory sensitivity such as aversion to a morning welcome song as evidenced by grimacing and covering one's ears, and you can see how difficult it becomes to participate in the activities of the day.

Every child is unique and may have different reasons for behaving in this way, whether it be social discomfort, sensory challenges such as discomfort sitting on the floor or seated too close to others, anxiety, or the aforementioned executive functioning challenge with shift/mental flexibility. While a quirky child's peer normative counterparts also experience stressors throughout the day, the quirky child will likely have a greater difficulty letting this stress go and moving on (a difficulty shifting away from the feeling of frustration or upset).

The good news, from a peer perspective, is that preschool children are fairly oblivious to such meltdowns, and although they may look in the direction of a student displaying an emotional outburst, they don't think about it much beyond the initial observation. Thus, a preschool child would not refuse to play with a peer because he had a meltdown in circle time. However, as children move to kindergarten and beyond, these types of events have staying power and can significantly and adversely influence the peer group's perceptions of the disruptive child. Children don't think about why this may be the case; they only know what is observable to them and they often refer to it as "bad" and may notify the child's parents about the behavior during pickup from school.

Repeated disruptions to the flow of the day can result in the other children resenting and even avoiding the child who behaves in a manner that undermines their classroom experience. Furthermore, the other children may not want to get into trouble or be associated with a child who tends to get into trouble, so they keep a safe distance. Children also begin to notice that the adults in the classroom may approach a quirky child differently and may question the fairness of this (e.g., a teacher allows a child to chew gum during quiet work to keep him from humming and disrupting the other students, but no one else in the class is allowed to chew gum). You will learn more about developmental milestones associated with each year of school from preschool through fifth grade and how achieving or failing to achieve these milestones influences the interactions of those around the child in Key 6.

Sample Quirky Profile

No two children within the normative category of development are exactly alike, and the same holds true for children who may be considered quirky. The normative–quirky–pathology continuum is dynamic, and thus children within the normative category may eventually experience enough stress and difficulty participating in daily activities or interaction that they ultimately enter into the pathology category.

Consider a fifth-grade child who becomes depressed because his best friend is diagnosed with cancer and passes away a year later. This child had been within the normative category prior to the loss of his friend, but the stress and grief became too great and took a toll on his emotional and mental health. The child is ultimately diagnosed with a major depressive episode and enters into the pathology category. With the appropriate counseling and treatment, he learns to cope with the loss and returns to the normative category. Pathology came and went.

Migraine headaches are another example. When you develop symptoms and receive a diagnosis of migraine headache, you enter into pathology. However, you only experience the pathology if you remain untreated (e.g., do not seek out an evaluation of your symptoms or do not take your medication as prescribed) or when the headache symptoms emerge. Otherwise, you remain within the normative category. Although the depression example could result in remaining in the pathology category throughout the day for weeks or months or even years, the migraine example may only result in pathology for a few hours a day, three to six days a month.

A quirky profile can also be dynamic within the category itself, with some of the STRESSED characteristics coming and going. Because a child is determined to be within the quirky category at one time does not necessarily mean he or she will always be quirky. Many individuals channel their quirks into socially acceptable areas of interest like the arts. I find deadpan stand-up comics to be some of the funniest people because they make you laugh with hilarious jokes, but their affect is flat and dry. The nonverbal messages are not congruent with the verbal content of the jokes, but it works. I think part of why this is the case is that people often laugh when they are uncomfortable or experiencing dissonance and the deadpan comic creates this dissonance in a way that makes laughing acceptable despite the dry or flat approach. When this type of comedian is on stage, this approach works and he or she can be very successful and make a nice living. Once the comedian is off the stage, the quirks, if they are truly a part of the his or her delivery and not just a part of the act, can be result in social distance or misunderstanding. The context is so important.

For the quirky child who is aware of his dissonance and wants to be able to fit in more with the normative group, instruction is required to increase his awareness of what is normative and how to behave in a way that is consistent with that information. If the child is successful, he shifts more toward normative. If he is not successful, he remains in the quirky category or might experience enough stress, anxiety, or mood challenges to move toward pathology.

It may not be until the child is exposed to other children in a structured setting like school that quirky characteristics from the STRESSED model emerge. To help you conceptualize what this might look like during a child's early development, consider the example presented next. The STRESSED categories that the child in this example experiences are identified. The child in this example begins in the quirky category, but as the school year goes on, ends up in the pathology category.

Anthony was the first child born into his loving family with parents who were excited to welcome him into the world. Around 24 months of age, Anthony quickly developed an affinity for words and essentially taught himself to read by watching children's educational television programs and looking at picture-word books (smart/social imbalance). Around his third birthday he began using apps on his parents' smart phones to teach himself phonics and learned how to sound out unfamiliar words, or he would simply ask his parents for clarification. He especially enjoyed using letter refrigerator magnets to spell words. His parents were excited. Here was their child with an innate desire for learning. Relatives or friends of the family who would visit the family home were often in awe of Anthony's ability to sustain an adult level of conversation, despite his young age.

Over the next year, however, reports began to come in from Anthony's preschool that he was often off by himself during free choice/play time while the other children played nearby or with each other. The other children were interested in each other, but Anthony was only interested in what *he* was doing, which involved looking at books (disinterest in imaginative play/depth seeking). Anthony became frustrated with the transitions in school and often protested against an activity if it interfered with his exploration of the classroom reading area (transitional stress). If the teacher could facilitate a transition to the group's circle time morning meeting, he often insisted on bringing a book with him.

Anthony would scream or cry for 20–30 minutes at the beginning of each school day when his mother dropped him off (emotional reactivity). This was going on months after the initial and developmentally appropriate separation anxiety of the peer group had subsided. Anthony began to experience stomach pains because he would not use the bathroom at school due to the loud flushing sound of the toilet (sensory sensitivity). His family struggled to get him dressed and out the door in the morning. On the evenings before school, Anthony began to have difficulty sleeping because he was now "afraid" to go to school (emotional reactivity).

His parents began to look for explanations. The school began keeping a behavior log each day that they sent home in Anthony's backpack for the parents to review. The school suggested using this to track behaviors and look for triggers because Anthony was now fleeing from the room or was hitting other kids (regulatory difficulties). Other parents were staying after school to complain to the teacher about Anthony's behaviors and express concerns about their child's safety.

His parents felt more and more dejected while reviewing the behavior sheets, which only described what Anthony was doing wrong. The feedback that was designed to better understand his challenges began to feel like daily punch in the gut. Evenings at home were spent recuperating and attempting to discuss appropriate behavior and occasionally even punish him for the behaviors he demonstrated while in school, even though it had no effect on his behaviors there. Anthony could always tell his parents what he did wrong and what he should have done instead, but the behaviors continued almost as if he forgot everything he had discussed at home upon arriving to school each morning (executive dysfunction).

Anthony's difficulties became so challenging to manage that the school discussed their concerns with his parents, who agreed to a school evaluation to determine if he would benefit from educational support services. Despite being an advanced reader, Anthony was classified as having a "developmental delay" (i.e., one of 14 categories of special education eligibility to be reviewed in Key 6) given that his behaviors and coping style were delayed relative to what was expected for a child his age. Indeed, his peers, who exhibited development consistent with the normative category, were asked to participate in the same routine and did so without much disruption. Specialists from the school district, including a speech pathologist, social worker, and occupational therapist were assigned to come into the classroom and propose some changes to the staff's current approach to Anthony while also providing him with some coping strategies. Anthony began to adjust, and then he began to thrive.

In this example, Anthony morphed from a quirky child who was an early reader to a child that was highly anxious and struggling to remain in the classroom and participate in the structure of the day. With the necessary and appropriate supports, his comfort and confidence increased and his educational support plan was discontinued when he entered the first grade.

Not all cases like this have such a happy ending, but the example illustrates how a combination of factors can come together and result in a quirky categorization that intensifies into the pathology category of development. Once Anthony's profile was properly addressed, his developmental profile fell within the normative category.

SUPPORT BRAIN FUNCTIONING

The brain is an unbelievably complex and amazing organ. I must admit some bias here because it's all I think about when I'm at work (and sometimes at home), and thus I am quite fond of all that the brain can do while also trying to determine what might be interfering with the brain doing what it should be able to do. Every time I think to myself that the brain is the most important organ in the human body, I chuckle because of course my brain would tell me to think that! Despite my bias and all of the amazing things that the human brain is able to accomplish, neuroscience has yet to fully understand everything there is to know about this delicate and complex organ. Although neuroscientists have mapped out brain structures and locations, we still seek explanations about how and why people experience developmental delays, often despite having intact structures. This chapter presents Key 3 to raising the quirky child: support brain functioning.

The brain is the command and control center for the human nervous system, which is a complicated and elaborate communication system. The brain interprets and processes sensory input received from throughout the body, regulates numerous bodily functions (e.g., balance, respiration), facilitates muscle tone and movement, creates feelings and thoughts, controls mood, and controls all behaviors.

The fundamental unit of the brain's circuits is a specialized cell called a *neuron*, which conveys information both electrically and chemically. The function of the neuron is to transmit information: It receives signals from other neurons and, in turn, transmits signals on to other, adjacent neurons.

When babies are born, they have almost all of the neurons they will ever have—more than 100 billion of them. Although research indicates some neurons are developed after birth and well into adulthood, the neurons present at birth are primarily what we have to work with as we develop into children, adolescents, and adults.

During fetal development, neurons are created and migrate to form the various parts of the brain. As neurons migrate, they also differentiate, so they begin to "specialize" in response to chemical signals (Perry, 2002). This process of development occurs sequentially from the bottom up, that is, from the more primitive sections of the brain (the brainstem and midbrain, which govern the bodily functions necessary for life, such as feeding and respiration) to the more sophisticated sections (the thinking and reasoning sections; Perry, 2000).

A typical neuron consists of a main cell body (which contains the nucleus and all of the cell's genetic information), a large number of branches or offshoots called *dendrites* (typically 10,000 or more per neuron), and one long fiber known as the *axon*. At the end of the axon are additional offshoots that form the connections with other neurons.

When signals are sent from one neuron to another, they must cross the gap at the point of connection between the two communicating neurons. This gap is called a *synapse*. At the synapse, the electrical signal within the neuron is converted to a chemical signal and sent across the synapse to the target (receiving) neuron. Synapses organize the brain by forming pathways that connect the parts of the brain governing everything we do from breathing and sleeping to thinking and feeling. This is the essence of postnatal brain development, because at birth, despite having more than 100 billion neurons, very few synapses have been formed. The synapses at birth are primarily those that govern our bodily functions such as heart rate, breathing, eating, and sleeping to facilitate survival.

The chemical signal sent across the synapse to the target neuron is conveyed via messenger molecules called *neurotransmitters* that attach to special structures called receptors on the outer surface of the target neuron. The attachment of the neurotransmitters to the receptors consequently triggers an electrical signal within the target neuron. Up to 100 different neurotransmitters have been identified in the human body (Snyder, 1986).

Neurotransmitters may have different effects depending on what receptor they activate. Some increase a receiving neuron's responsiveness to an incoming signal—an excitatory effect—whereas others may diminish the responsiveness—an inhibitory effect. The responsiveness of individual neurons affects the functioning of the brain's circuits, as well as how the brain functions as a whole (how it integrates, interprets, and responds to information), which in turn affects the function of the body and the behavior of the individual. The accurate functioning of all neurotransmitter systems is essential for normal brain activities.

The Role of Dopamine

Dopamine is one of the approximately 100 neurotransmitters in the brain, and it plays an important role in the control of movement, cognition, motivation, and reward (Di Chiara, 1995). High levels of free dopamine in the brain generally enhance mood and increase body movement (motor activity), but too much may produce nervousness, irritability, and aggressiveness. Too little dopamine in certain areas of the brain results in the tremors and paralysis that occurs with Parkinson's disease.

Various activities result in a release of dopamine throughout the brain. We know that certain medications, illicit drugs, and even activities such as playing video games affect the levels of dopamine in the brain. Natural activities such as eating and drinking activate an area of the brain known as the nucleus accumbens, resulting in increased communication among the brain's neurons. This internal communication leads to the release of dopamine. The released dopamine produces immediate, yet brief feelings of pleasure and elation. As dopamine levels subside, so do the feelings of pleasure. If the activity is repeated, dopamine is released again, and more feelings of pleasure and euphoria return. The dopamine release and the resulting pleasurable feelings positively reinforce such activities and motivate their repetition. The brain circuit that is considered essential to the neurological reinforcement system is called the limbic reward system (also called the dopamine reward system or the brain reward system).

Given that there are up to 100 other neurotransmitters in the human brain, we might wonder what is so special about dopamine. The answer is that dopamine is a key neurotransmitter when it comes to reward, motivation, reinforcement, interest, excitement, pleasure, and attention. By understanding the role of dopamine in your child's brain, you can begin to interact with and engage your child in a manner that takes advantage of this naturally occurring chemical messenger and results in outcomes that favor his or her overall development.

Neuroscience has demonstrated that an increased level of dopamine is released within your child's brain when he is rewarded. Tolerance for boredom is related to what is referred to as the dopamine agonist hypothesis, which states that people who are experiencing addiction-like withdrawals go through a process in which the brain demands more and more stimulation. The removal of what had previously stimulated that brain (e.g., a video game) only serves to cause a cyclical reaction of events that brings the person right back to it unless they can get away from it long enough to find stimulation, or dopamine release, by participating in other activities. To better understand the role of dopamine in the brain of a quirky child, we need to investigate how it's likely to be released in greater amounts so as to avoid the addiction-like withdrawal experience from occurring.

Depth Seekers versus Breadth Seekers

As described in the depth seeker/disinterest in imaginative play characteristic of the STRESSED model in Key 2, a child within the quirky category of development is likely to be a depth seeker. A review of depth seekers and breadth seekers is provided here to better understand the role of the brain in this way of relating to the world.

Children within the normative category of development are generally intellectually curious about their world and those around them. Indeed, the majority of children progress through their development as breadth seekers and continue this throughout their lives. I use the term *breadth seekers* to describe individuals who like to experiment with a variety or interests and explore topics of interest that are not always their first choice. They exercise their curiosity across a wide variety of interests and people with whom they choose to explore these interests. This is essential to healthy social, emotional, and academic development.

Breadth seekers protect themselves from anxiety and boredom with novel tasks because they see these tasks as an opportunity to explore and learn more about themselves, others, and the task at hand. As a result, breadth seekers give themselves more opportunities to release dopamine in their brains, which increases the likelihood that they will retain knowledge from and perhaps even return to that experience at a later time. Breadth seekers will certainly engage in many things that they determine to be too difficult or of little interest to them and they eventually move on. But the process of the approach and the experience itself are enough that they have released dopamine in the brain, learned something, and thus have developed. It may not be so much of a dopamine release that they must come back to it and do it again, as would be the case for a person abusing or addicted to a substance such as cocaine, but it was enough for information to be considered and even placed into long-term memory storage.

This is my neurological argument for why children whose development is deemed normative are able to learn so much about themselves and others simply by participating in a variety of experiences with a variety of people. The social skills literature supports this view. A review of the available research literature on social skills development states that children need exposure to as many different children in as many different contexts as possible (White et al., 2007).

Thus, when dopamine is released during an experience, we remember information from that experience. When dopamine is not released, either because it is not readily available in the brain or because the experience was not exciting enough to us to trigger that release, then all of the information is essentially gone. This process is central to learning in general. The brain takes in new information and if it determines that the information is relevant or important, it holds on to it. If not, the information is forgotten. I consider this to be the key neurological reason that teaching social skills to depth-seeking children is so challenging. The breadth-seeking experiences are simply not exciting or rewarding enough for depth seekers to want to retain the experience. As a result, unless we can develop an approach to social skills intervention that activates the dopamine reward system of the brain, we essentially start over each time we are faced with a new situation and we don't have enough previously learned information or context to be successful.

Children within the quirky category of development, as well as those with significant and persistent enough social challenges that may necessitate a clinical diagnosis (e.g., pathology category such as autism spectrum disorder), tend to be depth seekers. Depth seekers like to cut their losses and stick with what they know and do best. They protect themselves from discomfort by exploring a highly selective set of interests or perhaps just one interest at a time before moving on to another one, a process that could take years per interest, while they gather as much knowledge and experience as possible about the topic, activity, or interest. Depth seeking results in a significant social disconnect because essentially nothing else can compete and provide the same level of stimulation in the brain that results from a depth-seeking activity or interest.

This model has tremendous implications for teaching, learning, and treatment of individuals who are depth seekers by nature. How do we compete with the large amount of dopamine that is being released, resulting in a strong feeling of pleasure and excitement, and thus reinforcing participation by the depth seeker when they engage in in a narrow, often solitary area of interest? How can we engage depth seekers in a wider variety of activities when we now know these experiences will not result in the same levels of pleasure and excitement, but are so critical to the child's future success because they provide the necessary foundation for learning and development?

The key to answering these questions is twofold. First, you must encourage and teach desirable behaviors with excitement, novel methods, and rewards. Second, you must do everything in your control to keep the trend toward depth seeking from becoming a pattern. Depending on how much of a depth seeker your child has already become, this is a hard sell. The dopamine release that has been occurring in the brain each time the child is depth seeking has resulted in a heightened sense of well-being, excitement, pleasure, and even euphoria. By taking this away, the result (temporarily) is dysphoria or a feeling of emotional and mental discomfort that can result in discontentment, restlessness, dissatisfaction, malaise, moodiness, anxiety, or indifference.

Furthermore, prolonged participation in depth-seeking activities can affect a child's sleep, nutritional intake, and socialization. Each day becomes a cycle of achieving the euphoric rush of the dopamine release associated with the depth-seeking activity and a dysphoric crash when that activity must stop. Once the rush begins, behaviors such as socializing, eating, and sleeping serve only as distraction, allowing less time to spend on the depth–seeking activity. The ramifications of this cycle can be profound.

Controlling the Dopamine Release

As a parent, of course you want your child to feel good and experience joy and excitement. If the only way for the child to experience this feeling is from depth seeking, then you have a problem. You wrestle with the idea of limiting or even eliminating these activities or interests from your child's life. You ask yourself, how could I take away the one thing that my child looks forward to each day?

Let's use video games as a depth-seeking example. In our current society, video games are readily available in most households and are a multibillion-dollar industry for game developers. Your child loves video games and is now exhibiting an approach to them that is consistent with a pattern of depth seeking at the expense of most everything else. If you substituted video games in this example with an addictive drug like cocaine, your response to the depth-seeking behavior would obviously be very different. You would work to eliminate the child's access to the drug and you would provide treatment for the withdrawal symptoms while also exploring ways the child could experience life without the drug.

Debates about whether video game addiction is a possible form of addiction aside, what is occurring in your child's brain (as observed during brain imaging studies) when he plays video games is similar to what occurs when an addict uses cocaine. Namely, dopamine levels increase in the reward center of the brain and pleasurable feelings result. There may be few other times in the child's day in which that same feeling is achieved. That serves a major difference between breadth seekers and depth seekers.

Certainly, breadth seekers also participate in specific activities that result in an increased production of dopamine and thus increased feelings of pleasure. However, because they are able to experience pleasure in other activities (although perhaps not to the same degree or intensity), the need or craving to get to a depth-seeking activity is not as strong. This pattern occurs for many children during the school day. One class period may result in little release of dopamine because the topic is not interesting, or it's so challenging that there is little reward. However, the topic shifts to something of interest, or the child has an engaging and energetic teacher during the next class, and the child is suddenly reengaged because dopamine is released.

I surmise that depth seekers crave that dopamine release throughout the day but have significant challenges achieving it during everyday, routine activities. As a result, they become distracted either by counting down the hours or minutes until they can get do the preferred activity , or by fantasizing about the activity in their mind until they can actually get there. Children may also demonstrate their desire to obtain that pleasurable dopamine release by persistently asking when they can get to the depth–seeking activity or by attempting to get you to agree to give them more access to it once they have started (e.g., "just five more minutes!").

The depth seeker's peer group, comprised mostly of breadth seekers, is fond of variety while the depth seekers are fond of immersion. Thus, the breadth seekers are able to fluidly move in and out of a variety of social contexts involving a variety of people because they are open to many ideas and interests, and they have experienced enough variety to be able to blend in during different activities with different people. The depth seekers, on the other hand, are limited to a marginal number of people who may share the same interest because the topics are often specialized or because only breadth seekers are available for social interactions and breadth seekers want to move on and explore something else. Indeed, breadth seekers often find sustained focus on only one activity to be boring, while depth seekers find exploration of a variety of activities to be boring.

Often, the depth seekers choose an activity or interest that does not require social involvement, such as reading, video games, or topics of specific knowledge such as military weapons, the *Titanic*, or dragons. If there is a social opportunity to connect with others, depth seekers attempt to draw others into their expert topical world, one with which the breadth-seeking peer counterpart has minimal experience. The depth seeker finds it boring if not stressful to engage in a variety of activities with others, whereas the breadth seeker wants to move on to other things and becomes bored when hearing everything there is to know about one particular topic. These two approaches do not work well together, and the two groups eventually go their separate ways.

Quirky children are depth seekers by nature. Unless they come into contact with another person who shares a similar interest, there may be little more to build on in terms of connecting with that person, or they may not know how to connect. Thus, parents and other important adults in the child's life (teachers) must work to encourage exposure to a variety of situations and topics of interest while also working to keep the child from spending too much time going deeper with their particular interest(s).

Video games (often a case example in this book due to the quirky child's propensity toward this activity) provide a good example. By limiting access in terms of how much time is allowed to be spent on the game each day, you can help the child from seeking too much depth in this area. Depth seeking becomes harder to control if the child continues to talk about or fantasize about the games. The key to interrupting depth seeking is engagement and containment (discussed in the depth seeking characteristic of the STRESSED model in Key 2). It's not enough to offer the child an alternate activity suggestion or attempt to change the subject. You must get the child actively engaged in something else or they will often continue to seek depth in their interest mentally, even when it's not available physically. Some children I treat will explore YouTube for videos of other people playing their favorite video game when they are unable to play it themselves! You contain the depth seeking by only allowing access to the activity on specific days or by only allowing a predetermined amount of time to engage in the activity. Sometimes it has to go away altogether.

How Did I Get This Way?

As children develop more insight and self-awareness about how effectively they relate to and connect with the world and other around them (e.g., the "switch" phenomenon described in Key 4), they may begin to question why they think the way they do. The scientific information that researchers have gleaned thus far regarding brain development has helped define the roles that genetic as well as environmental factors serve in terms of how development is played out. Genetics play a role in terms of predisposing us to develop in certain ways. However, many of us are predisposed for things that never play out.

Some of us may be predisposed to various psychiatric conditions due to family history (bipolar disorder, schizophrenia, etc.), but we grow up in low-stress environments and thus these predispositions are never expressed. This is often referred to as the "diathesis-stress" model. This model asserts that if the combination of a genetic predisposition and environmental stress exceeds a certain threshold, a person will develop a disorder.

Research is also pointing to the fact that many capabilities, believed to be fixed at birth, are actually dependent on a sequence of experiences combined with heredity factors. Both heredity or genetics and environmental interactions are essential for optimum development of the human brain (Shonkoff and Phillips, 2000). Thus, some children who are born with tremendous potential but are not stimulated to express the potential never develop the skill.

For children with questions about their development or why they are having difficulty, if can be useful to have a name for what is making life more challenging. When I am working with a teen with a traumatic brain injury (TBI), for example, I can help him better understand the injury and its effect on his current level of functioning. In the case of TBI, there is a name for it and a reason life can be difficult to navigate at times. For a quirky child, however, there is not a label other than "quirky," which may not be useful to the child. I encourage you to focus on the specific characteristics of the STRESSED model that are part of the child's profile. These characteristics have names and can be defined and understood. Furthermore, knowing that other children experience similar challenges can provide a sense of relief. I find it to be equally comforting to both parents and children that there is an existing awareness and understanding of what you are experiencing difficulty with, and with that knowledge you can begin to develop an approach to help produce the desired outcomes.

Lack of Stimulation

For children to master social, emotional, and cognitive development, they need opportunities, encouragement, and acknowledgment from their caregivers. If the child is delayed in these areas (and intervention, guidance, and stimulation are lacking during the child's early years), the weak neuronal pathways that had been developed in expectation of these experiences may wither and die, and the children may not achieve the usual developmental milestones.

In the case of a child within the quirky category of development, the brain may not be interested in the interactions that stimulate growth and development in these areas, or it may not be tuning in enough during the critical windows of development. The child may miss the cues that the typically developing brain may instinctively pick up on. He or she may also be so absorbed in an activity of their interest (depth seeking) that it becomes difficult to engage them in the variety or interactions required to fully develop.

For instance, the child may be promoting his own visual–spatial reasoning by building with blocks, setting up elaborate train tracks, or working on puzzles for lengths of time, or he may develop incredible word knowledge and reading ability by focusing intensely on books. However, these are not social experiences because they do not require input or interaction with others and thus the neurons in the social and emotional regions of the brain begin to weaken and even die.

For example, babies need to experience face-to-face baby talk and hear countless repetitions of sounds to build the brain circuitry that will enable them to start making sounds and eventually say words. If babies' sounds are ignored repeatedly when they begin to babble at around six months, their language may be delayed. Babies who fail to babble or who do not orient toward their caregiver's speech and nonverbal interactions such as eye contact and touch often do not show the rapid growth that normally occurs in language development at 18–24 months (Scannapieco, 2008).

Thus, a failure to acquire language often has nothing to do with a parent not trying. It may be more related to the child not possessing the necessary attention or instinct to find these cues important, or the brain may not be ready to interpret these cues during the critical window of developmental opportunity. These types of delays may extend to all types of typical development for certain children who lack the developmental readiness to benefit, including their cognitive, behavioral, social, emotional, and physical development. If there is a noticeable developmental delay that your child is experiencing, then early intervention is essential. The early intervention approach is described next, along with information about the role of neural plasticity in the developing brain and how you can use this to your advantage to maximize the child's growth during early intervention.

Early Intervention

Intensive, early interventions are key to promoting development in children who are not progressing at the expected rate. Because brain functioning is altered by repeated experiences that strengthen and sensitize neuronal pathways, interventions cannot be limited to weekly therapy appointments. They must address the totality of the child's life, providing frequent, consistent replacement experiences so that the child's brain can begin to incorporate a new way of relating to the world. This is why I stress to families the importance of checking things out early if there is any doubt or concern. Consult with developmental specialists and follow your instincts if you believe something is wrong with your child's development.

Knowing when to seek an evaluation is tricky because the "wait and see" approach can often result in the child catching up. Perhaps a "better safe than sorry" approach is indicated for many children. Also, if the child is your first or only, and you do not have much background in child development, it can be challenging to know if there should be a cause for concern. Extended family members, spouses, or partners may try to ease your concerns and make you feel better by reassuring you, but if your instincts are telling you otherwise, remember: If there is a doubt, check it out.

Your pediatrician or local school district can help if you are interested in pursuing early intervention. A developmental specialist like myself can also be consulted to determine what, if any, early intervention services may be required. Early intervention services are generally available to children beginning at the age of 18 months and can continue until the child reaches preschool or even kindergarten age. If the child qualifies for educational support services through the school district because of developmental delays, the provision of intervention services can follow the child through school, if necessary. Early intervention is especially effective to address developmental delays because it provides intensive services during a stage of a child's development in which his brain is capable of making tremendous gains. The reason for this is neural plasticity, which is be explored next.

Neural Plasticity

Neuroscientists use the word *plasticity* to describe the brain's ability to change in response to repeated stimulation. The extent of a brain's plasticity is dependent on the stage of development and the particular brain system or region affected (Perry, 2006). For instance, the lower parts of the brain, which control basic functions such as breathing and heart rate, are less flexible than the higher functioning cortex, which controls thoughts and feelings.

Although cortex plasticity may lessen as a child gets older, some degree of plasticity remains. In fact, this brain plasticity is what allows us to keep learning into adulthood and throughout our lives.

However, the tremendous rate in which a person can acquire new information and adapt slows down beginning around the age of six years. This does not mean that you are out of luck if you want to effect change in a child older than six. Instead, you need to understand that the gains you are seeking will not come as fast and furious as those that can take place in the first six years of life.

The developing brain's ongoing adaptations are the result of both genetics and experience. Our brains prepare us to expect certain experiences by forming the pathways needed to respond to them. For example, brains that develop within the normative category are wired to respond to the sound of speech; when babies hear people speaking, the neural systems in their brains responsible for speech and language receive the necessary stimulation to organize and function (Perry, 2006). The more babies are exposed to people speaking, the stronger their related synapses become. Although we don't yet have quantifiable neurological research to support the following assumption, it would be probable that the more children of all ages are exposed to a variety of people in a variety of social situations, the stronger their related synapses become as well.

If the appropriate exposure does not happen, the pathways developed in anticipation may be discarded. This process is sometimes described with the adage "use it or lose it." Through these processes of creating, strengthening, and discarding synapses, our brains adapt to our unique environment. Some children, such as those with an autism spectrum disorder (ASD), may not tune into these experiences in the same way as their normative counterparts, and thus children with ASD miss out on the critical window of language development. This results in children who are either completely nonverbal or those who are slow to develop language and thus require explicit instruction in speech and language. It's almost as if we need to say to the child, "Hey, listen to me! Pay attention and remember these words! This is important!" The same principle applies to children who require social skills support. Merely exposing them to social contexts and a variety of people is not enough. We need to help them to tune into what is important and coach them in terms of how they respond to various social situations.

The ability to adapt to our environment is an indicator of normative development. Children growing up in cold climates, on rural farms, or in large sibling groups adjust, adapt, and learn how to function in those environments. Regardless of the general environment, all children need stimulation and nurturing for healthy development. If the child's brain is not instinctively adapting or reaching the expected and necessary developmental milestones, brain development may be impaired and explicit instruction and guidance in these areas are required. Thus, you should consult with your local school district or pediatrician if you have concerns that your child age 18 months to 6 years is not developing at the expected rate in a particular area or areas and determine whether early intervention services are indicated.

The Executive Functions

In the introduction and Keys 1 and 2 of this book you were introduced to the STRESSED model. The first E in STRESSED refers to executive dysfunction that many quirky children experience. The phrase "executive function" is used by psychologists and neuroscientists to describe a loosely defined collection of brain processes. Controlled by the frontal lobe of the brain, located behind the forehead, executive functions are responsible for planning, cognitive flexibility, abstract thinking, initiating appropriate actions (e.g., starting schoolwork without prompting), and inhibiting inappropriate actions (e.g., refraining from hitting someone when upset). Invariably, children with neurodevelopmental delays or diagnoses such as ASD, attention-deficit disorders, and learning disorders experience executive dysfunction. These difficulties are also commonly experienced by quirky children, which adds to the child's overall quirky manner of approaching situations.

The frontal lobe is the chief executive officer or CEO of the brain and is responsible for mediating ancillary brain processes. Think of a ball rolling into the street. First, the child's visual cortex sees the ball go into the street, and the motor cortex prepares the legs and arms to move so that she can run after it. The frontal lobe's job in this example is to tell the child, via a thought process, "Wait! Look both ways! There might be a car approaching!" When this system is underdeveloped, these messages may get through too late or not at all, and responses are based on impulses (the primitive brainstem) rather than thoughts (the sophisticated cerebral cortex).

The current neurological consensus is that the frontal lobe is not fully developed until a person reaches their mid-twenties, which may explain the impulsiveness and poor decision making often present among young adults. It may also explain some of the challenges associated with trying to teach various social skills, which are dependent on frontal lobe development, to children. The specific executive functions are described next.

Shift/Mental Flexibility

Although all executive functions are critical to success in life, the ability to shift or be mentally flexible is a notable challenge for a quirky child. Shift is the ability to adapt or change when faced with a setback, obstacle, mistake, or new routine, task, or information. Children who are considered to be mentally inflexible will almost always have difficulty with transitions. Consider the following strategies to help:

- Establish a daily sequence of routines (e.g., get up, brush teeth, get dressed). Document this in a user-friendly manner (picture chart, daily planner, electronic organizer). Experiment with different ways to complete routines (e.g., try driving the child to school using various routes).

- Allow a few minutes of down time or relaxation between the end of one activity and the beginning of the next. This can ease the stress of transitions.
- Note any changes in scheduled activities in a daily planner or address them with a preferred problem-solving strategy.
- Develop a response for when the routine changes. The question to be answered is, "How do I plan to deal with a change I was not expecting?"
- Pay attention to others and observe how they adjust to change.
- Establish an escape plan with the child, such as a code word or signal, that allows them to communicate stress associated with an unexpected change and get away for a set time period to regain composure, use relaxation strategies, and so on.

Emotional Control

This executive function refers to the ability to control emotional expression by thinking rationally about feelings. An example would include a second-grader who screams and cries for five minutes because he did not get to be line leader in class. Most children his age might be disappointed if they did not receive a classroom job they had hoped for, but they approach the situation rationally by remembering that there are lots of jobs to do, and there will be another chance to be line leader in the future. Consider the following strategies to help a child with emotional control difficulties:

- Check in with a peer or adult to determine if your response was appropriate to the situation. This might include an adult who is available to inform the child how his behavior affected others and how that will ultimately have an effect on him.
- Think logically about a problem as a means of keeping your emotional responses more controlled.
- Learn and practice healthy strategies (e.g., walk away, agree to disagree, take a break, deep breathing) for dealing with situations that result in strong emotions.

- Consider short breaks or calm-down periods to think about your response to an event or situation. This approach works best before frustration occurs.
- Demonstrate stress with the child by blowing into a balloon to represent their stress each time you fill the balloon with air. Note that there is only so much room for stress in the balloon before it will pop. Thus, you need to let some stress or air out occasionally before you can add more stress.

Inhibition/Impulse Control

Inhibition is the ability to stop one's own behavior at the appropriate time, including stopping actions and thoughts, or impulse control. The opposite of inhibition is impulsivity. If you have difficulty stopping yourself from acting on your impulses, then you are impulsive. Consider the following strategies to help a child with impulse control difficulties:

- Use "behavior-stopping" techniques. Strategies such as counting to five or ten before responding or reacting to a situation can provide the necessary time to think about your response and the possible consequences.
- Identify responses that may or may not be helpful as you approach a particular task or activity. For example, it may be helpful to ask for help when frustrated or confused, but it may not be helpful to crumble up your worksheet and throw it on the floor while feeling this way.
- Take periodic attention breaks (that preferably include some physical activity). Determine the most effective time intervals for taking breaks (e.g., every ten minutes).

Planning/Organization

Planning is the ability to think ahead and prepare for future tasks and their demands. Consider the following strategies to help a child with planning and organizational difficulties:

- Have the child verbalize a plan of approach at the outset for any given task, whether it is an everyday chore or routine or an academic activity. The plan can be broken down into a series of steps, arranged in sequential order, and written down as a list. The plan can be guided interactively with the parent or teacher to achieve sufficient detail and to increase the likelihood of success.
- The child might plan to approach a writing assignment by starting with the introductory paragraph, but could also plan to start with a detailed outline and write paragraphs for the body of the text first, then write an introduction.
- It may be helpful to begin learning strategic planning by practicing with only a few steps, then increasing the number of steps and the amount of detail gradually.
- Teach the child to develop time lines for completing assignments, particularly for long-term assignments such as projects or term papers. The child may need assistance in budgeting time to complete each step or phase in larger projects or tasks. Break long-term assignments into sequential steps, with timelines for completion of each step and check-ins with the teacher to ensure that he is keeping pace with expectations.

Initiation

Initiation is the ability to get started or begin a task or activity and generate ideas, responses, or problem-solving strategies without much prompting or assistance. Consider the following strategies to help:

- Create to-do lists or goals related to accomplishing activities. Topics or activities that a child finds particularly interesting will be easier to begin with.
- Provide incentive or rewards to help begin tasks. For example, if the child begins homework without reminders, then he can stay up an extra 15 minutes at night (or a later curfew for an older child).
- Be specific about how to begin working on a task and what steps

to follow to overcome difficulties getting started. Break things down into manageable steps.

- Peers can often help serve as models to help the child get started on tasks. Working in pairs or in small groups may be helpful, as peers will serve as external cues. Cooperative projects may be most useful because the interaction with peers will help keep the child on task.

- Some children benefit from having time limits set for completing a task. Use of a timer may facilitate increased initiation and speed of task completion.

Organization of Materials

Organization of materials requires being able to order and arrange materials necessary to successfully complete work and play and also to reduce clutter in one's work or living space. Consider the following strategies to help a child organize materials:

- Keeping an extra set of books at home can be a powerful tool for helping a child with organizational difficulties, as it alleviates a need to remember what books to bring back and forth and provides ready access to materials at school and home.

- Ask the child to restate the overall concept and structure of the information or task following a lecture. This will provide an opportunity to ensure accurate understanding as well as an opportunity to correct any misunderstanding.

- Students with difficulties keeping track of their assignments may benefit from learning to use an organizational system, schedule book, or daily planner. Use of such a system can help facilitate many aspects of organization and planning, but requires effort on the part of the student, parents, and teachers.

- Many teachers prefer different organizational and planning systems. This can be confusing for children with organizational difficulties. It is best for children to learn one system that is sufficiently flexible to be used for all or most subjects and can be maintained or expanded as needed over the years.

Self-Monitoring

This executive function is the ability to keep track of a personal behavior and the effect it has on others. This also involves recognizing and assessing your performance while completing a task or activity so that the approach can be modified accordingly. For example, task-monitoring involves recognizing when you make a mistake, such as a spelling error, and you correct it. A child who rushes his work and does not notice that he is writing an answer in the space on the page that is designated for another question is likely experiencing a task-monitoring difficulty. Consider the following strategies to help with self-monitoring:

- Encourage the child to identify his strengths and weaknesses for specific tasks or activities. Ask him to predict his performance (e.g., "How well do you think you will do?") and then complete an after-the-activity evaluation ("How well did you do?"). Create your own five-point rating scale of how well you did.
- Record an activity or situation to watch for specific behaviors as well as reactions to situations and interactions. For example, if a child hums during silent work in class, record this behavior and review the video or audio footage with the child to increase awareness and negotiate replacement behaviors that may serve the same purpose (e.g., hum inside head, chew gum, use stress ball).
- When completing a task, try to ask, "What works?" and "What doesn't work?" or "What am I doing?" as self-monitoring tools.

Working Memory

Working memory is your ability to hold information in your memory while completing a task. Remembering a phone number until you can write it down requires working memory. Children with working memory difficulties struggle to complete multistep directions such as, "Go to your room, get your coat, and put your dirty clothes in the laundry on your way downstairs" without reminders. Children with ADHD and other neurodevelopmental diagnoses often have working memory difficulties. The following strategies can help:

- Instruct the child on how to quietly talk herself through a task. Referred to as subvocalizing, sometimes processing information in a soft volume (speaking under your breath) can assist in concentration and ultimately in task completion.
- Create a written checklist of steps required to complete a task and approach larger tasks one step at a time.
- Ask others to repeat instructions or new information to assess understanding before getting started.
- Use mnemonic devices (memory strategies) or try to combine information into chunks (e.g., instead of remembering 2, 7, and 8 separately you can memorize the numbers as "278").
- Rehearse material to help store it in your memory. This involves practicing, via repetition, the information to be retained. The more that a person practices using new information and rereads it, the more likely it will be stored in memory.

Take-home points:

- Children within the quirky category of development tend to be depth seekers. Depth seekers protect themselves from discomfort by exploring a highly selective set of interests or perhaps just one interest at a time before moving on to another one, a process that could take years per interest, while they gather as much knowledge and experience as possible about the topic, activity, or interest. Depth seeking results in a significant social disconnect because essentially nothing else can compete and provide the same level of stimulation in the brain that results from a depth seeking activity or interest.
- How can we engage depth seekers in a wider variety of activities? The key to answering this question is twofold. First, you must encourage and teach desirable behaviors with excitement, novel methods, and rewards. Second, you must do everything in your

control to keep the trend toward depth seeking from becoming a pattern.

- Depth seekers crave a dopamine release throughout the day but have significant challenges achieving it during everyday, routine activities. As a result, they become distracted either by counting down the hours or minutes until they can get do the preferred activity, or by fantasizing about the activity in their mind until they can actually get there.

- Breadth seekers are fond of variety and expansion while the depth seekers are fond of similarity and immersion.

- The keys to interrupting depth seeking are engagement and containment. It's not enough to offer the child an alternate activity or attempt to change the subject. You must get the child actively engaged in something else or he will continue to seek depth in his interest mentally, even when it's not obtainable.

- Executive functions are responsible for planning, cognitive flexibility, abstract thinking, initiating appropriate actions (e.g., starting schoolwork without prompting), and inhibiting inappropriate actions (e.g., refraining from hitting someone when upset). Invariably, children with neurodevelopmental delays or diagnoses such as autism spectrum disorder, attention-deficit disorders, and learning disorders experience executive dysfunction. These difficulties are also commonly experienced by quirky children, which add to the child's overall quirky manner of approaching situations.

OPTIMIZE SOCIAL SKILLS

In Keys 1 and 2, you learned that social interaction challenges are the most notable characteristic of a quirky child's unique developmental profile. The child may be experiencing a host of social challenges, whether it be disinterest in others, a lack of understanding the nuances of social communication, hesitation or difficulty when initiating interactions with others, or other social communication challenges.

Teaching a child with social interaction challenges to navigate the social domain effectively can be like teaching a child a foreign language. Quirky children can struggle to read between the lines of social exchanges and miss or misinterpret the subtle nuances of social communication. Effective social communicators instinctively know how to make inferences and adjust their approach based on the information they are gathering during each interaction. A quirky child may not pick up on or accurately interpret these signals, and this creates stress in the communication.

Imagine you run into someone in the grocery store who you have not seen in a while, but you are in a hurry to finish your shopping because you need to get across town to an appointment. You quickly begin to mentally rehearse how you can exit this exchange gracefully so as to leave the person with a good impression of you and, more important, not hurt any feelings. In this type of scenario, you have a variety of possible responses. Which one do you choose?

A. Pretend you didn't see the person and quickly walk down another aisle.
B. Tell the person, "I'm really in a hurry. I can't talk."
C. Engage with the person and allow yourself to be a little late to your appointment.
D. Warmly greet the person. Have a brief exchange, and then apologize that you have an appointment and tell them that it was great to see them.

The obvious choice is D. Perhaps you would find an approach not offered as one of the above choices. The point here is that any time you are entering or engaging in a social exchange, you constantly mentally review options. You consider a multitude of variables, options, and approaches with a general focus on presenting yourself favorably and making the person feel good about the exchange. You accomplish this with a combination of the right things to say and friendly, approachable demeanor, tone of voice, and body language. If you think about social exchanges in this manner, you would be within the normative category of social development. A quirky child may be unaware of the importance of these approach variables and also lack the awareness and understanding of how to effectively be social in the first place.

Given the roles that social development and social skills play in a person's life success, and knowing that children in the quirky category experience most of their challenges in the social domain (even if other characteristics of the STRESSED model are also present), we need to understand how to promote social development in a child who has not yet achieved normative levels of social functioning. To begin to understand how to help, we need to understand the science behind social skills intervention. The next section explores some of the social skills research to date.

Social Skills Research

Researchers interested in social skills development have identified several elements that seem to contribute to a worthwhile social skills training program. White et al. (2007) reviewed 14 studies and identified a number of "promising strategies":

- Increase social motivation (foster self-awareness and self-esteem; develop a fun and nurturing environment).
- Increase social initiations (provide more opportunities for the child to interact with others through activities, play dates, etc., and facilitate initiations and subsequent interactions as indicated).
- Improve appropriate social responding (use modeling and role–playing to teach skills).
- Reduce interfering behaviors, such as tantrums or personal space invasion (teach emotional control and coping skills and make social rules concrete; e.g., "Stay one arm's length away from the other person" to maintain appropriate personal space).
- Promote skill generalization by orchestrating peer involvement, using multiple trainers, involving parents in training, providing opportunities to practice skills in naturalistic settings, and assigning "homework"—having children practice between sessions.

Another key issue for social skills development is the need for interventions to require interacting with as many different kinds of people as possible. One-on-one direct teaching or therapy is important to social skills training, but to truly practice a social skill requires creating a social situation or using a preexisting one. The more a person practices and the more people he practices with, the greater his likelihood of improving skills. This point applies to learning in general. The more that a person uses and practices newly acquired knowledge in a variety of contexts, the more likely this knowledge and skill set becomes ingrained.

Matson et al. (2007) completed an evaluation of numerous

social interventions (79 studies in all) for children with social difficulties, with participants who displayed a wide range of functioning in other areas of development (e.g., language, intelligence). Despite some wide-ranging individual differences, the authors suggested that effective intervention programs include the following:

- Parent training and education so that intervention can occur for younger children with the goal of improving skills and generalization to various settings.
- Treatment to address interfering behaviors or emotions, such as disruptive behaviors or anxiety.
- Early start (the younger the identification of difficulty the better).
- Social skills must be practiced and coached while in the school setting.
- Differentiation and accommodation of the child's needs within the approach (i.e., address basic versus more advanced skill development needs).
- Consistent use of some sort of quantifiable rating scale to assess if children are meeting their specific goals over time.

Thus, an effective social skills program should include a number of variables, many of which seem like common sense. It is easy to assume that the more you practice (with a variety of people and in a variety of locations), the more you promote success. There are other interventions identified in the research literature that many families cannot receive because they do not have an educational support plan in place for the child. These include providing social skills instruction, modeling, and coaching in the general education classroom or school setting, such as a lunchroom or playground. The age at which a family begins intervention is also important; as with most things in life, the sooner you begin, the better. Finally, addressing behavioral or emotional issues associated with social skills difficulties improves outcomes.

Understanding Social Development:
The Windows of Opportunity

Any parent attempting to remediate a quirky child's social difficulties needs to have a basic understanding of child development. Parents of a quirky child must be especially aware of what to expect and when to expect it. There is no need to memorize this information, but you should review it as questions arise. It may be useful to consider development from various specific theoretical perspectives, two of which are outlined in this chapter.

There is one important neurodevelopmental factor that I cannot stress enough: Each and every time you experience *sustained* gains in any area of social functioning, another stage of development will begin. You certainly deserve to pat yourself (and your child) on the back for making it this far; however, your child will wake up, seemingly the very next day, and begin to experience a new set of difficulties related to a new stage of development. It is critical that at these transitional times or stages, the child's presentation not be interpreted as regression. Indeed, new challenges are often misinterpreted as new delays. Certainly the gains that you and your child have made up to that point will contribute to the ease with which you approach and complete the next stage of development. View this change not as a setback but as a marker of success, and don't panic! Recharge your energy if needed, keep humor and affect high, and keep the creativity in your approach flowing.

Chronological versus Developmental Age

One of the most difficult aspects of social skills training, beyond how much persistence and effort is required, is the need to alter the approach according to how the child is progressing through each stage of development. Furthermore, it is essential to remember that a child's chronological age is based on birth date, but a child's developmental age is based on progress through anticipated stages of development, which will be covered in this chapter.

Although a child may be expected to progress through a certain stage when they are chronologically six years old, for example, they may need assistance with developmental tasks, such as social initiations (i.e., starting a conversation) that most four- or five-year-olds can complete.

If you prepare yourself and keep this book as a reference, you can alleviate a lot of stress associated with where you think your child should be developmentally compared to where they actually are. It is essential to work with a child at their current developmental stage to make social gains. I encourage you to use the information about each stage to determine whether your child is developmentally progressing through a stage, regardless of his or her chronological age. If a child gets pushed forward into the next stage of development without having achieved the necessary foundation in prior areas of development, further progress will not be supported, the child will become stuck, and you will become frustrated.

Preparing for Your Social Journey

Several guiding principles are of note before you begin this journey toward social skills development with your child. First, this is a marathon approach, not a sprint. Teaching a child to be social is a 24-hours-a-day, seven-days-a-week job because it requires you to manage everything else in the child's life, including his diet, sleep, behaviors, emotions, sensory profile, and more to achieve the best outcomes. If this sounds like a lot of work, it is. Second, this marathon will require you to remain connected to others and use social supports such as friends, family members, youth groups, religious organizations (if applicable), and so on as supports throughout your journey. It truly does take a village to raise a child. Finally, it has been estimated that it takes anywhere between six and ten years to become good at something. That's about 10,000 hours of practice. If you are leaving the playground feeling dejected after one hour of play because an unfortunate incident occurred, remember that you now are an hour closer to the amount needed, even though it didn't go the way you would have hoped. Keep calm, and carry on.

Theories on Social Development

As a psychologist who counsels children and their parents on social development, I use the work of two developmental theorists, Jean Piaget and Erik Erikson, to inform what to expect from children during each stage of development. Piaget focused on cognitive development, and Erikson was interested in how children socialize and how this affects their sense of self. Both theories are essential to understanding how to help a child make improvements in social functioning.

Probably the most cited theorist regarding the cognitive development of children is Piaget. As with all stage theories, Piaget's *Origins of Intelligence in Children* (1952) maintains that children go through specific stages as their intellect and ability matures. They start with rudimentary interactions, such as grabbing and mouthing objects, and eventually progress to highly sophisticated skills, such as scientific observation. A chief tenet of Piaget's theory is that these stages do not vary in order, cannot be skipped, and should not be rushed. The age range for each stage, however, can vary from child to child. Thus, you must determine if your child is developing according to the chronological age markers specific to each of Piaget's stages as covered next or whether there are developmental gaps that place the child in an earlier stage of development. Piaget's work in child cognition has revolutionized science's way of thinking not only about children but about learning, intelligence, and the nature of knowledge. His work serves as a powerful tool to help understand how to teach a child social skills based on his current stage of development.

Note: All of the stages described in the following sections indicate what you can expect to occur if the child is developing according to normative growth patterns. Thus, you should read through these stages with an eye toward what is normative or expected of a child based on chronological age and consider what your child is able to do relative to each of these stages to determine if and how much of a delay is occurring. Thus, you will begin to further understand your child's development relative to his chronological age.

Piaget's Cognitive Development

Sensorimotor Stage: Birth to Two Years

During this stage, the child learns about himself and his environment through motor and reflex actions. He interacts with his environment using physical means (sucking, pushing, grabbing, shaking). These interactions build his cognitive brain structures that aid him in understanding and interpreting the world and its functions as well as how to respond to the physical overtures of others. Object permanence is discovered (i.e., things still exist while out of view, such as putting a ball behind your back and the child crawls around you to get it). Teaching a child during this stage is best accomplished via the senses (vision, hearing, touch, smell, and taste). You can modify behavior by using the senses-based cue such as a frown (visual senses) or a stern voice (auditory senses) to alert a child to their inappropriate behavior (e.g., saying "no" in a firm voice while demonstrating a furrowed brow in response to a 12-month-old biting you on the shoulder during a hug). Furthermore, the way you initially begin to connect with your child, other than talking to him, is to physically play with and hold him.

What we know about play from the very earliest stages, whether we look at this in the animal behavior literature or among human beings, is that we play using our *bodies* initially (Brown and Vaughan, 2010). Through physical play, brain development is improved as well as our relationships with each other. We make our first contact and connection with one another via physical means. Infants grab at objects as they begin to develop. They roll on their stomachs. They hold their heads up. They crawl. They have innate reflexes that allow them to feel the sensation of falling, and they have depth perception. The Moro reflex, for example, is a hard-wired startle response that, from birth, results in the infant responding with a specific physical movement (arms flinging out sideways) and even crying in response to loud noises or the sensation of falling. They begin to explore the world for its sensory properties, often by touching objects and putting objects in their mouths.

Infants enjoy bodily physical play, which includes having their faces covered with a blanket and then pulled away in a game of peek-a-boo, being tossed in the air, or having "raspberries" blown on their bellies. These are examples of the ways we first connect and bond with one another from a social standpoint. Thus, our initial social overtures with children are physical and involve bodily interactions given that expressive language is not yet present. Although we talk to our children to model language, we also model interactions with each other through our play. Sharing is modeled when we roll a ball on the ground and then pass it to the child so that he can have a turn to roll it. We might also clap together when we sing or listen to songs or to cheer on a particular behavior. These are the early building blocks of two-way communication that set the stage for advanced social communication in later years.

Preoperational Stage: 18 months to 7 Years
This is the stage in which most children begin to talk. Some children who are at risk for experiencing social difficulties may experience language delays (e.g., autism spectrum disorder). The child who is beginning to speak during the early stages of this developmental window applies her new knowledge of language and uses symbols to represent objects or themes. Thus, pretend play emerges with toys used both for their intended purposes as well as their imaginary value (e.g., a toy car can "drive" on the road as expected but can also fly through the air like a spaceship as the child makes rocket noises). She is also better able to think about things and events that are not immediately present and make inferences (e.g., seeing a toy in a store and exclaiming, "I have that toy at home!").

Oriented to the present, the child in this developmental stage has difficulty conceptualizing time. Trying to discuss plans in advance such as what will happen next week, or understanding how much time remains following a five-minute transition warning, is nearly impossible for her. Her thinking is influenced by fantasy, the way she would like things to be, and she assumes that others see situations from her viewpoint. Thus, perspective taking is difficult.

The child is not yet able to form abstract conceptions and must have hands-on, in-the-moment experiences to form basic conclusions. Typically, experiences must occur repeatedly before the child grasps the cause-and-effect connection. This is why behavioral modification requires repeated efforts, and also why many parents believe that their behavioral attempts are not working when the child does not quickly respond. Repetition of all teaching moments is necessary for learning to occur, no matter how intelligent the child.

The more that you teach this child in the moment, the more ingrained the learning will be and the greater the likelihood that these lessons will generalize to other situations. Knowing that children during this stage of development learn best from hands-on experiences, exposing them to social interactions (as opposed to just talking about social skills) is necessary for improvement to occur. This is consistent with research findings that indicate practice and exposure in real-world scenarios lead to better gains in social skills (Bellini et al., 2007). Furthermore, exposing a child to novel situations with a variety of kids (with whom they can practice new and recently familiar skills) promotes generalization and dopamine release (recall Key 3). Thus, when your child begins to spontaneously share during a play date with a familiar friend, you want to praise and reward the sharing behavior so that they feel good about it and will want to continue to do it in the future. You could then take the child to a public location or play group and look for an opportunity to reward her again for using the sharing behavior in a new context that involves different, perhaps unfamiliar kids.

Concrete Stage: 7–12 Years

During this stage the child develops an ability to think abstractly and make rational judgments about concrete or observable phenomena, which in the past she needed to touch and manipulate physically to understand. When teaching this child, giving her the opportunity to ask questions and explain things to you allows her to mentally manipulate information. Thinking becomes less self-centered, and the child can now account for the perspectives of others. The child attempts more sophisticated explanations and predictions for events. She engages in abstract problem solving such as mental math, but still understands best when educational material refers to real-life situations. Children who are mentally inflexible and have difficulty with perspective taking begin to experience increased challenges while trying to interact with their peer group during this stage. Play remains an important aspect of interpersonal functioning and relationship development.

The Importance of Play

Perhaps the definition of the word *play* changes as we get older, but as we mature and develop, the amount of time in which we are engaged in play should remain consistent. As young adults grow older and become parents, hopefully they evolve into the type of parents who want to play with their children, which will encourage the cycle of play to continue through generations. Play is more than just fun, it promotes creativity, it encourages problem solving, and it improves social functioning and relationships.

If you are reading this book and you are the parent of an older child, the importance of play applies equally, although the content and the quality of pretend play is certainly dramatically different among younger children than it is among middle school children, teens, and young adults. At a very early age, we learn about our world and our social environment by watching/modeling our parents and through play. Regarding the latter, adults and children play differently in some ways, but similarly in many other ways.

Many of us are reminded how similar our approach to play can be when we have our own children. With young children, espe-cially boys, many parents engage in rough-and-tumble play. It comes naturally and easily to both parties, and this style of interac-tion is mutually enjoyed. Something begins to change in our body chemistry and emotional status as we play this way: We connect with the child on a deeper level than if we just sat and watched the child play. The noticeable effect of this approach is that you begin to feel young again yourself, you bond with your child, and your mood improves from the physical exercise involved in this type of play.

Try your best not to become too stressed or focused, initially, on the quality and content of the play with a child. Your primary objectives are:

1. Put in the time. Parents should play with kids whenever the opportunity presents itself (and work to create the opportunities if spontaneous play opportunities don't present themselves enough).
2. Have fun. If you are genuinely concerned that you don't play "well" as a parent, seek some guidance. Most play therapy train-ing in psychology is simply about following the child's lead, help-ing him build on his ideas and have more fun, and commenting on what he is doing rather than asking him questions.

You want to play with your child as much as possible because through play the child solves problems, generates ideas, and works through dilemmas in a safe and socially acceptable manner. It may be easier for some children to use action figures or puppets to resolve real-life conflicts than it would be for them to address the same issues during a face-to-face conversation.

Formal Operations: 12 Years–Adulthood
This is the Piaget's final stage of cognitive development and it extends throughout the adult years. The individual no longer requires physical/tangible objects to make rational judgments. At this point, he is capable of hypothetical and deductive reasoning. Thus, this individual can make a prediction to the question, "What

might happen if you whisper to someone while another child is watching you?" Teaching approaches for the adolescent may be wide ranging because the child is able to consider many possibilities from several perspectives. Thinking becomes more abstract, incorporating the principles of formal logic.

As children grow older, the focus tends to shift from what I do when I'm playing with others to whom I play with. Play becomes more focused on relationships as opposed to topics of interest. Play remains just as important at this stage. Indeed, teenagers are quite skilled at playing with ideas even though parents and teachers may not always agree with them or may not think they are realistic in their approach to solving the world's dilemmas. Nonetheless, it remains important that we allow adolescents this cognitive flexibility to be able to play with their ideas.

As adults we can model for kids that playing is fun and there is always time and opportunity for it. Adults can find ways to play in conjunction with family life whether it's taking on a hobby or coaching sports. Play changes in structure, shape, and form as we age, but the benefits remain. The amazing thing about play is that it is fun, kids love it, and playing as an adult not only helps improve your relationships with your kids but also lowers stress.

Recall from the STRESSED model of the quirky child presented in Key 2 that the D stands for depth seeker and disinterest in imaginative play. Thus, a quirky child may remain most comfortable with tangible approaches to play that provide immediate and easily interpretable feedback. He frequently finds comfort in the fact that if the Lego instruction manual is followed correctly, the result is that the pieces will be put together to look like the picture. If the quirky child pushes the correct buttons on the video game controller using the proper sequence and timing, points will be achieved and the game will advance. In the video game example, if the timing and sequence is off, the game resets and you can try again. If the timing and sequence is off in a social exchange, you may offend or alienate the person you were interacting with, and perhaps even incite a bullying incident, and there might not be a chance for a do-over.

Erickson's Psychosocial Development

Like Piaget, Erikson maintained that a child's development occurs in a predetermined order. Instead of focusing on cognitive development, however, he was interested in how children socialize and how this affects their sense of self. Erikson's life-stage virtues (1963) consist of eight distinct stages, each with two possible outcomes. For example, progression through one stage referred to as Industry versus Inferiority results in the person either becoming industrious (learning or developing new skills) or feeling inferior (feeling incompetent or like a failure). According to the theory, successful completion of each stage results in healthy personality development and successful interactions with others. Failure to successfully complete a stage can result in a reduced ability to complete further stages and a diminished sense of self, resulting in lowered self-esteem. These stages can be resolved successfully at a later time.

Infancy: Birth–18 Months

Erikson referred to infancy as the period of development in which the adult focus is on positive and loving care for the child, with a strong emphasis on visual contact and touch. This is consistent with Piaget's theory in this stage of development, which emphasizes the importance of physical contact with the child for bonding and learning to occur. For a child to pass successfully through this period of development, he or she must learn to trust that life is generally comfortable and have basic confidence in the future. If the child fails to experience trust and is constantly frustrated because his needs are not met, then he may end up with a deep-seated sense of worthlessness and a mistrust of the world in general. The questions to be addressed during this stage are whether the child determines that his caregivers are reliable and whether the caregivers consistently respond to his needs. Thus, social, intellectual, and emotional development begins at birth and is significantly dependent on how our caregivers respond to and interact with us.

An important disclaimer is in order here. Erikson did not include a caveat in his model of development for children with neurodevelopmental diagnoses or quirky children. Thus, he would not argue that a child's innate developmental challenges are the result of how a caregiver did or did not respond to the child. However, he would argue that once a developmental delay has been identified, parents do possess the ability to interact with a child in a strategic manner to promote developmental gains for the child.

Early Childhood: 18 Months–3 Years

During this stage children learn to master skills by themselves. They learn to walk, talk, and feed themselves during this time; They also learn fine motor development as well as toilet training. Children are working to build self-esteem and autonomy as they gain more control over their bodies and acquire new skills, such as learning right from wrong. One of the child's newfound skills during the "terrible two's" is the ability to use the powerful word *no*! It may be frustrating for parents, but it develops important skills of the will. It may sound strange, but there may be cause for concern if the child is not opinionated or if the child is overly agreeable or willing to just sit back and watch during this stage. Children with social difficulties tend to remain in the social periphery well beyond this stage as active observers or parallel players. Some children with social challenges appear completely disinterested in other children during the first three years of life.

Parallel play is still acceptable during this stage, although two- to three-year-olds begin to have brief and even sustained reciprocal interactions with each other. Not referencing other children at all is always cause for concern. Even children as young as ten months will crawl to another child at one point when they are in the same room. Children who enter a playroom at this stage and are only interested in the toys without at least some regard for the other kids may be at risk for experiencing social difficulties.

Also during this stage, kids can feel vulnerable from an emotional standpoint. If a child is embarrassed or shamed while learning important skills, as sometimes occurs in the process of toilet training, he can doubt his capabilities and suffer low self-esteem as a result. An example of this would be scolding a child for having an overnight wetting accident during toilet training or for missing the toilet during urination. Thus, parents and caregivers must provide an appropriate balance of patience and understanding while also encouraging the child to approach new aspects of their development, especially in the area of social interactions.

A child may present as shy or nervous and even avoidant due to feelings of vulnerability secondary to not knowing how to interact with others. Having a trusted and supportive adult in the environment to facilitate interactions can alleviate much of this stress and encourage future, repeated attempts.

The most significant relationships are with parents during this time. Although adults may begin referring to other children as "friends" of the child, the primary social interactions still come from caregivers. The child needs encouragement, opportunities, and support exploring the world, especially while he is pursuing social relationships.

Play Age: 3–5 Years

During this stage of development, children experience a desire to mimic or copy the adults around them and take initiative in creating play situations with adults as well as other children. Children make up stories with dolls, talk into toy phones, make engine noises with miniature cars or animal noises with animal toys, and experiment with "grown-up" life via role-playing and dress-up. Children also begin to use that wonderful question for exploring the world that often has adults stumped: "Why?" Formal early childhood education begins during this stage and uses play as the first approach to teaching children.

The most significant relationships during these years are with the immediate family. Thus, the primary play partners continue to be parents and siblings (and extended family, such as cousins), but families are strongly encouraged to expand the child's playmates to neighbors, children of friends, and peers the child meets during activities, play groups, or early education programs. This is consistent with the social skills research cited in the beginning of this chapter that recommends variety among the people with whom a child interacts.

The "danger" associated with interactions around highly familiar children such as siblings or relatives is that these interactions become comfortable and repetitive over time. Thus, children highly familiar with the child having social challenges may adapt in a manner that keeps the child comfortable and able to sustain interactions but will not promote the child's flexibility with future playmates.

Exposure to varied groups of children, situations, and environments is essential for overall social skills success. This recommendation is not easy to follow. Social accidents are inevitable. The child may experience stress and frustration, and other children may avoid the child due to his style of play, whether because he's quirky or perhaps aggressive. Other parents, who do not know your as child well as you do, may chastise you as a parent or your child because of his social challenges. Your child continues to look to you for reassurance, direction, and guidance during these formative stages of development. If you begin avoiding social exchanges due to your own or your child's discomfort, you child will happily develop a solitary style of depth-seeking interaction close to the family home that keeps all involved comfortable, but does nothing to promote further social development.

School Age: 6–12 Years

During this stage, that concludes with the so-called 'tween years, a child is capable of learning, creating, and accomplishing numerous new skills and knowledge, thus developing a sense of industry. The child begins to identify more strongly with the parent of the same sex and has increased interest in friends of the same sex, participation in clubs, adherence to the latest trends and styles, and hero/role-model figures (e.g., professional athletes, pop stars). Children during this stage have wonderful entrepreneurial ideas that with proper adult supervision and support not only boost self-esteem but can also generate some spending money.

As the child's world expands beyond the family home, their most significant relationships occur with the school, neighborhood, and community. Parents are no longer the ultimate authorities they once were, although they remain very important to the child's overall development. In conjunction with the expansion of how the child sees the world is an increased awareness of the realities of the world. Thus, children experience real-world fears and anxieties that can interfere with social success. For example, a child might not want to go to the school carnival because it is tornado season and there could be a storm.

As the child begins to focus on connecting with other kids from school or his neighborhood, having adults available to facilitate these relationships remains essential. Because parents cannot be available during the school day, and having parents around is becoming increasingly embarrassing for a child this age, school professionals should be responsible for facilitating social relationships during the school day. Furthermore, using peer mentors and supports can be a means of removing the immediate adult facilitator and instead allowing adults to supervise the peer supports from a distance. Peer mediators, coaches, mentors, and buddies (these are mostly interchangeable terms depending on the school's approach) are critical to the social progress of a child during this stage.

The focus on topics during conversation (recall topics, personal, private from Key 1) is in sharp contrast to the 'tween years of development that occur between 9 and 12 years of age in which children begin to depend on the peer group more for enjoyment and connection, and interests must be developmentally appropriate or the child risks being rejected. For example, continuing to love trains in the fifth grade may not provide the same strength of relationship glue to keep a child connected with his peers that it did in the second grade. Although there may still be a few peers just like the child who continue to enjoy playing with trains, the majority of the peer group is making a developmental shift into relationships based on feelings, opinions, and perspectives about various situations and on connecting with each other on a more personal level. Indeed, this is the stage in which functional play and topical discussion is replaced by companionship with others. Children connect more on a feeling level ("I feel happy when I spend time with him") rather than an interest level ("We like the same toys").

The "Switch" Phenomenon of the School-Age Years

This is a very social stage of development, and if unresolved feelings of inadequacy and inferiority are experienced, the child can experience serious problems with competence and self-esteem. A central component of this stage of development, which I have observed over the years of working with children in this stage, is what I refer to as the social "switch" that seems to turn on in a child's brain sometime between the 9th and 11th birthdays. This involves the child beginning to experience heightened insight and self-awareness, and it often results in the child having more interest in having friends and engaging social interactions, provided he is not too much of a depth seeker by this time.

If you are reading this book and your child is younger than nine years but exhibits depth-seeking behavior, now is the time to use my strategies of containment and engagement described in Key 2. If the child is older, it's not too late to use these strategies, but you should be prepared that containment may not be possible and you may need to consider elimination of the depth-seeking interest or activity, depending on how much of a challenge it presents to achieving the social goals.

For the child with social skills challenges, the experience of the switch (heightened insight and social awareness) can be a frustrating and stressful time of development given that the desire to connect is now active but the skills needed for successful connection remain dormant or do not yet exist. Thus, parents, teachers, caregivers, therapists (if applicable), and the child need to be prepared for this time with a variety of strategies so that self-esteem can improve and be maintained to encourage continued social exercise.

Adolescence: 12–18 Years

Prior to adolescence, according to Erikson, development mostly depends on what happens to the child. In other words, the child is a passive recipient of development. During adolescence (ages 12–18 years), development depends primarily on what the child (dare I say, young adult) *does*. This means that the child must now actively work on development and will make gains according to her self-directed efforts. Although adolescence is a stage in which children are transitioning between their childhood and adulthood, life is becoming more complex as children attempt to establish a sense of identity, experience difficulties with social interactions, and debate moral issues.

For successful development to occur, the individual must differentiate (become someone who is separate from the family of origin) and integrate as a "contributing" member of society. Unfortunately for those around the child, as the child navigates this stage she may go into a period of withdrawing from responsibilities, which Erikson called a "moratorium." This is one reason people often refer to teens as lazy or unmotivated. Furthermore, if an individual is unsuccessful in navigating this stage, she will experience role confusion and upheaval (i.e., emotional stress or difficulties due to not having a sense of where she "fits" or belongs in the world). The result can be frequent arguments between parent and teen about motivation, drive, goals, and direction of life.

A significant task for adolescents is to establish a philosophy of life. In this process, teens tend to think in terms of ideals (how it *should* be), which are conflict-free, rather than reality (how it *is*), which is not. The problem (and the reason adults and teens often argue during this period of development) is that teens do not have much experience and find it easy to substitute ideals for experience. Parents, on the other hand, have experience in the real world and thus tend to put the brakes on a teen's idealistic thinking, which upsets the teenage brain. Teens also develop strong devotion to friends and causes. Thus, it should come as no surprise that the teen's most significant relationships are with peer groups, who just so happen to use and value this idealistic style of thinking.

This is a period of development in which many teens take on volunteer work or begin to participate in organizations for the greater good. Erikson believed that if parents allow and encourage the child to explore, he will conclude his own identity. However, if the parents continually push him to conform to their adult views, the teen will face identity confusion, which results in not being able to make a successful transition into independent adulthood.

Young Adulthood: 18–35 Years

In the initial stage of adulthood, most of us seek companions and love. As we try to find mutually satisfying relationships (primarily through dating, marriage, and friendships), we generally also start a family. Today, the age at which one begins family planning is later than in the past, with many waiting to start families until their thirties. If negotiating this stage of development is successful, intimacy is experienced on a deep level.

If a person is unsuccessful at finding companionship and love, isolation and distance from others may occur. When it is difficult to create satisfying relationships, the world can shrink; in defense, Erikson believed that individuals may begin to convince themselves that they are superior to others. Some quirky young adults with social difficulties who have been unsuccessful in significantly improving their level of social functioning may cite their "superior intellect" or the "boring interests" of the rest of the world as an excuse for why they don't have friends ("Why would I want to sit down and listen to a bunch of imbeciles talk about sports?"). It is often more effective, in the interest of self-esteem preservation, to blame everyone else for one's difficulties than it is to acknowledge one's own limitations.

Now that you have a clearer understanding of the various stages of child and adolescent development, you are probably asking what can be done to promote social competence. In the sections that follow, various approaches to promotion of social development for a quirky child are explored.

Scaffold According to Development

It is essential to find the ideal time in development in which a child is ready to accomplish something and determine that they have an adequate foundational skill set to do it. The preceding sections were written to help you understand what occurs during various stages of a normative child's development so that you can plan your approach accordingly. If you are attempting to support a quirky child, you probably noticed his developmental progress was delayed using chronological age to compare the child to the normative group. Now that you have that information, you can begin to develop your approach based on your child's developmental needs and where you would like him to be relative to what is normative or developmentally expected for his chronological age. Teaching a child a new skill at the opportune time in his development sets him up for positive experiences and positive emotions. It is extremely rewarding when a child makes developmental gains, and he will get there if you keep supporting and encouraging.

Walking the Tightrope

Parents must remember to challenge the child throughout the process of development for the child to continue to make gains. Be aware of the tightrope walk that family members experience. Many families ask me, "How do I know when to push, and when I am pushing too hard?" I respond, "When you ask a child to execute a social skill or interaction and he successfully completes it without help, he could already do it. He has learned nothing. You need to raise the stakes. If he is completely overwhelmed, then we need to reevaluate the goals or address whatever may be getting in the way (e.g., anxiety or mood difficulties)." It is important for parents to gradually hand responsibility over to the child until the social skill can be executed independently, as explained next.

Scaffold According to the Child's Development

Once the switch turns on in the child's brain and he is intrinsically motivated to improve his social skills, the parent is now presented with a critical opportunity to engage with the child and begin to scaffold the child's social development. Prior to the switch phenomenon, parents are encouraged to provide supervised and facilitated opportunities for social growth and development such as play dates, social interactions at school, after-school clubs or activities, and participation in parent-child play groups.

The *scaffold* (Vygotsky, 1978) is the term used to describe the environment the parent or adult creates, the instructional support, and the processes and language used to help improve social skills with the child. Please be aware, however, that this approach can and should be used for younger children as well, even if the switch of self and other awareness has yet to turn on in their brains. The primary difference is that the younger child may not have as much motivation, typically due to little self-awareness of the importance or relevance of acquiring new social skills. However, this does not mean they cannot learn something new. Younger children will require more assistance on the ancillary issues that could interfere with their social skills progress, such as helping them with sensory sensitivity, emotional reactivity, transitional stress, depth seeking, and regulatory difficulties (all detailed in the STRESSED model in Keys 1 and 2).

There is a strong focus on early intervention for children with developmental delays (e.g., limited expressive language) because of the significant effect it can have in helping the child make necessary gains. In terms of addressing the social challenges characteristic of the STRESSED model, however, I consider the child's eighth year of life to be the beginning of the early intervention period for quirky children given that the child's motivation to make gains in this area does not truly begin until this time. It requires at least six years or approximately 10,000 hours to become good at something, so this intervention window provides ample time to work with the child and prepare them for the high school and college years and beyond.

Scaffolding should include what is near to the child's experience or what they can already do well, and build toward what is farther from their experience, or what they should or need to be able to do. A number of steps are involved to effectively scaffold a child. An adult cannot simply create a scaffold and expect the child to "climb" it on his own. Instead, the adult needs to build the scaffold with the child and ASSIST the child by following these steps (Stone, 1993):

- **Arouse** interest in a new social skill or build on a social skill that already captures a child's interest. Engage the child in such as way that you trigger a dopamine release in their brain (see Key 3).
- **Simplify** the skill, helping the child complete certain steps or aspects of the skill.
- **Scaffold** the skill so that it is within the child's ability, perhaps by being part of the interaction or arranging the environment so that success is possible.
- **Interpret** the interaction with the child so that the child's cognitive understand and reasoning will facilitate skill mastery.
- **Solve** problems and anticipate mistakes and guide the child to avoid or correct them.
- **Teach** enthusiasm by encouraging the desire to achieve and by keeping the child interested and keeping confidence high by praising success.

Quirky children can and will develop new social skills and abilities when adults lead them through interactions. Depending on various factors, an adult will lend various levels of assistance over different iterations of the interactions. The goal is to allow the child to do as much as she can on their own, and then intervene and provide assistance when it is needed so that the task can be successfully completed. This allows the child to learn the particular skill, build the necessary confidence, and further promote her overall social skills development.

An example of ASSIST in everyday practice would be helping a child with a jigsaw puzzle. To arouse the interest of the child, the puzzle might need to involve a theme or one of his favorite characters (e.g., Thomas the Tank Engine or Toy Story). You would then simplify and scaffold by arranging pieces by type, such as outer edge pieces, and then helping the child find pieces and even doing some hand-over-hand completion. Talking aloud while completing the puzzle helps interpret and improve the child's cognitive skills ("This piece has a blue edge so it probably fits in the top part of the puzzle where there is sky"). Solving would involve troubleshooting any difficulties along the way, such as moving on to find another piece after trying to force a different piece into a section that is clearly the wrong size. Finally, praising the child's persistence and success completing the puzzle helps build esteem and encourages future interest in the activity (i.e., teach).

Engagement

Although this book covers a wide variety of strategies to help promote development for a quirky child, engagement with others is arguably the most important approach and could fill up an entire book by itself. You will recall that engagement is one of the methods (presented in Key 2 and Key 3, along with containment) required to help a quirky child avoid too much depth seeking and make successful transitions.

Children who experience difficulties connecting with others socially often gravitate toward topics or areas of interest to occupy their time and bring them happiness. Whereas most children share similar interests in the same topics as quirky children at some point in time, they often outgrow them and move onto others. Furthermore, most children seek others out to increase their satisfaction in a particular activity.

Consider play among preschool children. Most children walk into a preschool classroom full of toys and begin to look for toys of interest (e.g., baby dolls). However, once they locate the toys they like, they begin reference the other children to see what they are interested in and perhaps discover a way to play with toys that they had not yet considered. Although parallel play is still developmentally expected during the preschool stage, children quickly learn that playing with their favorite toys is even more enjoyable when they do it with others.

When I evaluate a child's quality and quantity of engagement, I begin by asking the question, "What do you like to do for fun?" If the child is not old enough or able to answer this question, I ask the parents. This not only allows me to understand the child's interests, it also allows me to determine if there is a theme regarding their interests.

Let's assume I ask 11-year-old Jackson this question, and he replies, "I like the iPad, word searches, video games, reading, and building Legos." The theme here is that all of these activities can be completed without any interaction or engagement with other people. I then ask, "What do you like to do for fun with other people?" Jackson appears puzzled, seems to think for a moment, and then replies, "I don't know." He clearly has some challenges with engagement. What is often frustrating for children like him is that they may enjoy people and want to interact more, but because of challenges doing so successfully in the past, they may have developed more solitary interests to pass the time and find enjoyment.

Parents often ask how to help a child who tends to engage in more solitary interests. I have learned that telling a child to "stop" what they're doing or offering suggestions of alternative activities (e.g., "How about if we do [activity]?") is not effective. Parents can become quite frustrated when these attempts are unsuccessful.

Consider the example of video games. One of the reasons I theorize many children gravitate toward video games is that it is perhaps one of the only areas where they can successfully receive feedback and respond accordingly. The child interacts with the game and the game provides immediate feedback whether in the form of a score, points, or a product of whatever he did when he is interacting with the game.

If you are not able to pick up on the subtle feedback cues (e.g., sighs, eye rolling, look of boredom, bodily tension, attempts to interject) that are abundant during a social exchange, you may have to rely on the more obvious clues that do not occur as frequently (statements such as "You're weird!"). Thus, you may continue to pursue a social approach that causes stress or tension among those with whom you interact. A video game, however, provides immediate feedback. A video game character gets points for each object acquired and loses energy or levels of the life meter when injured. If only social interactions were this obvious.

To effectively promote engagement, we need to engage individuals more not only in conversation but in reciprocal interactions of play. To accomplish these goals, we need to find more opportunities for exposure and growth, away from depth-seeking activities.

Accomplishment Outside of the Home

Building on the "What do you like to do for fun?" question is the recommendation that with your assistance and encouragement (and possibly mandate), your child pursue at least one activity or interest outside of your home where they are accomplished. When I ask quirky kids, "What are you good at?" they typically respond with an activity they complete from within the family home (reading, video games, Legos). The problem with this is the solitary accomplishment. That's not to say that we should not be excited for a child who accomplishes something that is solitary in nature. However, when we are trying to improve a child's social development, the child needs to participate and become accomplished in at least one activity that involves other people.

Boy Scouts or Girls Scouts are possibilities. You might begin to pursue this recommendation by taking what a child loves to do for fun and look for opportunities to do this with others outside of the home. Thus, a child who loves to read might enroll in a book club that meets to read together or talk about books. A child who loves video games can join a gamers club or enroll in a class about video game design. George Lucas, the creator of *Star Wars* and an idol to many quirky children, said it best: "Everybody has talent, it's just a matter of moving around until you've discovered what it is."

Show-and-Tell

If you spend as much time around quirky children as I do, you begin to notice that they often engage with you in a show-and-tell style of interaction. In other words, they tend to feel most comfortable teaching others about their interests, perhaps with minimal consideration of whether their audience has any interest. This is why I compare it to show-and-tell, which is an incompatible social approach style that was introduced in Key 1.

Recall from your time in school when it was your turn to bring a show-and-tell item in to the class. This was your chance to have a captive audience with whom you could demonstrate your favorite toy or game while explaining everything you knew about it. Your classmates were then encouraged to ask questions about your item and you could elaborate further. Some of your classmates were genuinely interested in knowing more, while others tried to appease the teacher by participating and asking a question even if they really didn't care. This forced style of interaction is comforting to a child who wants others to know more about what he or she finds interesting.

Imagine if show-and-tell ended, however, and the student continued to tell you or even try to teach you about their interest. A quirky child may approach social interactions as if they are a show-and-tell activity. Due to perspective taking challenges, a quirky child thinks, "I like this, so therefore he must like this, or I want you to like this as much as me, so I'm going to do you a favor and tell you everything you need to know," even if the other child is not asking for more elaboration.

A quirky child can find so much joy in his areas of interest (e.g., depth seeking) that it is often challenging to understand that others may not share that level of joy. This show-and-tell approach lacks the reciprocity essential for social relationship formation. It feels forced and almost scripted. It's very much an approach of "I am going to tell you, and then I will wait for questions."

This is often why a quirky child will do quite well in a question-and-answer format of interaction. Adults and older children often engage younger children in this type of interaction, which is why a quirky child may relate better to adults and older children than to same-age children. Notice that show-and-tell does not allow other children in the class to share their interests. It's only about the child who is presenting. In this context, this style of interaction is expected and thus acceptable. In a social context, however, this way of relating to others is unexpected and the outcomes are not good. By encouraging breadth seeking (as described Key 2) and accomplishment outside the family home, we can begin to expand the child's ability to discuss and experience more variety so that he does not need to rely so much on the show-and-tell approach.

Embarrassment, Shame, and Humiliation = Social Avoidance

Although some quirky children inherently lack the social interest to actively pursue social interactions with others, many become conditioned to avoid social interactions due to the experience of strong, uncomfortable emotions. These emotions are typically not experienced until the child is self-aware enough (after the "switch" phenomenon previously described in this chapter has occurred) to determine how others are negatively responding to his overtures.

There are so many layers to a social exchange. People must approach each other, take turns, ask and answer questions, modulate voices, maintain personal space appropriate to the relation-ship, and read nonverbal cues. For children who are eager to connect, they may come on too strong by blurting out comments, beginning a conversation mid-thought as if the others had been experiencing the same thought all along (i.e., perspective-taking challenges), invading personal space, or speaking too fast or too loud.

Imagine a group of children are playing out a predetermined game on a snow pile at recess during the winter months, a popu-lar activity in my home state of Michigan. Another child wants to join the play, so he jumps onto the pile and interrupts what the others had been doing. He was eager and excited but did not suc-cessfully time the entry into play, did not assess whether inclusion was an option, and did not consider what the others were doing at that time and try to fit into the current theme. The other children begin to berate him for interrupting and spoiling the momentum of their play and yell at him to leave and then make comments to each other about how "weird" he behaved. The child may retali-ate and try to further agitate the others due to an "eye for an eye" mentality. After all, the other children had just "mistreated" him. In this example, the child did not consider why the other children reacted the way they did but only considered how "mean" they were while attempting to play with them.

When a child fails to recognize her own contribution to strong reactions from other children, she can begin to feel strong emotions of shame, embarrassment, and humiliation. Boys who struggle socially may react aggressively toward those who have "mistreated" them, whereas girls who struggle socially may take the approach of avoiding those children again in the future to spare themselves the experience of those intense and uncomfort-able emotions.

Children, and even their parents, often experience the cycle of embarrassment, shame, and humiliation leading to social avoid-ance. What begins with avoidance as a means of coping quickly becomes comfort. The child learns: If I avoid social situations, then I won't be uncomfortable. True, perhaps, but then he also won't be able to be social or interact with others, and thus his social development will stall.

Fear is something we all deal with—whether it is something as seemingly small as the fear of not being liked or as significant as fearing for our lives. Being able to cope and act in the face of fear builds character and strength. Shrinking or retreating in the face of fear leaves us immobilized and powerless. Courage is not a lack of fear; it is taking action in the face of and despite the fear. The goal is to experience the feeling of worry or fear and approach the situation anyway. This is the essence of exposure, or putting oneself in unfamiliar or uncomfortable situations, which is an essential element of social skills development.

In the long run, this confrontation of fear will lead to the most progress. We need to support children to "hang in there" and perhaps gradually reintegrate them into social contexts by choosing more structured activities or interactions first before sending them into the lunch room, onto the playgroup, or away to camp to figure it out and fend from themselves without support.

Fantasy World

When you either don't like the world you live in, you can't relate to the world, or you just need a break from reality, you may be inclined to seek out a fantasy world. This is common among individuals who gravitate toward sandbox or massive multiplayer games as well as cosplay (dressing up in a costume to resemble your favorite fantasy character), reading fantasy books, and reading or writing fan fiction (fictional stories that fans of a particular character or theme create using those characters or themes). In a true sandbox video game, the player has tools to modify the world according to his own plan and control things. Examples of sandbox games include Minecraft, Terraria, and the Sims.

Consider the psychology of these interests for a moment. Quirky children may need to escape into fantasy due to stress, sensory overload, and/or social challenges. Once they enter this virtual world, they are in control. Everything is on their terms and they can create and interact with what they want, when they want, and how they want. For children who struggle to navigate their everyday real-world environments, why not enter into a world where they control what happens? Children in the normative category of development, who successfully navigate the real world, may still enjoy playing these games or engaging in some fantasy, but they don't *need* it. Indeed, fantasy is necessary for pretend play, and it's interesting that many quirky children struggle during their younger years to engage in the amount of fantasy needed to successfully pretend play (see the D of the STRESSED model in Key 2) given how much fantasy they often seek out later in life. I think the primary reason for this is that the early childhood fantasy requires you to create or develop your own themes because you have not yet been exposed to ready-made fantasy themes. Once children discover that themes have already been established, such as fantasy books or certain video games, they now have an idea or theme that they enjoy and they can build on. Perhaps it's that little head start of establishing the theme for the play that they need to be able to take the play to another level rather than beginning with a blank slate.

The Generalization Error and the Social Code

Long before children are able to verbally express themselves, they are interacting with the world. During this time, adults rely on receptive language to guide the child's behavior, such as praise for accomplishing a new skill ("Good job, sweetie!") and redirection ("No, no . . .") for engaging in an unwanted behavior. Adults may physically reward or redirect, such as hugging a child for an accomplishment or removing a dangerous object from her hands. In general, children not only commit these experiences to memory, they also learn to generalize them to other situations.

When children are first learning language, they overgeneralize. For example, they learn the word *dog* to describe the family pet, but then they characterize all animals with four legs as "dog." They may also refer to every adult male or female they see as "Dada" or "Mama." Adults will redirect these errors such as "That's not a dog, it's a *cat*," or "That's not your Mama, *I'm* your Mama." It also helps that there are numerous picture books available that depict various objects, vehicles, and animals, and parents often review these books with the child as they learn to label each item accurately. If only social skills could be taught this way and this easily.

One problem is that social skills are generally not concrete and quantifiable. Consider a ball, which is often depicted in many early childhood picture books. It is usually a beach ball, but it can be a basketball or a rubber ball. These objects all share "round" or "circular" as a common property, but they differ in color, size, and texture. The child learns "ball" first, but then he begins to differentiate a basketball from a beach ball. When he sees an orange piece of fruit, he may initially refer to it as a ball because of its circular shape, but with correction he learns that it is, in fact, an orange. Thus, just because an object is round does not mean it's a ball. The child is able to visually represent this and commit it to memory so that every time he sees a round object, he also looks for other characteristics to determine whether it's a ball or something else. Social interactions are not so easy.

Consider laughter. How does one learn that someone laughing is not insulting them but humored by them? This requires context and perspective taking. If I have never experienced this situation before, or I have experienced it before but was not really paying attention to the experience, I don't have enough context to know why others are laughing. I have witnessed young children begin to cry when adults laugh following something cute they did. Just like if I had never been shown a picture of an orange piece of fruit, I may have to apply what I know: it's round and thus it must be a ball. Thus, if my exposure and knowledge base so far is that people laugh when they are making fun of you, then I assume this is the case anytime someone laughs in my presence.

Another social situation where this generalization error can play out is when others are roughhousing near a child who has not yet learned the social code, or what often referred as the hidden curriculum (the unwritten rules of social interaction that are not explicitly taught). A quirky child may interpret this behavior only on a superficial level, similar to all animals with four legs being labeled a dog. He sees two children pushing each other. The only experience he has to date is that when he pushed another person, he was in trouble. The child thinks that the two children are hurting each other, so he jumps in and tries to separate them, and even punches the one child perceived to be the aggressor. If he fails to consider the context and lacks the experience of variability, an error in judgment and responsiveness occurs. In this case, the child only saw that two children were grappling and roughhousing, which was an isolated portion of the interaction. The child failed to notice that the children were smiling and laughing. Furthermore, he failed to consider the context that the other boys were close friends and had not been arguing about anything prior to the roughhousing interaction.

Here's where it gets tricky. Seeing two boys roughhouse, even when you know they are close friends, does not mean that they are not mad at each other and really fighting. The social code requires that you consider all of the variables before deciding if and how to respond. Some quirky children interpret the social code accurately but struggle with impulse control. Thus, a quirky child may understand that these boys are just playing around, but then impulsively jump in and begin shoving them because their behavior excites him. Other children may understand that friends sometimes play rough with each other, but lack the necessary attention to look at the affect variable in terms of the emotions they are displaying (i.e., smiling versus grimacing) while engaged in this behavior. Others do not know how or when, or fail to search for this critical variable before deciding how or when to respond.

A quirky child may respond inappropriately due to one or all of these errors: attention, impulse, or inability/failure to detect the critical variable(s). Quirky children who struggle interpreting the social code need assistance gathering the necessary information to accurately identify what the interaction is, and then they need to learn how to respond based on what they have determined. The best way to do this is to get the child into various social situations with various people and begin to interpret and discuss the code with him before asking him to interpret it himself.

Social Group Techniques

Tell and Ask (TASK) Approach

I use the acronym TASK (T for tell, then ASK) to help students remember this drill. This is a great exercise in the early training stages of social interaction. It simply directs that for every piece of information you tell someone, you must then ask them for some information. Obviously, to do this consistently during social interactions would appear robotic and would not go over well, but in social training it needs to be exercised in a black-and-white manner before it can eventually be finessed into a fluent, gray area of thinking approach.

Turn Off Your Filter

This is an exercise I have developed over the years while facilitating social skills groups. When I introduce this technique, I tell the students that I am going to be turning off the filter in my brain for a portion of time. This means that I will speak any thought that I am having as the group members are interacting with each other. I like to warn the group that I will be doing this because, first, it protects them from the interpreting my comments as being mean or critical. I want them to be aware that I am doing this to help them. Second, it directs their attention onto what I may be thinking, which is important, especially for students who don't read nonverbal cues well. When they hear me saying something about them, they tune into me, and I immediately see their behaviors shift.

I also tell the group members that if they hear something good, they should keep up whatever they are doing. If they hear something that is not as positive, I want them to try doing something different and see if they can influence my comments toward more positive feedback. If they are stuck, I coach them toward an approach that they can try to get back on track. I don't want members apologizing if they receive some negative feedback, I simply want them to try something else until they begin hearing comments they prefer to hear. Simply put, I am thinking my thoughts aloud. I am not actually speaking directly to the group members; rather, I am offering a third-party perspective from what just so happens to be my brain.

An example of this would be the following:

JEREMY: I like to play Minecraft!

DONOVAN: I hate that game!

ME: Uh oh! Jeremy was trying to share an interest with Donovan, but it didn't work. Jeremy did a nice job, but Donovan may have hurt his feelings.

Note: If Donovan were to try and speak directly to me to justify or explain his comment, I would not engage in this conversation. Instead I would watch to see what Jeremy did next and comment on that.

In this example, I am essentially narrating or providing commentary as the story unfolds. This is similar to a technique used in Parent-Child Interaction Therapy (McNeil and Hembree-Kigin, 2010) where parents are trained to narrate their child's play as it happens, similar to the way a color commentator will provide commentary throughout a sports broadcast. What begins to happen with this approach is that the child, the subject of the commentary, begins to shift his behavior so that he receives the commentary he prefers.

Some children will be silly with this for a short time and

behave in a way to get the adult to narrate silliness, for example. This usually gets old quickly, but if you try this approach, be sure that you keep those comments as matter-of-fact and bland as possible so as not to further encourage the child to continue behaving that way, or you can simply choose to stop narrating when the child is behaving badly. If you need to stop the exercise to directly address any unwanted behavior, then do so.

What I enjoy most about this approach is that you are not only helping the child shift his behavior without any redirection or prompting, you are also demonstrating what others hear when the child lacks a filter. I think the power of this exercise lies in the fact that you are giving the members of the group insight into what others think when they behave in a certain manner. This allows the group members to begin to realize an important concept, which is that people are having thoughts about you when you are interacting with them and you can influence the thinking of others about you when you modify your approach to the interaction. Children in my social skills groups need to be told not to try this activity when they are with other children at school. This is only an exercise we use to practice our skills in the group.

At-Home Strategies

The preceding strategies are ideal for use in social groups with several children, although they can be modified and used in your home or during outings together as a family. The next sections explore additional home strategies to help promote social skills for children from two years old through adolescence.

The Five-and-Five Exercise

I developed this method primarily for parents of children ages eight and younger who are rigid or inflexible in their play. This inflexibility can be in the form of wanting to play in a prescribed fashion with select objects or toys of interest, such as only wanting to build with Legos. The five-and-five exercise, introduced in Key 2, is also well suited for children who try to control play, such as telling others what to do or what to say (during pretend play), or those children who become frustrated when play does not go their way. The five-and-five exercise is simplistic in design, but may be difficult in execution, at least initially. This is one of the main reasons that it is set at just five minutes.

To do this exercise, you tell the child you want to play with him a little differently than you usually do. For the first five minutes, the child is going to have to play a game that is *your* idea. When this time period is up, you will stop and the child is allowed to play something that is *his* idea. When you are first introducing this, it is helpful to use a timer. I suggest that the parent go first because it will be easier to stop the parent's play and move onto the child's than if the child had to stop and play something different during the first exchange. Even if you are having fun during the first five-minute segment, you must stop and move on to the child's portion of play. Some parents choose to keep the items they were using during their play out in the event that they are going to repeat the exercise and would like to return to their idea.

Some children like the first five-minute play led by the parent so much that they choose to keep it going for their five-minute portion. This is great! The parent may then choose to keep it going or they may change the theme or direction of the play during a future interval. The parent must decide how long to keep the exchange going. If things are going well, you are having fun, and you have the time, then by all means keep going. Over time, many parents choose to change the five-and-five exercise to ten–minute segments, and sometimes even longer. If you want to try this with an older child, you may want to begin with a longer interval such as 10 or 15 minutes.

For parents who may be less comfortable with play, the five–and-five exercise is less anxiety-producing and easier to execute than a recommendation to "just play more" with the child. The goal is that over time, the timer goes away and the child becomes more flexible in his play because he has been introduced to other ideas and variations of play that he learns to love. This exercise also helps the child adjust to transitional demands by asking that he stop and shift his play at each specified interval. This is an area that many quirky children have challenges with, so it helps to exercise transitions in a fun manner with the five-and-five exercise.

Boundaries

The issue of boundaries comes up in a variety of situations. Most often, this involves difficulty related to physical or personal space. Children with boundary difficulties are often referred to as "space invaders." For example, they may give hugs at inappropriate times or to inappropriate people, such as strangers or when meeting people for the first time.

When I'm discussing this issue with children I will (depending on their age) try to use visuals to help explain physical space. For younger kids, it is useful to illustrate a comfortable distance between two people by extending your arms straight out to measure one arm's length. This is accomplished by having the child extend her arms like a mummy or zombie to get a sense of how far she should be standing from others. You can also lay a hoop on the floor and stand in the middle. Tell the child to stand outside the hoop as you have a discussion with her. She can walk around the hoop but cannot go inside of it. After she practices this enough, she will begin to acquire a sense of the space and won't have to put her arms out while talking to others.

Another silly, yet effective approach (depending on the sense of humor of the child) is the "taste of your own medicine" or "stick to you like glue" exercise. This involves staying as physically close to the child as possible, in a playful way, as she walks around the room to give her a sense of how this feels when she invades the personal space of someone else.

Older kids can understand that the average comfortable distance between two people in American culture is approximately three feet. Another way to visually demonstrate distance and personal space is to get a roll of masking tape and make two boxes on the floor or create two X's (placed about two to three feet apart) as a demonstration where each person should stand during a conversation. Once the child seems to understand the physical boundaries, you can remove the X's and continue to practice without the visual aid.

Read, Watch, and Discuss

The read-watch-discuss approach helps promote a child's social skills development. Children can read fairy tales and short stories, for example, and look for details that illustrate how the characters feel. Children can also compare and contrast characters in different stories. For example, how is the wicked Mother Gothel in *Tangled* different from the wicked stepmother in *Cinderella?* Why is Shrek so upset that others are in his swamp? Why doesn't Anna want Kristoff to tell Olaf that he will melt in the summer? Children can search for examples that demonstrate the characters' various personalities. When working with fiction texts, encourage the child to draw on prior knowledge and his own experiences to make connections with the characters as they read. As kids get older and their interests change, so does the content of what they want to read. The activity, however, remains the same regarding the discussion of themes, feelings of the characters, and so on. Thus, instead of discussing Disney characters, you begin to discuss *Hunger Games*, Harry Potter, Percy Jackson, or *Twilight.*

I also recommend that a parent watch movies or TV shows with the child or as a family activity. Try muting the television for selected portions of the show or movie, and try to guess what the characters are thinking and feeling based on their mannerisms and gestures. Mute the commercials and use that time to discuss what just happened. If you limit the child's screen time as a family rule, then you might agree that he can watch an extra show as long and he watches and discusses it with you. Whether it is with books or watching certain TV shows, try to spend at least some time documenting the thoughts and feelings of the characters.

Play Dates

Perhaps the most challenging aspect of this exercise to improve social interaction is finding the necessary play partner. The decision of whom to have a child interact with plays a role in the overall social development of the child. The choice of play partner and the context of the play are equally important to help a child with social skills difficulties. For example, having the child play primarily with siblings or other relatives (e.g., cousins) certainly helps establish foundational skills at a younger age (the toddler years), but ultimately familiarity reigns supreme and the quality of these interactions is not as dynamic as it would be with non–family members or unfamiliar individuals, such as an unrelated play partner. Thus, parents must give thoughtful consideration to whom the child will play with prior to the point at which the child can make those decisions for himself.

It is still common and appropriate to help select playmates prior to the child's entry into first grade. If you are like most parents, you will want to take advantage of this rare time in a child's development in which you have almost exclusive say over whom they interact with. It is only be a matter of time (hint: teen years) before this selection of peers becomes a point of contention.

I frequently give parents a play date assignment to help promote their child's social skills. The goal is to schedule play dates with non–family members as often as possible, in one-to-one ratios and in groups (ranging from small to larger, structured play groups). Parents often struggle with this assignment and are plagued with questions: How old should the play partner be? What should the skill set of the play partner be? How long should the play visit last? What should occur during the play visit? Where do I find a play partner for the child?

Regarding the age of the play partner, older children are more proficient play partners, but the general guideline is to select a play partner who is approximately the same age or in the same grade as the child. In terms of skill sets, the partner must be able to model appropriate social interactions and be patient with the child who requires some assistance, while not doing all of the work. This is where parents and other adults serve a crucial role as they mediate these interactions, helping the children strike a balance between giving and receiving help, for example.

When training to run in a race, coaches often recommend finding a running partner who is slightly faster so that you will work harder to keep up. The same principle applies to children with social skills difficulties. The child should always have appropriate peer models so that social skills can be modeled upward. Kids will work harder to match the peer model's skills and keep up. We just don't want them to have to work so hard that they give up. Furthermore, the greater the variety of peers that the child is exposed to, in as many situations as possible, the better the outcomes.

Play visits should alternate between the homes of the children involved and neutral locations, such as playgrounds, libraries, or other kid-friendly locales. Neutral locations allow more spontaneous and flexible interactions to occur such as another, perhaps unfamiliar child joining play. The length of the visit is often dependent on a variety of factors, including the activity and the age/attentional capacity of the kids. A good starting point is to keep it time-limited to about an hour, allowing flexibility to play longer if things go well. My recommendation is to quit while you are ahead and still having fun and end the play visit on a positive note. No parent wants to end a play date with a tantrum because the children are tired or frustrated. Ending the visit while everyone is happy helps promote excitement and interest in a future play meeting.

What should occur during play visits is also dependent on the child's developmental level, age, abilities, and interests. A general principle is to begin with structured activities (e.g., board games, physical play such as hide and seek, a snack) and actively supervise and mediate the play. As kids demonstrate fluency in interactions, the adult involvement can decrease as the kids' involvement increases. Remember that social skills do not improve if the kids watch a TV show together or do any other activity that is not interactive. Furthermore, allowing one child to play with Legos in one room while the other plays with action figures in another room is not interactive either. Although the entire play session does not have to be interactive, and breaks are okay, it is important to encourage as much interaction as possible, especially during time-limited play opportunities. Breaks are nice because they provide unstructured opportunities for interaction and can be used to help facilitate small talk and conversations and assess for conversational competence.

The answer to the question of where to find a play partner for your child can be tricky. Depending on where you live, you may have more options. Families that live in rural areas, for example, may be limited in terms of their built-in neighborhood network of kids. The more opportunities you have to be out and around other people, the greater your chances of meeting various children who could be possible play partners, as recommended by the research regarding social skills improvement (White et al., 2007). Good places to find other parents and kids include the library (they usually offer a story time activity for kids), reading time at local bookstores, community classes, dance, karate, religious services, youth group, public or club swimming pools, local parks, and organizations (e.g., Boy Scouts).

Many play dates develop out of play groups with several parents who connect. Creativity and an open mind are essential here. If one play partner does not work out, keep trying. As you work through the strategies outlined in this book, you increase the chances of repeat play dates. If you find yourself truly at a loss for where to find play partners, consider looking for postings on the Internet such as Meetup.com or even create your own Yahoo! Group or similar online group to begin establishing play dates. These sites allow people to meet in public locations as a group so that all parties involved are safe and comfortable. Individual play dates can be established based on the participants' levels of comfort with each other. If your child is in school, you may want to ask the teacher what children might be a good play partner for your child and try to connect with that child's parents.

Take-home points:

- One of the most difficult aspects of social skills training, beyond how much persistence and effort is required, is the need to alter the approach according to how the child is progressing through each stage of development. Furthermore, it is essential to remember that a child's chronological age is based on birth date, but a child's developmental age is based on progress through anticipated stages of development, which were covered in this chapter. Although a child may be expected to progress through a certain stage when they are chronologically six years old, for example, they may need assistance with developmental tasks, such as social initiations (i.e., starting a conversation) that most four-or five-year-olds can complete.
- Teaching a child to be social is a 24-hours-a-day, seven-days-a-week job because it requires you to manage everything else in the child's life, including his diet, sleep, behaviors, emotions, sensory profile, and more to achieve the best outcomes. If this sounds like a lot of work, it is.
- A social "switch" seems to turn on in a child's brain sometime between the 9th and 11th birthdays. This involves the child beginning to experience heightened insight and self-awareness, and it often results in the child having more interest in developing friendships and engaging in social interactions, provided he is not too much of a depth seeker by this time. The switch phenomenon can be a frustrating and stressful time of development given that the desire to connect is now active but the skills needed for successful connection remain dormant or do not yet exist.
- Quirky children can and will develop new social skills and abilities when adults lead them through interactions. Depending on various factors, an adult will lend various levels of assistance during various iterations of the interactions. The goal is to allow the child to do as much as she can on her own, and then intervene and provide assistance when it is needed so that the task can be successfully completed. This allows the child to learn the par-

ticular skill, build the necessary confidence, and promote her overall social skills competence.

- To effectively promote engagement, we need to engage individuals more not only in conversation but also in reciprocal interactions of play. To accomplish these goals, we need to find more opportunities for exposure and growth, away from depth-seeking activities.

- A quirky child will do quite well in a question-and-answer format of interaction. By encouraging breadth seeking and accomplishment outside the family home, we can begin to expand the child's ability to discuss and experience more variety so that he does not need to rely so much on the show-and-tell approach to social interaction.

- Quirky children who struggle interpreting the social code need assistance gathering the necessary information to accurately identify what the interaction is, and then they need to learn how to respond based on what they have determined. The best way to do this is to expose the child to various social situations with various people and begin to interpret and discuss the social code with him before asking them to interpret it himself.

KEY 5

RESPOND EFFECTIVELY

Parents who are raising a child in the quirky category of development share something other than the love they feel toward their children. The common thread is that they seek to understand how the child thinks and how to successfully parent him or her based on that information. There may be conflict between parents (regardless of whether they are unmarried, married, separated, or divorced) regarding the approach that will yield the best results. Generational input such as "It worked in my day!" or "All my parents had to do was give me 'the look' and I behaved appropriately!" may also play a role in a parent's approach prior to consultation with a behavioral specialist. I often hear parents insist, "No matter how many things we take away from him, it doesn't seem to matter." Parents need to fully understand what is driving a child's behavior to respond appropriately and help the child achieve success in the future. The fifth key to raising the quirky child is to understand the ABCs of behavior and respond effectively.

Developmental and behavioral specialists like me analyze children's behaviors according to the A-B-C model, which stands for antecedent-behavior-consequence. There are whole volumes and even certifications dedicated to this model; a brief overview is presented here. First, the antecedent is essentially the environment, situation, or event that occurred before a behavior was displayed. Behavioral specialists are often puzzled when hearing from an adult who asserts, "Jonny hit the other kid, and it was totally unprovoked." Indeed, every behavior has an antecedent, even if the antecedent is that Jonny's brain synapses misfired and an erratic neurochemical input resulted in an impulsive motor response in the form of hitting.

The child's environment is often the antecedent. To better understand the impact of environment on certain behaviors, consider this hypothetical exercise: Enroll in an advanced calculus class before you learn how to add and subtract and see what happens to your behavior, your mood, and your thought process. You may begin wiggling in your seat, doodling in your notebook, getting up to leave, chewing on your pencil, and feeling frustrated. Your behavior is a by-product of your environment (this class is unfamiliar and others seem to have more of a foundation), your past experiences (you have not yet acquired the foundational knowledge to support advanced calculus), and what you are being asked to learn (the content of the class is too difficult based on what you currently know). So while your behavior appears distractible and restless, it is a by-product of the situation.

Thus, if a child can sit through most other classes or activities without any difficulty, then environmental changes can be made to assist with the behaviors in question. In the aforementioned example, this would involve either withdrawing from the advanced calculus class and enrolling in an entry-level math course to establish a foundation in the subject, or hiring a tutor to acquire more knowledge about the material. By doing so, the problematic behaviors should decrease or even go away completely.

Another antecedent to a child's behavior can be that he has never learned how to handle a particular situation or how he should respond. Young children who have not had many opportunities to be around other kids may behave in a manner at home that, although inappropriate, may not concern the parents. Especially in the case of boys—parents, extended family, and even pediatricians in some cases look at some behaviors as "Boys will be boys," "He will grow out of it," or "Give it some time and he'll figure out what to do." If these assertions turn out to be accurate, then the child was only exhibiting a transitional behavior that would not be demonstrated after a certain period of time.

A general rule of thumb for children under nine years of age is to monitor a questionable behavior for two to three months before deciding to complete a behavioral analysis or seek out a developmental evaluation. This is due in part to the transient nature of many behaviors in children in this age range. Consider the example of tic behaviors (e.g., throat clearing, snorting, blinking). Although not all children exhibit tic-like behaviors, they are quite common in children ages five to nine years. Most developmental specialists will advise adults to ignore the behaviors (i.e., do not tell the child to "stop" or otherwise raise awareness when a child demonstrates the behavior), but instead monitor when the symptoms appear (i.e., time of day and situation) and how intense they are.

Common tic behaviors are eye blinking, nasal snorting, or throat clearing. These can intensify during times of stress or anxiety, and they also have a tendency to flare up while watching television or interacting with other screens, such as a computer or video game system. If the tics were triggered or intensified while watching a screen, exposure to the screen would be the antecedent, and the tic would be the behavior. If a parent told a child to stop doing the behavior, this would be the consequence. Once you can accurately identify what is motivating a behavior, you can establish a plan to modify it.

Thus, if the tic (behavior) was only observed while the child was watching television (antecedent), we would reduce or eliminate exposure to the television (change the antecedent) and the tic would stop (consequence), resulting in no demonstration of the original tic behavior.

The preceding example not only demonstrates how behaviors can be fully understood and addressed, it also demonstrates that the term *consequence* does not mean "punishment." In the A-B-C model, consequence simply means what occurs after the behavior is demonstrated or the antecedent is changed.

When working to address or correct a child's behavior, it is important that the A-B-C model be fully understood to modify any behaviors that are causing concerns as well as to help encourage appropriate or prosocial behaviors. Although many children will effectively and quickly adjust their behaviors secondary to consequences being administered (such as removal of privileges), a quirky child is less likely to benefit from a consequence-driven approach. This is a key point that will save parents a lot of stress once they understand this about their child. The reasons consequences are not generally effective when parenting a quirky child are explained in the next section.

The Problems with Consequences

Parents have often remarked to me that no matter how much they punish their quirky child, he does not seem to behave any differently. The child does not seem to learn from his mistakes and instead continues to repeat the same inappropriate or problematic behaviors.

The key to parenting a quirky child is to focus your energy and approach on the antecedent(s) to the behaviors you wish to address or correct. Consider the advanced calculus example earlier in the chapter. Knowing what you know about that person's background in math, would that person perform better in class and receive a higher grade if you focused on the consequence of the A-B-C model and punished him each time he failed an exam? Of course not. The same problem applies to a child in the quirky category of development. The main reason quirky children experience the challenges associated with the various characteristics of the STRESSED model is that they never learned the skill or never had the ability in the first place.

Consider a fourth-grade child who is quite skilled in geography but rushes through his geography tests in school so that he can get out a book that he likes and read for the remainder of the testing time. He is failing these tests, so his teacher decides to keep him in from recess so that he will learn a lesson. He is happy because he can stay in, avoid stressful social interactions (and thus not develop more coping via exposure), and read some more!

His test grades continue to remain at the same level despite the consequence. If this were a child in the normative category of development, this type of consequence would probably work well because he would miss the opportunity to be with his friends and thus he would change his approach to test-taking.

If the teacher would have simply eliminated the possibility of getting out a book to read once he handed in his test, the child would learn that there is no incentive to rushing through the test and begin to use a more controlled and thoughtful approach to responding to the test. Another option would be to expect that the child, who was a strong geography student already, achieve at least 85 percent correct on the test, and then he would be allowed to read for the duration of the test period. The teacher would make a special arrangement to grade the child's test immediately and give it back to him, without indication of what he needed to correct if it was less than 85 percent right. This approach would also promote self-monitoring or checking for mistakes and revising answers.

When you use a consequence-driven approach with an individual who lacks the necessary development to be successful in the first place, you add insult to injury. Thus the antecedent approach to the social challenges characteristic of the STRESSED model, for example, is to provide guidance and promote the child's social competence. For a child who has a disinterest in imaginative play, containing his interests in depth seeking activities like video games does not result in the child immediately wanting to explore a variety of other activities. Instead, you must engage him in various activities that might appeal to him, albeit not as much as videos games might, to increase his comfort levels and the likelihood that he will want to return to those activities in the future.

It is a key parenting strategy and true that you will have increased success while parenting a quirky child if you address the antecedent or the precursor to the actual behavior in question. You must teach the child to do what it is you want them to do rather than punish them for not being able to do so independently. That being said, you still need to administer punishment or consequences when aggressive, dangerous, or damaging behaviors such as destruction of property occur. Indeed, you would not look the other way if a child hit someone or damaged some personal property. However, in anticipation of a future occurrence such as this, we can learn from that experience and work to determine what the trigger or antecedent for the behavior was. Once we have identified the antecedent, then we can work to set the stage for the child's future success by potentially preventing problematic behaviors from reoccurring.

Let's use the example of the child who frequently leaves class to use the bathroom during language arts class. The teacher becomes upset because the child is "messing around" in the bathroom and not returning to class. The behavior in this example is the student leaving the room and spending extended periods of time in the bathroom. The consequence, or what follows the behavior, is that the teacher becomes upset and eventually begins to limit the amount of bathroom breaks the student is allowed during the day. However, we are missing the critical element of the model, which is the antecedent.

To accurately identify the antecedent, we must ask, "Why is this child leaving the classroom to use the bathroom?" In an effort to understand why, we ask the teacher to complete a behavioral log that documents the time of day the child exits the room to use the restroom and how long she spends there. Once we have that data, we realize that the child is exiting the classroom every day during language arts class (a challenging subject for her), as well as toward the end of the day (when the classroom environment becomes chaotic and noisy).

We use this data to determine that the girl is nervous about her classroom performance because language arts has become more challenging for her and she does not know how to organize her ideas during writing assignments. Furthermore, this child has a sensory sensitivity (recall this quirky characteristic from the STRESSED model in Key 2) that makes it challenging for her when there is a lot of movement and noise occurring in the room, as is often the case when children are packing up to go home.

The problem with applying a consequence approach to this child (e.g., not allowing her to use the bathroom) is that we do not address the underlying reasons she is trying to escape from the environment. The child is escaping from these situations because she is trying to avoid the feelings of shame, stress, and embarrassment during language arts work, and at the end of the day she is attempting to avoid sensory discomfort. Additionally, especially if the escape-avoidance cycle occurs long enough, she may develop additional symptoms or behaviors. Thus, it may only be a matter of time, if we are only relying on the consequence approach of limiting bathroom breaks, before the child begins to have toileting accidents at her desk.

Perhaps the child learns that if she cannot make an escape by going to the bathroom, then the next attempt is to act up or hit another student so she can be sent to the principal's office, which effectively allows for a break from the situation. Being sent to the principal's office now serves as the most effective way for the child to obtain the needed escape or break from those feelings, and what we have just inadvertently done is reinforce and condition her to act in an aggressive fashion in order to get a much-needed sensory break or to avoid the feeling of embarrassment in class. Now we have just added another undesirable behavior to the child's escape behaviors: aggression in the form of hitting.

Once you understand the A-B-C model, you can see the power at your disposal to make a significant impact on your child's daily functioning. In the aforementioned example, once we begin to assist this child with her language arts difficulties and allow her to pack up her things and exit the classroom five minutes before the peer group (to buffer her sensory sensitivities), the child no longer needs to take bathroom breaks for long periods of time. Instead, she now only uses the restroom one or two times a day when she really needs to go. Thus, if you only target disruptive behaviors without understanding the underlying causes, you may end up preventing one undesirable behavior but another is destined to replace it.

At home, an example of the importance of focusing on the antecedent rather than the consequence might involve a quirky child experiencing a significant challenge completing the evening bedtime routine, such as putting on pajamas and brushing his teeth. You remind him several times before you begin yelling, "How many times am I going to have to tell you?!" I can easily answer that question for you. You will have to tell him *many* times and it still won't help. You make your next attempt and tell the child, "No iPad tomorrow!" No matter how much you take away or threaten to take away, he still cannot complete the evening hygiene tasks independently.

Clearly this child has both transitional stress and executive dysfunction characteristics from the STRESSED model, and no amount of reminding, repeating, yelling, or removing privileges is going to fix this. You must complete the routine with the child and act as his surrogate frontal lobe (explained in Key 3) because clearly he does not have the ability to complete these tasks alone. As frustrating as it may be to have to help, it's more frustrating to yell every night and not get any results.

From parents of older children, especially fathers, I often hear, "He should be able to do this on his own by now!" I agree. Children older than six should be able to independently complete the bedtime routine with minimal reminders and assistance. Children who can complete these activities independently are more likely to fall within the normative category of development. Therefore, the argument that the child should be able to complete the routine is moot. He's not able to do it alone, so therefore he may not fall within the normative category and we must consider his developmental profile as a contributing factor for his challenges rather than citing his chronological age as a reason he should be successful.

With my surrogate frontal lobe approach of remaining close to the child as he completes the routine, the child eventually learns to do it himself and may even insist that you let him do these tasks independently because he wants the responsibility and ownership of the accomplishment. I can't tell you how long it will take for your child, but if you do the tasks with him, he will eventually have enough exposures to commit the routine to muscle memory and be able to do it alone.

In case you were wondering if this approach enables a child or makes them dependent on you, rest assured. That would only be the case if the child was within the normative category of development and could generally complete these activities independently. It's only enabling if a child could already do it but you do it for or with them anyway.

The Trilogy of Behavior

Once you have identified a behavior you would like to address, you can complete the aforementioned A-B-C analysis to understand why the behavior is occurring and the response that is likely to be the most effective at addressing it. Recall that for a child in the quirky category of development, focus on the antecedents or why the behavior is occurring in the first place and helping the child build the necessary skill set to be successful is key. The exception to this is if the child is engaging in dangerous, destructive, or aggressive behaviors. In these cases, an immediate consequence is indicated (to keep the child and others safe and allow the child to regulate and reset) followed by a focus on the antecedent, such as emotional control techniques and calming strategies, so that future aggressive acts can be avoided.

Teaching a quirky child the skill necessary to benefit from the antecedent approach requires time, energy, and patience. It's more like a marathon than a sprint. However, there are numerous behaviors that occur throughout the day as part of family life that parents need to respond to quickly. Time cannot be spent completing an A-B-C analysis of each and every behavior a child demonstrates, nor is this approach necessary for most of these behaviors.

Hundreds of times a day, parents observe their child demonstrating a variety of behaviors. A simple model to follow is to divide behaviors into what I call the trilogy of behavior: good behaviors, bad behaviors, and ignorable behaviors. This structure divides behaviors into three categories and allows you to quickly and effectively respond to any behavior that a child may display.

Although this approach is highly effective for any parent, I often introduce it to families who have a child with developmental delays or a quirky profile. The reason for this is that many of these parents attempt to understand whether the child understood what he just did, and this deliberation clouds the parent's judgment and decision-making ability in terms of how to best respond to the behavior.

Many parents ask me whether punishing a child for hitting is appropriate—for example, if the child does not seem to understand that hitting is wrong. Behavior modification for aggressive or dangerous behaviors is the job and responsibility of every parent, regardless of the child's developmental profile. Hitting requires action. If a child slaps his brother, for example, saying, "Don't do that!" or "Be nice!" will not change the behavior.

If you believe that your child cannot help his aggressive behavior, does not understand what he's doing, that he doesn't mean to behave that way because he has X diagnosis or a quirky developmental profile, please accept the challenge to remain focused on the behavior itself and remember that you are working on the aggressive behavior out of love for the child and not to be mean or make him more uncomfortable. Indeed, the fact is that you love the child too much to put up with or stand idly by and watch as he exhibits aggressive behavior.

You are never helping a child by looking the other way or ignoring a dangerous or aggressive behavior. I tell families that if a child is in a wheelchair and hits someone, the behavior is still hitting. You cannot feel sorry for the child, nor can you make excuses or exceptions. You simply look at the behavior and determine whether it falls into the good, bad, or ignorable category (to be explained in the next section) and respond accordingly. You owe it to the child to respond, correct, and thus demonstrate what is acceptable behavior and what is not. Otherwise, you will be caught in a trap of trying to determine the motivation and understanding of each behavioral display, and it will paralyze your parenting and fail to teach the child how to behave appropriately.

If you want people to respect you and spend time with you, then you cannot hit them. There needs to be a consequence for that. If your 11-month-old crawls over to your new laptop computer with a sippy cup and proceeds to dump the liquid over your keyboard, are you going to sit back, watch, and calmly say "No, sweetie," or think to yourself, "Well, he's just a baby. He doesn't know any better"? My hunch is that you would be out of your chair redirecting the child both physically (picking him up) and verbally (telling him "no") while also modifying the environment (moving the laptop computer to a different location or a tall table out of the child's reach). Immediate reactions and appropriate responses are important, and the trilogy of behavior approach will help you be prepared to respond quickly and effectively.

When your child behaves well or appropriately (a good behavior), you should react as quickly as possible by rewarding him. This will guide him to behave appropriately more often. One good thing you can do that does not cost you any money is to pay attention to him. A child will work very hard to get attention (e.g., verbal praise) from a parent. In fact, sometimes children will behave badly to get attention! After all, some attention, even in the form of disapproval, can be better than none at all, especially if the child is feeling ignored or that his parent is too busy with other things (e.g., constantly checking email on a smart phone when the parent could be playing with or watching the child).

You may notice the power of attention when interacting with children and you lose your temper. Many children will almost smile at the reaction you are having because, in that moment, they realize that their behavior has tremendous power to get you to react. Toddlers, and many older children for that matter, love cause and effect! Parents often think that giving "bad" attention, like lecturing the child or showing them how much you mean it by raising your voice, will make the child behave more appropriately. However, sometimes to a child, any attention is good. This means that if you respond to a bad behavior with any attention (like lecturing or yelling), the bad behavior might increase. After all, they get lots of your attention when you lecture, and they love to see that they can get a reaction out of you. They also tune you out if all you do is yell or lecture. The rule to remember is that if a behavior (good or bad) is immediately followed by any type of attention, that behavior will occur more often.

An easy way to remember the trilogy of behavior is that good behaviors please you and should be followed by some feedback so that the child knows you noticed him being good or doing something well. Bad behaviors are aggressive, dangerous, or destructive and require immediate redirection such as time out (explained later in this chapter) or loss of a privilege. Finally, ignorable behaviors are generally any behaviors that annoy you but are not dangerous or destructive. They simply wear you out. These might include nagging you with requests, whining, or talking back. Whenever possible, you can attempt to ignore these behaviors.

To effectively address an ignorable behavior, you must not (1) look at the child, (2) talk to the child, or (3) have any physical contact with the child (i.e., if you are touching a child to move him back into time out, you are not ignoring him effectively). Ignoring can be very effective as a means of eliminating a behavior, but many children are persistent and try to push you to your boiling point to get some attention. If this describes your child, then I would strongly advise you set limits on these types of behaviors so that he does not get that reaction out of you. If the child succeeds in getting a rise out of you, then you reinforce their desire to behave this way again in the future because they learn that it works. One of the most effective ways to address persistent behaviors that are difficult to completely ignore is with the 1-2-3 Magic approach (Phelan, 2010).

Let's imagine you took away your 11-year-old's video game console for one week after he received a detention in school. On day 4, your child begins to remind you of how "good" his behavior has been the past few days and asks if he can have the console back early. You remind him that he lost it for a week, but he continues to try and discuss it. You try to ignore this, but he's very persistent and cannot seem to move past it. If your child is generally persistent in this manner, you would want to avoid any attempts to ignore and go immediately to the 1-2-3 Magic counting method. If his persistence is a new phenomenon and you are trying to ignore but he won't stop, and you are losing your cool, then you should immediately move to the 1-2-3 Magic method.

To do this method with your child, it would proceed like this:

PARENT: "The gaming console is locked up until Friday. You may have it back then."

CHILD: "But Mom, I've been doing good. That detention was bull anyway. That teacher is mean!"

PARENT: "That's one."

CHILD: "I'm serious. I promise I'll never get a detention again!"

PARENT: "That's two. If I get to three, I am keeping the console another week."

CHILD: "Fine!" (Child walks away feeling defeated but ceased persisting with the request.)

The nice thing about this approach is that it allows parents to avoid bringing more emotion into the situation, which only serves to escalate things further. It also allows the parent to keep the discussion to a minimum by keeping to the counting, while giving the child fair warning that they are approaching a consequence if they cannot stop their persistent behavior or request. Once children are familiar with this approach, provided you consistently use it, they quickly learn that a parent counting means they need to stop their current approach or suffer the consequence.

I hope that the trilogy of behavior and associated strategies described in this section allow you to make quicker, more effective decisions regarding your response to a child's behavior, because essentially all behaviors can be categorized into one of these three domains. Once you know what type of behavior it is, you will be prepared to respond accordingly and achieve good results.

Many parents experience the most difficulty and stress responding to the bad behavioral category. Thus, the next section of this chapter explores various parenting approaches to address bad behavior so that you can make an informed decision of how you plan to respond to your child when he or she demonstrates one of these behaviors. An important note here is that the term *bad* should only be applied to the behavior and never to the child. The moral here is that you love your child, but you don't like the bad behavior he is demonstrating.

Spanking

Some parents question whether physical punishment in the form of spanking would help keep their child from demonstrating a bad behavior (i.e., aggressive, dangerous, destructive) again in the future. The debate regarding whether to spank a child is not new. In fact, I find myself in this debate at least a few times each month with families I am counseling for the first time.

Is spanking an effective form of discipline? My professional stance, in conjunction with the research that supports it, is that spanking is actually punishment (not discipline) and is only effective in the short term. Try telling that to the old-school parent who swears, "It worked on me when my father spanked me!" I often reply, "Well, my great-great-grandfather had a horse and it worked for him, but I prefer a car." With a little more investigation during history gathering with parents who believe that spanking was effective during their childhood, I am often able to discern that although it may have garnered their attention as children in the short term, it fueled resentment or fear toward the parents who were spanking them over the long term and potentially had a negative influence on the parent–child relationship.

Unfortunately, spanking models that aggression is how adults solve problems. This child thinks to himself, "Well, Dad hits me when he doesn't like something I did, so that's what I will do when someone else does something I don't like." The act of spanking also causes the child to focus more on the feeling of being spanked rather than on what needs to be done to correct the behavior that caused the parent to spank him.

Furthermore, the child also quickly learns that as long as he can be sneakier about the behavior and not get caught, he won't get spanked. This results in modifying his behavior in the presence of the adult who might use spanking. It's the same thing that occurs when adults are driving. We speed down the road, but quickly press on the brake pedal when we see a police car. We pass by the police at the appropriate speed limit and once we are far enough out of sight, we resume speeding.

Some parents who use spanking with their child have asked me, "Why does my child not seem to be worried when he knows that he is going to get a spanking?" My response is, "Do you really want your child to fear you as means of getting your point across?" I believe that the majority of spanking is in fact a form of a parental loss of control and demonstrates that the parent lacks an effective discipline strategy. This is why having a preestablished parenting approach, using strategies discussed in this chapter, is so important. Without a plan, there will be confusion, frustration, and a loss of patience that often leads to a loss of control (i.e., physical discipline). If you are well versed in behavioral strategies such as those outlined here, there should not be a need to spank your child.

In the event that you are still convinced that spanking is an effective means of behavioral modification, take a moment to consider some research on it. Research indicates that spanking makes children anxious (especially toward the parent who is executing this method) and can lower his or her self-esteem (Straus, 1994). A report endorsed by the American Academy of Pediatrics (Gershoff, 2008) looked at 100 years of research on spanking and concluded, "There is substantial research evidence that physical punishment makes it more, not less, likely that children will be defiant and aggressive in the future."

As stated previously, spanking often occurs when parents are at a loss for how to respond more effectively to their child's behavior.

I know that most parents I meet who acknowledge spanking their child are good parents who either don't have a plan or the one they have is not working. Hopefully the strategies outlined in this chapter and this book will help aid in the development of an effective approach. If you need more assistance, you are encouraged to consult with a developmental specialist to develop an effective parenting and behavioral plan based on your child's unique needs.

Parents who are not quite ready to scrutinize themselves in a therapist's office are strongly encouraged to read books such as *1-2-3 Magic* (Phelan, 2010), *Raising an Emotionally Intelligent Child* (Gottman, 1998), and *Positive Discipline* (Nelson, 2006). These books provide practical and effective strategies designed to prevent frustrated and exasperated parenting. The result can be an improved relationship with your child as well as a decreased incidence of undesired behaviors.

Aggressive, Destructive, Dangerous Behaviors and Time Out

Aggressive, destructive, or dangerous behaviors are those that need to be addressed immediately. They cannot be ignored or redirected. When the child demonstrates or displays aggressive behaviors such as hitting, kicking, pushing, biting, slapping, shouting, or destruction of property, I use the formula Aggression = Action, meaning that the child needs to be directed to a time out or other break location (i.e., aggressive behaviors exhibited by the child require action from any adult who witnesses the behavior and cannot be ignored).

I enjoy teaching families rhymes to use with their children that help the kids remember what they are expected to do, while also making it easy for the adult(s) to remember the effective method of responding to the behavior. Some effective rhymes I share with parents include:

- "If you hit, you sit."
- "If you throw, you go."
- "If you shout, you're out."

Beginning to use these rhymes while the child is in the toddler or early elementary school years allows for the child to quickly and easily memorize them. You may begin to hear the child begin to say them aloud, almost as a means of reminding himself or talking himself through what will happen if he acts out, and thus he regulates his behavior. These rhymes can also be effective for older children, although older children in the normative category of development are generally expected to be able to solve problems and negotiate conflict more verbally rather than physically. In the case of a child who struggles with self-regulation, such as one in the quirky or pathology categories, continuing to use these rhymes can be helpful. I tell parents, "Keep your approach simple and predictable (and be consistent!)."

An analysis of the traditional time-out procedure is important here because many parents create additional stress by trying to follow a prescribed time-out approach that often involves making the child sit in a predetermined location for a set amount of time (typically one minute for each year of life), while also expecting that the child adhere to some fairly rigid behavioral control (e.g., "You can't come out until you stop crying and are seated completely still!").

In my professional opinion, a time out can be helpful in the short term to help a child regulate and reset, especially for aggressive behaviors but does not usually result in much long-term change. Furthermore, trying to adhere to a rigid time-out approach might even escalate situations and result in increased stress for both parent and child. The farther a time-out location from the area in which the incident occurred, the more likely the child may continue to engage in aggressive behaviors that further escalate the situation. Thus, avoid having a predetermined location because you never know how far you may need to travel get to it.

My recommendation is to have the child take a time out where the incident occurred whenever possible.

I urge parents to consider time out simply as a quick break from any attention being delivered to the child. No attention (ignoring the child) means that you do not look at the child, talk to the child, or touch the child. Whenever possible, the time out should happen as close to where the incident occurred as possible. This is the ideal approach because trying to escort an aggressive or frustrated child to a remote location may only create more problems. Furthermore, to effectively ignore a child, you cannot touch him. Thus, if you have to physically move him to a location, you are giving him attention. Another thing I want to avoid is having a parent sit outside a child's bedroom door, holding it shut because the child keeps trying to come out. If you are doing this, then time out is not an effective approach for the child and ultimately you are in time out as well given that you have to sit there to make it happen.

Let's think about an example in which your son hits his sister. You would immediately say, "If you hit, you sit" (which is even more effective if you have already taught this rhyme to the child), and then gently direct the child either with a light touch on the shoulder or a finger point to sit on the floor near where the incident occurred and take a break. If you use this technique, children will learn very quickly that the time out will not last long and is simply designed to interrupt what they were doing so they can take a moment to calm down, reset, and think. Over time, children will learn not to put up much of a fight because the quicker they go into the time out, the quicker they will get out of it. You are sending a clear and consistent message that no matter how brief the time put may be, the behavior was not acceptable and it will be interrupted and addressed.

If the child is really struggling to complete a time out (e.g., they run away from you), you may need to spend some time practicing or role-playing a time out while the child is calm and not in any trouble. You would ask the child to demonstrate how they get to a time-out location and what the expected behavior looks like one they are there. This way there's no question left in the parent's mind that the child knows what they should be doing. Once the child is seated in that location, they are ignored (no looking at, no talking to, and no touching the child) for a brief period of time (e.g., one to two minutes). The amount of time spent does not need to be tracked with a timer. Use your best judgment of what is acceptable, short, and sweet.

Remember, the goal of this time-out method is to show the child that what he did was unacceptable and thus he needed a quick opportunity to calm down and reset. When the parent is satisfied that the behavior was successfully interrupted, the child is able to come out of the break and can be directed back into the situation to assess whether he is ready to reengage and whether any restitution such as apologies need to be delivered (telling his sister "sorry" from the previous example). The reality here is that any apology that comes after a time out is pretty sheepish and not very sincere. Thus, forcing a child to apologize is not required to exit time out. Besides, the sister is already feeling better knowing that her brother got into trouble!

During the time that you are reintegrating the child back into whatever activity was interrupted, your time and interaction with the child should be kept brief and matter-of-fact so as not to inadvertently provide the child with attention. This is because some children will engage in bad behavior to get parents to pay more attention to them, even if it means spending additional time with them talking through what they did wrong.

Time Out While Away from Home

Many parents ask me about time-out procedures while away from home. The procedure remains consistent with a time out that would occur in your home. Parents have to use their best judgment about sitting the child down in the location of the incident. This may involve sitting the child down in the aisle at the grocery store, for example, and standing near them while still following the no talking, no looking, no touching approach. If the child escalates further, you may need to leave your shopping cart and escort the child to your car in the parking lot to complete the time out. You would not be able to fully follow the ignoring protocol due to having to touch the child to escort him out to the car, but you have to respond depending on the situation, and you can continue to follow the no talking and no looking at the child rules. Having to leave a store or other location is not ideal, but as stated before, once the child learns that he will get out from the time out the quicker he begins it, the need to leave the store may never occur. If you do need to go out to the car, just remember that parenting is not always convenient, but it's worth it if you teach your child how to behave.

Escape Artists

Some children will act out and intensify their behaviors for the sole purpose of being removed from a particular situation. I refer to these children as "escape artists." Children in the quirky category of development may become escape artists in situations away from the home base. To effectively respond to this, you should recall the A-B-C model of behavior explained in the beginning of this chapter. For example, the child may be sensory overloaded (e.g., overwhelmed by too much noise in the environment) or have some other reason for escalating his behavior so intensely that the trigger or antecedent would need to be explored and addressed accordingly in the future. For example, a child who consistently runs off (i.e., regulatory difficulty of the STRESSED model) while you walk through the grocery store may need to sit in the cart or be given a list of items to help you look for to keep his brain focused on a task rather than what upsets him. A child who is sensitive to the acoustics and sounds of the shopping mall (sensory sensitivity of the STRESSED model) may be better able to tolerate the experience and refrain from escaping if he is provided with a pair of noise-canceling headphones to wear while at the mall. More extreme or challenging examples may require assistance from a developmental or behavioral specialist who can advise you regarding strategies specific to your situation.

Indeed, some children will throw a tantrum and act out for the sole purpose of being removed from a situation they don't like. Perhaps the child would rather be at home playing video games and hopes that a tantrum will result in you taking her home sooner. Whatever the reason, I recommend that any time you have to leave a location (and are not able to go back in because the tantrum continues or escalates), you remain absolutely silent, buckle the child into the car, and drive home silently, even turning off the stereo.

If your child screams during tantrums, you may want to keep foam earplugs in the glove box to help yourself remain calm and focused while driving. Note: If the child is so escalated emotionally that he is trying to get out of his seat, out of the car (while you are moving), is kicking the back of your chair, or is hitting others in the car (you, or siblings if they are present), then you will need to pull over. Ideally, you would place your child in a backseat location that make some of the behaviors impossible, such as seating him in the back row of the van so that he cannot kick the back of the driver's seat. You may need to remove the child's shoes before driving if kicking is an issue. If you need to pull over, use silence as your secret weapon. Keep a book in the car to read or check your email on your phone in complete silence until the child is calm enough for you to begin driving again.

If other adults are in the car, they need to be silent as well. Once you arrive home, escort the child to his room in a nonaggressive manner, and in as quiet and calm a voice as possible, tell him, "When you are calm and quiet, you may come out." No matter how angry you are and how inconvenient this approach is, you are establishing a precedent that will pay off tremendously in the future in terms of preventing more situations like this from happening. Most important, if the child was having the tantrum in an effort to return home to be able to complete a desired activity, he should not have any access to that activity until the next day at the earliest. If possible, you could return to the store and finish your shopping with the child, but this would need to be determined using your best judgment. Once the child learns that he will lose access to his desired activity by having a tantrum to get you to take him home, these occurrences should occur less frequently, if at all.

Encouraging Self-Control with a Break Area

Earlier you learned how to implement a time out when a child demonstrates an aggressive, dangerous, or destructive behavior. This section focuses on how to help a child practice self-control before he demonstrates aggressive, destructive, or dangerous behaviors. To do this, you must designate a location in your home where a child can retreat to calm down. Going to this break area is encouraged and rewarded, and thus the area should not be used for punishment.

Once you decide where to locate the break area, you and your child can name it if you would like (e.g., "Jillian's Island") and then begin to set it up with items the child can use to relax. This can include preferred items such as stuffed animals, books, and favorite toys. Make the area cozy with a blanket, beanbag chair, or a pillow. Explain to the child that the area is their space and others should not be allowed there unless the child allows it.

Next, explain that the child can use this place to relax after school or if they are feeling frustrated such as when a sibling might be annoying them or if they are frustrated during a complicated homework assignment. This place serves as an alternative to time out and when used correctly can prevent punishment from needing to be used while also teaching the child to make good choices by controlling his reactions to stressful situations.

Natural Consequences

Although antecedents often hold the key to successful behavioral management, especially for quirky kids, natural consequences can have a powerful effect on a child's behavior in the future. Natural consequences, or learning by experience, will generally be more effective than consequences administered by adults. Natural consequences are anything that naturally occurs without any intervention required. If you touch a hot stove, the burn on your finger is a natural consequence. Hunger would be a natural consequence of choosing not to eat your dinner. Natural consequences can also be a good thing—such as studying hard and getting a good grade on a test. For natural consequences to be positively oriented, such as good study habits, the individual must be highly motivated.

Provided that your child is not in any grave danger and is exhibiting a behavior that has a natural consequence, you may want to think twice the next time you want to step in on the child's behalf to redirect them. Children learn many things without being taught and without being punished, and natural consequences are the reason. Indeed, your child learns a significant amount about the world when you are not there to instruct him, and it's because of natural consequences.

Closing Thoughts

As with any new behavioral plan or approach, there is a high likelihood that the behaviors you are trying to stop will increase when you begin to execute the plan. This is the child's way of getting the parents to back off or persuade them that their plan does not work. Parents must dedicate the necessary time to modify behaviors and remain persistent. Once a consistent plan is established and properly executed, the goal is that the approach will become a part of everyday life.

When I hear from a parent that a plan stopped working, it is usually a result of inconsistency or an abrupt termination in the execution of the strategy rather than the plan itself not being effective (although this should be investigated to be sure). The idea is to shift the approach permanently, not simply use the plan briefly. Children will exhibit challenging behaviors throughout their childhood and adolescence. Some adults continue to exhibit challenging behaviors! The key is to establish a response style and stick with it while making slight modifications along the way that are based on the child's age and level of development. For example, a time out may be used when a toddler hits a parent, but the police may need to be called if your teenager assaults you. There is always a response to the behavior, but the response has to be appropriate for the specific behavior and the age of the child.

If you have or are now beginning to realize that that consequences don't work well with your quirky child, or you avoid disciplining him because you worry he doesn't understand that what he is doing is wrong, you need to reread this chapter. If the goal is to help the child improve his social skills, it is crucial to teach him appropriate behavioral control because it won't matter how good his social skills are if he is behaviorally disruptive. Be patient and consistent. Kind yet firm parenting results in the best outcomes for children as they become adults.

Take-home points:

- When working to address or correct a child's behavior, it is important that the Antecedent-Behavior-Consequence (A-B-C) model be fully understood to modify any behaviors that are causing concerns as well as to help encourage appropriate or prosocial behaviors. Although many children will effectively and quickly adjust their behaviors secondary to consequences being administered (such as removal of privileges), a quirky child is less likely to benefit from a consequence-driven approach. This is a key point that will save parents a lot of stress and improve parenting outcomes once they understand this about their child.

- It is true that you will have increased success while parenting a quirky child if you address the antecedent or the precursor to the actual behavior in question. You must teach the child to do what it is you want them to do rather than punish them for not being able to do so independently. That being said, you still need to administer punishment or consequences when aggressive, dangerous, or damaging behaviors such as destruction of property occur.

- Teaching a quirky child the skills necessary to benefit from the antecedent approach requires time, energy, and patience. It's more like a marathon than a sprint.

- An easy way to remember the trilogy of behavior is that good behaviors please you and should be followed by some feedback so that the child knows you noticed him being good or doing something well. Bad behaviors are aggressive, dangerous, or destructive and require immediate redirection such as time outor loss of a privilege. Finally, ignorable behaviors are generally any behaviors that annoy you but are not dangerous or destructive. They simply wear you out. These might include nagging you with requests, whining, or talking back. Whenever possible, you can attempt to ignore these behaviors.

TRACK YOUR CHILD'S DEVELOPMENT

A quirky child may not begin to experience challenges that adversely affect them until they face the increased social demands that accompany the elementary school years. Typically, children with speech and language delays are identified earlier, during the preschool and kindergarten years. Many quirky children can get by under the academic radar until first grade. Some other quirky students may be able to get to third grade, or even beyond in some cases, without any identification. Others, especially girls, can go through to high school graduation without access to services.

In the most recent revision to the *Diagnostic and Statistical Manual of Mental Disorders* (DSM-5; American Psychiatric Association, 2013), a section of the criteria for a diagnosis of autism spectrum disorder states, "The onset of the symptoms is in the early developmental period (but deficits may not become fully manifest until social communication demands exceed limited capacities)." When and if this happens varies depending on each child's unique profile which involves how quirky he is as well as how he copes with the demands he faces.

If a student who is quirky and is beginning to experience challenges is not failing in school (and many children in the early grades are not graded, so would not be identified as failing) or does not meet the school's criteria for educational support following a school-based evaluation, what should be done to help? For those quirky students who often fall within the gray area of several possible diagnoses but do not receive definitive explanation for their behaviors, it is only a matter of time before difficulties may arise. Although I can accept that schools must establish and follow criteria to determine who is eligible for support while at school, I can also assure you that quirky students require as much prevention support as they do intervention support.

To know what to look for in terms of expected social and emotional development, the following sections of this chapter provide you with an outline of what most children (normative category) should be capable of during various stages of their development. Information regarding special education assessment and accommodations are presented later in the event that you think your child would benefit from additional supports while at school.

Social and Emotional Development: Three-Year Olds

A preschool child is experiencing tremendous developmental growth. This is the age when children still need plenty of help from adults, but they begin to assert themselves and desire some control and independence in their lives. Parents are wise if they take advantage of a child in this age range's desire to help and learn new tasks. Preschoolers love to help around the house and take tremendous pride in completing tasks and receiving praise. The following are some developmental milestones typically achieved among three-year-old children both at home and in a preschool setting:

- Follows simple directions; enjoys helping with household or classroom tasks
- Begins to recognize her own limits and asks for help when needed
- Likes to play alone, but near other children
- Does not cooperate or share well

- Able to make choices between two things
- Begins to notice other people's moods and feelings
- Copies adults and friends
- Shows affection for friends without prompting
- Takes turns in games
- Shows concern for crying friend
- Begins to absorb knowledge about himself and the world around him

Consider the following strategies when interacting with your three-year-old child:

- Transitions are difficult at this age. Provide warning of changes so your child has time to shift gears: "We're leaving in ten minutes." You may need to use a visual representation of the time left, such as a sand timer or digital countdown timer as many children do not yet understand the concept of time and how long five or ten minutes really is. Further, you may need to be close in proximity to the child when informing them of a transition. For example, a child may be less likely to process the need for transition if you notify them from a different room. You may need to sit next to them while they are playing, join them in the play for a moment, and then look for an ideal opportunity to stop what you are doing together and then make the transition as a team rather than willing the child to do this independently.
- Rituals are important. Household routines and schedules give your three-year-old a sense of security.
- Point out colors and numbers when possible during everyday conversations: "You're coloring your picture orange" or "This ladybug has seven spots."
- Encourage independent activity to build self-reliance. Work with your child to begin dressing herself independently, putting on her own shoes and jacket, pulling up his pants after using the bathroom (if toilet trained), and so on.
- Provide lots of sensory experiences for learning and developing coordination—sand, mud, finger paint, puzzles.

Social and Emotional Development: Four-Year Olds

Silly, imaginative, and energetic, your four-year-old child loves to try new words and new activities. Use humor, when possible and appropriate, to spark your child's learning. Children who are happy are more likely to remain engaged and want to continue the interaction, which allows for more opportunity to connect. The following are some developmental milestones typically achieved among four-year-old children:

- Takes turns, shares, and cooperates
- Expresses anger verbally rather than physically
- Can feel jealousy
- Sometimes lies to protect herself, begins to understand the concept of lying
- Enjoys pretending and has a vivid imagination
- Enjoys doing new things
- Pretend plays "mom" and "dad" roles
- Is more and more creative with make-believe play
- Wants to play more with other children than just by himself
- Cooperates with other children
- Often can't tell what's real and what's make-believe (e.g., mascots, costumes)
- Talks about what she likes and what she is interested in

Consider the following strategies when interacting with your four-year-old:

- Four-year-olds crave adult approval. Provide lots of positive encouragement.
- Display calendars and analog clocks to help your child visualize the concept of time. Consider purchasing a *My Tot Clock* that represents time with color so that your child will know when it is time to be in his room or out of his room (e.g., yellow means "day" and the child can come out of their room in the morning, and blue means "night" and the child needs to remain in bed).

- Play word games to develop his growing vocabulary; overlook his fascination with bad or potty words ("poopy").
- Offer opportunities for sorting, matching, counting, and comparing with games, workbooks, and educational apps.
- Provide lots of play space and occasions to play with other kids.

Social and Emotional Development: Kindergarten

Kindergarten is a critical year in a child's academic career. I spend considerable time in my clinical practice helping families determine whether their child is ready for kindergarten. Some question whether an additional year of kindergarten is necessary to facilitate further development. The dilemma for a quirky child who is doing well academically (i.e., knows how to read) is whether they will be bored in kindergarten. If the child is struggling socially, they are likely to be bored regardless of the grade in which they attend. This is especially true if the child is a depth seeker (described in Key 2 and Key 3) given that he subscribes to a specific set of interests and often fails to recognize the importance of learning a variety of information about different topics.

When trying to determine kindergarten readiness or retention (an additional year of kindergarten) for a child in the quirky category of development, always consider the child's development rather than their chronological age. School district cutoffs for kindergarten readiness using date of birth criteria are set up with children in the normative category of development in mind. A quirky child, as well as a child with a neurodevelopmental diagnosis (autism spectrum disorder) in the pathology category of development, will require additional consideration regarding ability to enter school or progress through kindergarten depending on their specific developmental profile.

The milestones provided here should be reviewed to get a sense of your child's ability to complete the tasks and keep up with the social and emotional demands of each year of school. Consultation with a developmental specialist and school district personnel is indicated if you have concerns regarding your child's development and appropriateness of school grade placement.

By the end of kindergarten, most children:

- Follow class rules
- Separate from a parent or caregiver with ease
- Take turns
- Establish left- or right-hand dominance
- Understand time concepts like yesterday, today, and tomorrow
- Stand quietly in a line and respect the personal space of those around them
- Follow directions agreeably and easily
- Pay attention for 15 to 20 minutes
- Develop better self-control skills, such as sitting still and listening quietly
- Learn how to follow directions
- Become more skilled at cooperating with others
- Discuss families, holidays, and other things about their worlds
- Play make-believe and dress-up
- Emulate adults and seek praise
- Seek to play rather than be alone; friends are important
- Play with both boys and girls, but prefer to play with the same sex
- Want to conform; may criticize those who do not

Social and Emotional Development: First Grade

First grade is the first year in which students are not playing as much in the classroom and are instead expected to remain seated and complete work either at a table with other students or at a desk nearby other students. This is a big adjustment for some children who have become accustomed, during their years of preschool and year of kindergarten, to having plenty of time to play and move around the room. The first-grade year will inevitably bring about challenges for students who have difficulties regulating themselves. Many students who are inattentive, hyperactive, or impulsive are often identified during the first-grade year. Furthermore, the demands on fine motor control or handwriting, as well as reading and completion of other building blocks of academics, such as math facts, begins to allow identification of students who may have learning difficulties.

Socially, the peer group is beginning to cooperate with one another and interact more, especially during less structured times of the school day, such as lining up to leave the classroom, walking through the hallways, eating lunch together, and going to recess. A quirky student may have difficulties due to a variety of factors that may include behavioral regulation challenges, anxiety, and social awareness, making these times of the day quite difficult for them to navigate.

A quirky student may also demonstrate sensory challenges that make situations such as the lunchroom difficult to tolerate and can result in behavioral reactivity, such as a child who struggles with the smells of the cafeteria or the sound and commotion of a large group of students eating together in a large room. A quirky student may spend the recess portion of the day on his own either on the perimeter of the playground walking around trying to determine something to do, engaging in some fantasy play in his mind, or isolating himself on playground equipment such as swinging, digging in the dirt, or find another method of keeping to himself (e.g., reading a book). The peer group may not pay much attention to the quirky child who is off doing his own thing, but the child is certainly missing out on valuable opportunities to develop his social skills in these instances. For the child isolating himself, the family can consider requesting that he not be allowed to take a book onto the playground and that he participate in a peer support program so that others can engage and include him in recess activities.

The quirky child who draws negative attention to himself in school can begin to suffer socially because even in first-grade, students are beginning to have less tolerance and patience for others who are struggling in the social context, such as students who demonstrate behavioral reactivity that is disruptive to the classroom or who otherwise engage in quirky, "weird," or odd behaviors as determined by the peer group (e.g., tantrums out of proportion to the triggering event or sustained and intense emotional outbursts).

Parents often report to me that if they pick up their children from school, other students in the class may report to them things that happened throughout the day and even use labels such as "He was bad today" or explain other behaviors that made it difficult for the child to engage and connect with the peer group appropriately. Some children ask a parent of the quirky student for information about the child, almost as if they are attempting to learn more about the student because it was difficult to do so directly. To determine how your child is doing or if you need to know what to expect, consider the following normative milestones for first grade.

By the end of first grade, most children:

- Work independently at their desk
- Listen and sustain attention during longer sets of directions
- Complete homework and bring it back the next day
- Sit in a chair for a longer period of time without needing breaks
- Are able to see things from another person's point of view; this allows you to reason more with your child and teach her empathy
- Relate experiences in greater detail and in a logical way when discussing the events of the day
- Problem-solve disagreements
- Crave affection from parents and teachers
- Have some minor difficulties with friendships and working out problems with peers
- Are able to plan ahead
- Become even more adept at paying attention, following instructions, and exercising self-control
- Learn how to work together with classmates on a group project
- Become more attuned to the concept of fairness and justice; more important, children learn that the "eye for an eye" mental-

ity ("He hit me, so I hit him back!") is not the best way to solve problems and can actually create more problems

- Gain more confidence in expressing opinions and sharing stories, such as during morning meetings or check-ins.

Social and Emotional Development: Second Grade

Second grade in many cases is the last "insulated" year for a quirky child. The social demands may still be manageable, although the normative children in the quirky child's class are realizing that just because you are in a class with someone, it does not mean they are your friend, as was the case in previous years. Children are becoming more selective about whom they play with and why they seek certain people out versus others.

Academically, as the expectations for reading continue to increase during this year, a quirky student may begin to demonstrate reading comprehension challenges that are a by-product of social awareness difficulties. Indeed, if a quirky child does not have any challenges with reading (many are often fairly good or advanced readers), they typically do experience reading comprehension challenges that demonstrate the degree in which they have challenges interpreting or inferring the context and meaning that underlies various social situations.

The peer group is beginning to mature and understands the structure and behaviors required to be successful in the classroom. A quirky student, especially one who experiences regulatory challenges, may continue to push the boundaries seemingly unaware of the consequences that her behavior has. These consequences are important because they involve not only how the teacher is feeling about these behaviors, but also the degree to which it is preventing classmates from learning. Second grade is essentially an extension of the first-grade year with many of the same themes only becoming further intensified and thus exacerbated, which can create increased social distance between the quirky student and his or her peer group.

By the end of second grade, most children:

- Begin to reason and concentrate
- Improve their ability to process information
- Work cooperatively with a partner or small group
- Understand the difference between right and wrong
- Expand their vocabulary
- Read fluently with expression and are able to infer meaning, draw conclusions, and understand why characters in books think and feel the way they do relative to the storyline
- Develop close friendships. Friendships are now increasingly selective and no longer just the result of sharing a classroom together. Birthday party invitations begin to become more selective and include input on who should attend from the child having the party
- Are better able to concentrate on lessons for longer periods of time and demonstrate increased patience and self-control.

Social and Emotional Development: Third and Fourth Grades

The third- and the fourth-grade years are considered the high-- stakes years because the demands both academically and socially rise exponentially. Schools will obviously differ in terms of the degree of increased demands during the third-grade year, but if the child is still able to get by academically and socially in third grade, he will inevitably begin to experience some roadblocks in the fourth grade year.

I meet with many children for the first time during their fourth- grade year for academic and social concerns. These are the years in which the basic building blocks are assumed to have been established and the student must be able to apply new concepts to previously acquired foundations of knowledge. For a quirky child who is quite bright intellectually and doing well academically, these are the years in which the social demands increase so much that he may begin to suffer despite his academic and intellectual talents and abilities.

These are also the years that I begin to intensively treat many quirky students because their brains now have the capacity for insight and awareness (the switch described in Key 4) that allows them to be introspective about their situations and recognize the effect it is having on them when their peer group is stressed out or upset with their behaviors. This self-other awareness creates a catch-22 for many quirky children. As the child's treatment provider, I am excited that he is now motivated and capable of making some changes in their life, but at the same time this comes at a cost because he is becoming stressed, anxious, and upset that he is seeking connections with others but is unable to successfully create them. Instead, the child begins to report receiving negative feedback from the peer group on a regular basis.

A quirky student will often misinterpret the feedback from peers as being mean or being teased or bullied. In many of these cases, the manner in which other students provide feedback to the quirky child does resemble bullying, but there were often numerous attempts to try to give feedback to stop a certain behavior. Because the quirky child was not reading or responding to those cues accurately or quickly enough, the other students resort to becoming aggressive or verbally abusive as a last-ditch effort to get their point across.

Unfortunately, parents often hear about how another child was mean, rude, or nasty to their child. Although there are certainly instances in which this was the case, many times it is the result of the quirky student not being able to quickly and accurately interpret the earlier, more subtle levels of feedback and parents have to be careful to not overreact to situations until all of the details and information can be obtained.

In general, quirky children are more likely to walk around with a "bull's eye" on their back and be targeted by bullies because of their social, behavioral, and emotional challenges. While addressing bullying in schools is always necessary, it is equally important that the quirky student begin to learn what they may be contributing to the attraction of this bullying and correct their behaviors to make themselves less of a target.

By the end of third grade, most children:

- Work cooperatively and productively with other children in small groups to complete projects
- Understand how choices affect consequences
- Become more organized and logical in their thinking processes
- Build stronger friendships and seek connection with others outside of the school through activities, such as play dates and sleepovers
- Become helpful, cheerful, and pleasant as well as rude, bossy, selfish, and impatient
- Become more influenced by peer pressure because friends are very important at this stage
- Enjoy immediate rewards for behavior
- Focus on friends; friendships become more important, and many third-graders look forward to socializing and seeing close friends at school
- Become more adept at understanding and sharing jokes and riddles with friends
- Take on more responsibility for themselves (e.g., making sure they write down homework assignments, packing up their own belongings for dismissal)
- Work cooperatively on group projects such as science experiments.

By the end of fourth grade, most children:

- Begin to make more decisions and engage in group decision making
- Want to be part of a group
- Think independently and critically

- Have genuine empathy or concern for the well-being of others
- Show a strong sense of responsibility
- Are able to memorize and recite facts, although he may not have a deep understanding of them
- Increase the amount of detail in drawings
- Can work on research projects
- Write a structured paragraph with an introductory topic sentence, three supporting details, and a closing sentence that wraps up the main idea of the paragraph
- Use a range of strategies when drawing meaning from text, such as prediction, connections, and inference
- Understand cause-and-effect relationships
- Gravitate toward certain friends. Friendship preferences may become more selective in four grade. (The downside to this can be the formation of cliques, especially for girls; peer pressure; and labeling others [nerd, cool, etc.])
- Take more responsibility for organizing and prioritizing her work. (If she needs help with these skills, now is a great time to step in, before the demands of middle school require even more self-discipline)
- Are more emphatic about expressing preferences about things
- Demonstrate increasing competitiveness with peers.

Social and Emotional Development: Fifth Grade

As weary as this statement may make you, fifth grade marks the beginning of the end of childhood. Fifth-graders within the normative category of development are beginning to crave independence. They want to be with their friends. This is often the sole motivating factor getting them out of bed and out of the house on most school mornings. Longtime friends may begin to explore other friendships, which can cause stress and grief for children. Indeed, your child's social network of friends may be constantly changing. A friend may be close one day and off exploring other friendships another day. Your fifth-grade child will cling so tightly to a friend that you become concerned they are missing opportunities to make new friends. Both boys and girls can develop crushes during this time in their development, and when it is not reciprocal, they get their hearts broken.

Parents need to remain very involved in their child's life despite the child's desire to have more independence and freedom. For some children, being allowed to venture out on their bicycle may allow them the necessary freedom to visit friends and increase their accessibility to social outings (e.g., going to a gas station together to buy candy, riding to the local playground or park).

The social lives of today's fifth-graders play out largely on the Internet or through social media (e.g., Instagram, Twitter). If you haven't been asked to buy your child a smart phone or tablet computer yet, you will likely receive this request from your fifth-grader. Easy accessibility to the Internet and technology can be scary for parents, especially those who find the online world unfamiliar. I strongly recommend placing the home computer in the family room and prohibiting your child from using the Internet while in her room. This has become more difficult in the days of laptop computers, tablets, and smartphones. Thus, parents may need to be savvy regarding how to disable Wi-Fi access during certain hours of the day (e.g., after bedtime).

Allow your child have an email account but insist on knowing the password. If you allow your child to use social media such as Facebook, Instagram, Vine, or Twitter, which are typically only recommended for children at least 13 years old, then insist that she only accept friend requests from people she knows personally and require that you also be added as a "friend" to those accounts so that you can monitor what is being shared and discussed.

Keep up with online trends. If you hear other children or parents talking about different social media apps or websites, learn to navigate that world. Are they talking about sites you've never heard of? Go online and find out what they are all about.

The most important thing about allowing your child supervised Internet access is communication. What is she looking at? Why is she looking at it? Who is she talking to? Let your child know you aren't trying to lock her out of cyberspace but are concerned with keeping her safe. If you have more serious concerns, consider purchasing tracking software that allows you to track phone or Internet activity and tell them that you are doing this so that they can make good choices and resist peer pressure (e.g., "I can't look on that website because my parents track all of my website visits").

Continue rewarding your child for good behavior, often by giving her a little more freedom. If you see you've given her more freedom than she can handle, pull back a little. Let your child know you are always available to listen to whatever's going on in her life, but realize you can't force her to share all the details. As time goes on, your child will open up more.

By the end of fifth grade, most children:

- Are generally truthful and dependable
- Develop increasing independence
- Improve problem-solving skills
- Develop more advanced listening and responding skills
- Enjoy organizing and classifying objects and ideas
- Are able to read and concentrate for long periods of time
- Read complex text fluently and with good comprehension
- Research a topic using a variety of sources, and use the features of a book (index, glossary, appendix) to find information
- Identify conflict, climax, and resolution in a story
- Write an organized, multiparagraph composition in sequential order with a central idea
- Are more attuned to what peers are wearing, the music they're listening to, and so on
- Spend more time socializing with friends, texting, video chatting, and so on
- Face more time constraints as schoolwork becomes harder and they have to juggle friends and extracurricular activities.

Educational Support Plans

As I have discussed in the STRESSED model, many quirky students have good intelligence (smart/social imbalance). When a school is making a determination to provide accommodations and services within the context of the school day, they evaluate a child for eligibility under guidelines established by the Individuals with Disabilities Education Act 2004 (IDEA 2004). This involves 14 educational eligibility classifications that can be applied to a student in need depending on their profile. A quirky child may need to be evaluated under the following categories: speech impairment, other health impairment, autism spectrum disorder, specific learning disability, developmental delay, and emotional impairment.

You can imagine, or may have experienced personally, how difficult it can be for a quirky child to obtain support because they may possess traces of several or all of these eligibility classifications—but not enough to qualify for services. Remember that the school is evaluating for an academic eligibility. Your child may have a medical or clinical diagnosis that the school is required to consider, but they do not have to accept it. Instead, the school needs to complete their own evaluation to determine whether the child is demonstrating enough of a challenge secondary to their specific profile in school to qualify for support services. Consider a student who is highly intelligent and doing well in school academically, but is engaging in distracting behaviors and having social skills challenges that cause him to be chastised by the peer group and is strategically isolated in the classroom so as not to disrupt the others. This may be an approach that the teacher puts into place in the absence of an educational support plan.

Individualized Education Program and Section 504 Plan

The Individualized Education Program (IEP) and Section 504 Plan are formalized plans agreed upon by parents and the school to provide the child with some level of assistance or intervention over the course of the school day.

If you are informed by a developmental/medical professional that your child may be eligible for special education services because of a diagnosis that fits into one of the current special education classifications, or if you believe this to be true and the school refuses services, there are a number of options available to you. Although an in-depth discussion of how to navigate this process is outside the scope of this book, you are always encouraged to put all communication with the school in writing. If you want the school to evaluate your child, it is your right. You need to put this request in writing and date it because the school has a required amount of time in which they need to respond.

You are also encouraged to find a special education advocate to work with you, either by asking other parents who have used such a service or by completing a district or Internet search for educational advocates in your area. School districts keep the names of advocates on file if you feel comfortable asking them for assistance. You may also need to seek out an attorney to represent you or request mediation services, depending on the school's response to your requests. If you are interested in specific information on special education law, an excellent Internet resource is http://www.wrightslaw.com. There are also free apps on the iTunes Store pertaining to IEPs (e.g., IEP Checklist) that can be used in meetings, as well as books and guides that can be found at your local bookstore.

I often express my disagreement with schools after they tell families I am working with that their quirky child is "too smart" to qualify for special education services. One of the difficulties of encouraging the school to help the child succeed socially is that technically the school is completing its obligation to provide a free appropriate public education if the child is learning and doing reasonably well academically.

What I have learned over my years working with kids, and what I try to emphasize to schools, is that it is only a matter of time until academic performance suffers as a result of the child's inability or difficulty connecting with other kids and teachers. Furthermore, if the child begins to fear school because of feelings of social isolation, or he is being bullied or harassed, teaching this child anything (and sustaining his previously strong academic performance) will be much more difficult. Finally, shouldn't schools be invested in teaching the child to be successful, not only in terms of academics but also in life? While having high test scores is laudable, being able to connect with others, communicate, solve problems, function successfully as a member of a team, and engage with others socially are invaluable skill sets as the student seeks independent living and entrance into the job market. Indeed, in the absence of such social skills, academic achievement becomes almost irrelevant.

My general response to the school's argument that "smart" does not qualify for services is to ask, "What do you do with a person who is confined to a wheelchair but has an above average or superior IQ and achieves straight A's? Does that level of intellect and academic performance mean that you are not going to allow accommodations for the child's mobility issues?" Whether you can't get to school because of a physical disability or are avoiding school due to psychological stress and anxiety secondary to social skills delays, the end result is the same: you are not in school, you are not learning, performance suffers, and the risk for dropout increases.

You may wish to mention to the school official who tries to reject social skills support or other services that current law does not support this claim. According to Individuals with Disabilities Education Act (IDEA) regulation 300.101(c), a school must provide special education to a child with a disability even though the child has not failed or been retained in a course or grade, and is advancing from grade to grade. The word *disability* in this statute, however, indicates that the child must have a classification from the school to even begin the discussion of services.

Whenever it is possible (based on a valid psychological diagnosis or educational classification) to begin an IEP or Section 504 Plan to help implement social supports for the child, the better are the chances of future success. The IEP and Section 504 Plan are similar in that both require an eligibility classification by the school. It is important to remember that schools only classify (e.g., "autism," "other health impairment," and "specific learning disability"—there are currently 14 possible classifications) and do not provide medical or psychological diagnoses. Instead, their classification determines eligibility, and informs and ultimately determines the types of services for which the child is eligible. However, the school must consider any outside diagnoses and reports when determining eligibility for services and accommodations.

The IEP is a contractual document that requires annual meetings as well as assessments that, depending on the school district, are updated at specified intervals. IEP accommodations often include therapy services that are paid for by the school district (e.g., speech therapy, occupational therapy, social work). A parent is permitted to request meetings (always do this in writing) to amend the IEP throughout the school year. The Section 504 Plan provides a list of recommendations that do not require incremental costs but can be useful to the student throughout the course of the school day (e.g., preferential seating, additional time to complete a test).

In the meantime, while you are working to get the school to provide services, I encourage you to request social accommodations that do not involve incremental cost to the school district and do not require any formal special education plan or paperwork. These approaches include peer supports (discussed later in this chapter), which use the built-in community of peers in the child's school. Keep in mind that you will have no legal outlet to ensure that the provision of peer supports is consistent and sustained in the absence of a formal special education plan. Thus, you will need to have a positive relationship with school personnel and know how to keep the plan active via check-in and follow-up once it begins.

Keep in mind that if you are the parent of a quirky child who is having social difficulties but is doing well academically, it may be difficult during the earlier grades to get formal accommodations. It is typically not until the middle school years that schools begin to realize the extent to which these social difficulties interfere with academic performance.

Regarding school intervention, families should request that:

- Services are specifically described on the student's IEP, if you have one.
- Anyone responsible for implementing the social skills services must have knowledge about both social skills development and the specifics of implementing the services. You can offer school staff a copy of this book if you think it may be helpful in this regard.
- Services are provided at the necessary rate and intensity to be effective. One or two visits with a social worker each month will probably not meet necessary criteria. Daily contact may be required to meet necessary rate and intensity criteria. If staff are not available at the required rate, then the use of peer supports are indicated, with periodic staff check-ins and training of the peer group.
- Interventions are delivered in authentic locations such as playgrounds, classrooms, lunchrooms, rather than just in the social worker's office, social skills group, or a resource room.

Handwriting Help

Handwriting is an area where quirky students might struggle. Often this can be due to fine motor coordination issues. Consultation and assessment by an occupational therapist would be indicated if you are concerned about your child's ability to write properly. However, handwriting challenges can also occur beyond fine motor delays and instead involve an ability to generate ideas and get those ideas onto paper.

Some students will overthink and approach their handwriting assignments from a perfectionistic standpoint, where they are censoring and filtering themselves to the point that they create a virtual writer's block. Others truly do struggle to generate those ideas in more of the creative realm. While many quirky students can write volumes of material on topics of their own interest, teachers often note that once an assignment is delivered that is outside of their scope of interest, they essentially shut down and have significant challenges being able to execute the assignment properly.

Many school programs have increased success by allowing the child an opportunity to dictate their assignments or type their assignments. Sometimes the use of a dry erase board can also help with idea generation in a nonthreatening manner. Some students benefit from standing or being seated on a T-chair or exercise ball while writing to keep their attention focused, and some benefit from wearing a weighted vest while they write, using a slant board or handwriting modification grasp on their pencil or pen, or using a rocking board under their feet so they can shift their feet left to right or up and down while they are writing.

Further, some students become overwhelmed with the number of sentences required and have a difficult time conceptually knowing when it's going to end. I find that establishing the expectations in advance is especially important, even more so when students are learning editing skills. Indeed, many students believe that once they have written down the required elements of an assignment that they have completed it. However, the work may require significant editing and the student should be informed ahead of time that step one is writing the sentences down or outlining the paper, and step two would be the editing process. I also find that something as simple as a small pad of sticky notes can be effective for task completion and persistence.

For example, imagine you are working with a student who is trying to write a five-sentence paragraph. To use the sticky note method, you would stick five blank notes (preferably colorful and smaller sized) onto the student's desk or on a nearby wall. The student would then be allowed to peel off one of the notes after each sentence is written. This helps them visually represent how much they have left to complete and gives them an opportunity to get a sensory break after each sentence. This is accomplished by allowing the student to crumble up the note after each sentence is completed, stand up, and walk to the garbage can to throw it away, and then return to the assignment to write the next sentence. This can also promote the flow of creativity and ideas by allowing the student some movement in the middle of the exercise, especially if stress and anxiety are factors while completing writing assignments.

Homework: Content versus Process

A common debate that arises during my work with children (many of whom are highly intelligent, yet demonstrate social quirks or challenges) involves homework. Many families are befuddled as their highly intelligent child, who excelled in the early elementary years, now begins to progress toward middle school and essentially debates, argues, shuts down, or is oppositional when it comes to being presented with assignments or homework, especially if the assignment is outside of their scope of interest (i.e., depth seekers).

I hear the argument day in and day out that unless the child can figure out how a particular assignment is justified or how it will directly benefit them in the future, he sees no reason to waste his time on it. Unfortunately, this argument takes up valuable time and many families begin to experience extreme amounts of stress because, as well-intentioned parents, they understand their obligation to help their child complete the homework and have it turned in to receive proper credit. Some children may also struggle to complete the assignment as indicated, such as solving the problem in their head and writing the answer on the empty space provided rather than showing the operations and work during math problems.

Over the years I have found considerable success by contemplating and validating the student's concerns with him, while also helping him understand the importance of process versus content when it comes to approaching homework. I begin this approach by developing rapport with the student so that he realizes I'm not just trying to talk him into something or trick him in any way. Parents and teachers may attempt to use questioning as a means of understanding the resistance, but depending on the degree of stress, tension, argumentativeness, and strained history regarding homework or other task completion, these adults may want to turn this exercise over to a qualified professional who is able to engage the student from a neutral vantage point.

I spend considerable time validating the student's sentiments about how homework is tedious, and I go as far as to emphatically state that homework is boring and in no way, shape, or form am I suggesting that they should enjoy it. Once the emotional validation has been established and the student realizes that I am not going to try to talk him out of his feelings, I begin to then investigate his reasoning and thinking, and shift him away from his focus on the content of the assignment and toward the more important process of the homework completion.

Indeed, many of these students have a point in that they may never use a specific assignment such as a formula or algorithm in the future. However, I have treated incredibly intelligent students who I met for the first time only after they failed to make it through school because they could not get past this argument in their mind of how the material is relevant. Some students reassure themselves that they will become one of a very small percentage of individuals who are able to make a tremendous amount of money without a formal education to back it up.

The ultimate lesson for the student here is that the content of what they are being asked to do—whether it be science, math, or writing an English assignment—may not always relate to future goals, but the process of spending the time problem solving, thinking the assignment through, following directions, organizing oneself by writing down the information in a homework planner, and then ultimately turning in the assignment are the critical life skills that the routine of homework is attempting to promote.

Children in the quirky category of development often experience significant challenges completing a task when they are bored, and they also experience difficulty delaying gratification. Furthermore, many of these children have been taxed socially, behaviorally, and emotionally each school day and in terms of their executive functions. Thus, when they return home they want to relax and decompress, and often gravitate toward highly stimulating and preferred activities of interest, whether it be video games, reading, or other (often solitary) activities of interest. Furthermore, if these children are prescribed medication, homework time coincides with the time of day in which many medications, especially those in the stimulant class (prescribed for students with attention and distractibility issues) are wearing off. This adds insult to injury for the parent who may be attempting to help a student complete his homework.

Homework is a time of day that can bring about conflict, stress, and frustration. Homework difficulties are not necessarily unique to quirky children but are especially apparent among them. Even for the brightest students, the organization, planning, and execution of homework (i.e., executive functions) can be problematic.

Challenges typically begin with the daily planner, if one is even being used, and parents not fully understanding the assignment because the child has not provided enough information to determine what needs to be accomplished. Further, if the assignment has been documented properly, the student may not have all the materials necessary to complete the work, or in some cases the student completes the homework but then does not turn it in because it is misplaced, left at home, or shoved into the bottom of a backpack or locker and thus never turned in.

Many students like to unwind after a long day of school with a relaxing activity and a snack. However, when the relaxing activity involves screens such as television or video games, it becomes more difficult for the student to break away from the highly motivating, relaxing, and rewarding activity and shift back onto academic and homework tasks.

Because students have different homework requirements, such as completing a packet of information that is distributed once throughout the week or not having homework on certain days, parents are often at risk for having an intermittent schedule of reinforcement set up for the child not doing homework. Thus if you anticipate that your child is going to have challenges regarding the execution of homework, then it is strongly encouraged that you begin to establish blocks of time, preferably beginning in the third or fourth grade, in which homework is part of the afternoon and evening routine. This method will be described in detail in Key 8.

The Adult Magnet

Teachers and other adults who interact with quirky students need to be aware of a common occurrence. Quirky children may be more comfortable with adults, and thus they tend to gravitate toward them when there are unstructured or social situations. Adults are often polite and humor the child, so the child continues to come back for more interactions. This is something that I experience regularly during my social groups with quirky children. The problem is that interacting primarily or comfortably with adults prohibits the child from the necessary peer-to-peer experiences. Thus, a preferred adult in the school may need to work to be sure that the child is not only talking to him or her during social opportunities and that adult may even need to be summoned to help facilitate some interactions with the peer group.

Home Consequences for School Behavior

I frequently consult with parents regarding various behaviors that occur at school that cause concern for school staff and parents. Consider the kindergarten student who is hitting classmates, talking back to his teacher, or running from the classroom. The staff at school are frustrated because as they attempt to intervene after the child has hit a classmate, the child also swats at them. His parents receive daily phone calls informing them of the behavior and asking them to come to school to talk to him or take him home. What should this family do?

If the child has an IEP at the time of any aggressive incidents or safety threats such as running away, the family can immediately request a behavior intervention plan (BIP) meeting. This is an opportunity for the IEP team from school to meet with the family and discuss the behavior(s) of concern and propose a response plan. Thus, if a particular behavior of concern is demonstrated in the school in the future, the team will respond consistently as indicated in the plan. An important part of the development of a BIP may include a functional behavior analysis. This involves an observation of the student in the school environment to determine what situation might occur before a behavior as well as the response of the staff. A functional behavior analysis uses the A-B-C model of addressing problematic behaviors as described in Key 5.

Imagine that the school team is trying to support a child who has been hitting others while walking down the hallway at school. The antecedent (what happened before the behavior) would be the child walking down the hall to another classroom. During the functional behavior analysis, the child is observed pushing another student and laughing, which would be identified as the behavior. Finally, the staff tell the student, "Keep your hands to yourself," which would be the consequence.

During the functional behavior analysis, no other incidents of pushing or placing hands on another student are observed at any other times of the day, so the team determines that the antecedent or situation most likely to result in physical aggression involves transitions in the hallway from the classroom to another area of the school. Telling the child to stop or keep hands to himself does not reduce any future occurrences of the behavior, so the team decides to intervene at the antecedent level rather than continuing to try out different responses to the behavior or consequences. If the goal were to prevent the behavior from occurring, the team would be wise to intervene at the antecedent stage. In this case, until the child can demonstrate consistent behavioral control in the group, he is lined up at the back of the line with a staff member walking next to him, and the pushing behaviors stop.

Regardless of whether the child has an educational support plan, it is imperative to separate school and home behavior. Avoid disciplining a child for things that happened at school once the child returns home for the day. When it comes to consequences, it is important to remember: the longer that you wait between a behavior occurring and the administration of the consequence, the less effective the consequence. So if the child misbehaves at 10 A.M., arrives home at 4 P.M., and is disciplined at home, the connection between the early misbehavior and the late consequence is lost. As a result, the consequence will lack power and effectiveness and may fuel frustration and hostility toward family members who had nothing to do with the behavior earlier in the day.

The reverse logic would be downright silly. Imagine your child had a rough night and was misbehaving before going to bed. You drop your child off at school the next morning and say to the teacher, "Would you make sure that you discipline Jordan today and give her some extra work? She was really difficult last night." The teacher would look at you like you're crazy! Whenever possible, the school should manage behaviors while the child is still at school. Dangerous and threatening behaviors that call for suspensions and expulsions are obvious exceptions to this rule. However, nothing is more irritating than when a parent receives a phone call or email saying that the school doesn't know what to do about a child's behavior. That is both nonproductive and indicative of a lack of understanding of behavioral strategies, especially if there are supports (an IEP) in place for that child.

It is generally not appropriate for schools to request that parents come pick up their children because they are misbehaving, unless the behavior is dangerous. What happens during the school day should be addressed using the school's expertise. At the end of the day, concerns can be discussed in-depth with the family once all the data from that day has been collected.

Back-and-Forth Communication Log

Back-and-forth communication between school and home is essential and extends across all stages of school development. Effective two-way partnerships between home and school are built through input regarding the child's learning, sharing, and listening to concerns; inviting feedback about classroom and home activities; and, where appropriate, eliciting active support. This communication establishes a relationship of trust and support. Open and consistent communication helps to keep everyone in the loop and helps avoid any misunderstandings, while also providing home and school with reciprocal "heads-up" information.

One way to help facilitate this communication process is to keep a log. This can be as simple as a notebook that has columns for notes related to home and school. Parents can fill out the log in the morning before dropping the child off at the bus stop or driving the child to school. The parent may document things that went well, things that were difficult for the child at home, and other behavioral notes. At school, the teacher can help the child complete it (or complete it without the child) before dismissal each day. School feedback can include items like what went well, what was difficult, points earned, homework for the evening, missing assignments, and social skills practiced, to name a few. Some families have created their own systems with checkboxes and pictures to represent specific behaviors that were displayed on any given day. Only the parents and the school will know which system, from simple to elaborate, will work best.

Children find it useful to acknowledge something that has not gone well in the back-and-forth log, and also to verbalize what went well. I recommend a two to one ratio of good things that happened during the day to things that did not go well (sometimes called the two roses and one thorn approach). The child is instructed to list the "bad thing" or "thorn" first because children, especially those with social difficulties, can often easily identify something negative from the day. In fact, they often have four or five things they would like to list, but they should be required to pick the thing that really bothered them most about the day. The two other notes are positive things, the "roses," that went well. It can be something as small or simple such as, "Billy said 'Hi' to me," or, "I got to take a turn during a game at recess." It does not need to be a huge accomplishment, but the process is designed to remind a child to recognize and acknowledge that although things do not always go as planned or as well as he would have liked, the day was not all bad and some things can (and did) go well.

The back-and-forth log should not be a burden to the school when it is used properly. It should not take more than a few minutes to complete at the end of each day. Seek out the appropriate staff member to complete it each day and it will eventually become a comfortable and familiar part of the daily routine. Some schools have tried to use cartoons with a happy smile, frown, and straight line for a mouth (i.e., "okay" day) as their back-and-forth log. Emotional representations in graphic form may work for younger kids, but without any qualifiers or additional information, they are not particularly useful for parents. Thus, if the school uses a check mark, stars, colors, or faces as a way of documenting the day, written comments of substance beyond "good day" should be included. Furthermore, some children can become fixated on losing points or receiving negative comments on their behavior logs or in their back-and-forth books. If the use of this strategy causes more stress for the child, then email communication or an alternative check-in method may be indicated. My goal of a back-and-forth communication book is not to get the child in trouble or to make additional work for the teacher, but to demonstrate that we are tuning in and paying attention to this child's needs and that everyone is working in a collaborative fashion.

Positive Peer Supports

Consider using the power of the peer group when it comes to managing a classroom with a quirky child. For example let's say that there are a group of students in the class who always point out when a quirky child is misbehaving or doing something annoying. One possibility would be to correct those students; another would be to pull those students aside and use their attention on the student as a means of assisting your efforts in the class. Thus you can frame it in a positive way and put the potential bully student position into a position of coaching and assistance. One thing you might say is, "I can see how you always notice when Jimmy is annoying the class but instead of telling him to 'stop' you can tell him what he should be doing instead, which would really be helpful. Further, because I'm not always able to interrupt my lesson to do that, it would be really valuable to me and helpful if you could assist me by helping your classmate out."

The earlier you request the assistance of the peer group to help a fellow student with social skills difficulty, the greater the level of empathy, assistance, and support you can expect from them. The goal is to create a culture or a community of peer support that is not geared only toward kids with social difficulties. Imagine the ripple effect of that type of approach in which all kids begin to feel a part of a group. This globalized approach also works very well, especially with regard to reducing bullying, encouraging problem solving and teamwork, and encouraging inclusion for cooperative activities. It sounds like common sense that a problem-solving, teamwork-oriented approach increases and improves student relationships and school performance, yet some schools fail to approach their curricula in this manner. Instead, they continue to allow for an "every man for himself" style of making it through the day. This is likely the same phenomenon that plays out in very large families, where there are simply too many kids to permit the necessary individual parental attention. What often happens in large families, however, is that siblings support one another, and more advanced siblings teach those who have yet to learn the same skills.

Positive peer support begins by educating all students about individual differences. Students are then asked if they would like to take part in a program that can not only change the lives of oth-

ers but also benefit them in the process. School staff then schedule meeting times for the group to meet. This can be several times
a month during recess or a lunch hour. If students sign up to take
part in the program, they are expected to attend the meetings at
those predetermined times. Despite any negative experiences
your child may have had with mean kids in the past, you should
feel relieved that there are still really good kids out there who
enjoy making a difference in the lives of others. I think most kids
are good, but many get caught up in peer pressure and other
dynamics that make it challenging to stand up for what is right.
Having an adult-facilitated and organized forum for children to
relate to each other in a positive way is a trend that I believe most
schools should be steering toward.

Lunch Groups

Positive peer supports can become members of lunch groups often
referred to as a "lunch bunch." This is basically a group of kids
who agree to eat together daily. This can occur in the cafeteria or,
depending on the school layout, in a quieter environment (classroom or library), especially if there are sensory issues to consider
(e.g., noise sensitivity or aversion to crowds). In general, a lunch
group is a supportive group of people that connects with one
another over lunch and can get to know one another well by meeting during each lunch period over a period of months, a semester,
or a year. Some schools rotate participation in the peer group so
that all kids are involved and a particular child is not identified.
Having an adult facilitate and supervise these lunch groups provides the necessary feedback and facilitation, although some group
time without adults (depending on the age and level of the group)
is also useful. In the absence of a lunch bunch, supervision in the
lunch room is often useful, especially when provided by teachers
or staff who are willing to go around to tables and talk (or even
briefly sit) with the kids in their natural seating arrangements, making students feel more comfortable and possibly facilitating relationships in the process.

Recess

The playground can be an ideal place to practice social skills, provided there is adequate supervision and coaching. In the absence of coaching or mediation by adults or positive peer models, the child is not going to figure it out simply by exposure. Although I may want my child to be able to swim, I can't just throw him in the pool and hope that he will figure it out. The same logic applies to the playground. Supervision and coaching of social skills is essential. Recess is a wonderful opportunity each day to work on social skills and connections with peers. Unfortunately, it is also a time in which teachers attend to administrative matters, and schools typically cannot afford to have multiple playground proctors. If schools use a volunteer parent or staff member to be on the playground, their role is often focused on safety and basic supervision of the children (e.g., watching to make sure that strange adults don't enter the playground or making sure that kids remain on the school's property), and they rarely have the time or the necessary training to help with social interactions.

Students develop new social skills when a teacher (usually an adult, but possibly a peer) leads them through social interactions. A teacher can offer various levels of assistance over the course of numerous social interactions. The goal is to allow the child to do as much as he can on his own and intervene and provide assistance when it is needed so the social interaction can be successfully completed.

Having an available adult or peer mentor (who is capable of coaching) to guide a group of kids through the see one, do one, teach one approach is essential. The peer or adult mentor first models a new strategy in the appropriate context and has the child watch or "see one." As this is done, the mentor describes what the strategy is, when the strategy should be used, and how to go about using it. For example, assume a peer mentor chooses a board game as a tool to teach the child turn taking and problem solving. The first approach would be to model playing the game with another peer as they describe what they are doing and why. The peer mentor might say, "Okay. We are going to pick game pieces first. I will be red. What color would you like to be? The instructions say 'the youngest player starts.' I am older than you, so you get to go first." This example is specific to a younger child and would be adjusted according to the age of the child you are coaching. Depending on the child's profile, the mentor may need to repeat the see one step several times to provide the necessary modeling.

Once the child being coached is ready to move on, the next step on the continuum is for the mentor to engage in the task with the child. Thus, we now ask the child to "do one." In the board game example, the child now plays with the mentor. The mentor looks for opportunities to reinforce appropriate behavior and coach when necessary. The mentor is instructed to keep feedback statements positive and tell the child what to do instead of what not to do. Finally, give the child time to problem solve and generate solutions.

The third step is for the child to take over the task of using the strategy with the mentor assisting and intervening as needed. This is when it would be ideal for the child to try to play the board game with multiple peers. The child would be asked to explain the rules and facilitate the play (i.e., "teach one") with the mentor helping out as needed.

Finally, the child independently uses the strategies he has learned while the mentor watches. Thus, the children are allowed to play together with the mentor present but no longer an active participant in the board game. If a child experiences difficulty using a strategy in a particular situation, the mentor may have to move back a step by providing help or taking over the task and asking the child to help.

Don't be afraid to combine boys and girls together during peer support activities, especially during the younger grades, as girls are often excellent peer mentors for boys with social difficulties. Kids can even volunteer to be a group leader during a recess period and choose an activity they will teach the group. Adults can be available to supervise as the children attempt to complete the activity. The group members can then show the adults what they have learned as they teach one to the adult.

Consider beginning with the cooperative game of Sardines. This can be played anywhere, indoors or out. The goal is similar to hide and seek, except that "it" hides first. Everyone else then tries to find "it." When someone finds "it," they hide with "it" in the same spot. The game ends when everyone finds the hiding spot of "it."

Recess Board Game Club

I often work with quirky students who isolate themselves during recess at school. These children may be observed alone on the swings, underneath a play structure digging in the dirt, or seated by a tree reading a book. They may also walk around the perimeter of the playground area alone or be observed talking to themselves as they engage in a fantasy, pretend, or role-play games in their mind without any other participants. I don't have any problems with a child who needs a break spending a little downtime on their own, especially if they don't receive enough sensory breaks or opportunities to regulate themselves throughout the day. However, if we are structuring a child's day wisely, we are giving him or her ample opportunity to decompress throughout the day. Recess often serves as one of the only opportunities in a child's time at school to truly promote social competence.

I appreciate that logistically many schools are unable to facilitate interactions. Certain programs that employ social peer tutors create self-consciousness for the child that can often be detrimental. Thus, I prefer to employ a strategy that is more covert in its operation and uses things like board games and creates clubs for students. Indeed, unless one is intrinsically social or athletic, one is unlikely to have ample opportunities to engage with peers during recess. Game clubs allow for a structured activity that has clear parameters, such as a board game, to be used on the playground and invites opportunities for other students who may like a change of pace or enjoy the particular game to play with one another. Furthermore, the quirky child can remain fairly incognito as far as requiring social assistance by simply signing up for these clubs, which the teacher can create in the classroom and request participants for each recess period.

One Bad Moment = Reset Button

Please remember to emphasize to your quirky child that having one bad moment in a day does not ruin the entire day. I often encourage students to visually represent a reset button in their brain whereby we can help them understand that they can make a mistake or experience an "oops" or "uh oh" moment and still recover. Quirky students may believe that their entire day is ruined, and as a result there is no incentive for them to get back on track. I see this problem especially played out with poorly developed behavior plans in school in which the student must work for the entire day to achieve a desired reward. The problem with this type of approach is that if the student makes enough mistakes in the early portion of the day and thus they will not receive the later reward, they have no incentive to get their behavior back on track.

Thus an effective behavior plan with the quirky student (or any student for that matter) must involve blocks of time in which the child can earn the necessary reinforcer with the opportunity to get back on track. An example would be to divide the child's day into intervals for each class period or subject (e.g., 9 A.M. to 9:50 A.M. math class). Next, specify the target behaviors or what you expect from the child during that time frame ("Child will remain in desk and raise hand before asking or answering a question"). If the child successfully engages in the target behaviors that have been specified, then he would be allowed to read quietly for ten minutes before beginning the next interval, provided that reading is a meaningful reward. If the child was not successful completing the specific target behaviors during that time interval, he would not be allowed the reward of reading that time, but could then reset to try to earn the reward during the next interval. This is a much more effective way to achieve desired behavioral outcomes because if the reading or other reward were not until the end of the day, the child would already have lost the chance to earn it by 9:50 A.M. Thus, what is the incentive in trying hard to meet the target behaviors for the duration of the day?

Homeschooling

You may be reading this book as a parent who home schools your child or may be considering a home-schooling option. Many of the strategies explained here can either be used in a home school arrangement or modified to fit the child's specific context. Parents often ask me about the home school option as it pertains to a child who is struggling socially. They question whether educating the child in an environment without much peer contact is a good thing. I reply that there are pros and cons associated with sending the child to school as well as home schooling.

The obvious con to home schooling a child is that the opportunity to interact with as many different children in as many different situations as possible, per the social skills research on effective intervention, is significantly limited. However, many home school programs now offer weekly gatherings where other home-schooled children can get together and interact during a variety of activities. The bottom line is that you need to understand your child's specific profile and needs before deciding to home school. Some children thrive with such an arrangement, whereas others fail to exercise the necessary social muscle at the needed frequency and intensity to achieve the desired gains and outcomes. Consultation with a developmental specialist can help you make an informed decision regarding your child's schooling. If your child is already home schooled and experiencing social challenges, you will want to provide many outlets and opportunities beyond structured home school gatherings to allow for development. A developmental specialist can also be valuable to you in answering questions regarding what those social outlets should include and how frequently you need to seek them out.

Using a Paraprofessional
as Behavioral Pharmacology

Behavioral pharmacology is the phrase I use to describe assisting a child through challenging scenarios especially those that involve or tax executive functions. Thus, instead of using medication to assist a child's behavior, we use behavioral intervention, often with similar results. A common example of this is a child who receives additional services in a classroom and has access to a paraprofessional who is able to assist them, through certain times of the day or the entire day.

A paraprofessional is an adult in the classroom who operates under the direction of the teacher and can assist the child during the activities of the day. Although many schools attempt to argue that children can become overly dependent on these individuals, it is my experience that this is rarely the case, and paraprofessionals are often what help prevent a child from requiring medication. I think of paraprofessionals as "surrogate frontal lobes" because they are available to direct the child's attention onto what is important as well as prompt, support, and assist the child in areas where executive functions may be underdeveloped or require additional assistance.

Consider a child who is distractible and inattentive and experiences difficulty remaining on task. The paraprofessional is able to prompt the child to attend at the correct time and help them to reengage their focus during times in which they are distractible. Often, parents, professionals, and schools rely on medication to help focus a child's attention or regulate behavior. Medication by itself does not help the child attend to what is important and when; rather it is designed to improve the child's attention. Unfortunately, the child must still possess the ability to be able to assess what is important and tune in to the right things at the right time. Indeed, inattention requires attention.

Thus, behavioral pharmacology is essentially any plan, accommodation, or adult (or even peer) assistance that a student may receive throughout the day that can provide them with the additional supports to help beyond medication approaches. Granted, some children require the use of both behavioral intervention and medication. I am also not suggesting that every child who struggles with executive functioning would qualify for a paraprofessional, but in more extreme cases or at least during the early formative developmental years, paraprofessionals can truly effect tremendous change on the child's overall outcomes.

Take-home points:

- Special education support in school through a Section 504 Plan or Individualized Education Program (IEP) may be necessary to provide your child with accommodations or intervention during the school day.
- Lunch groups, peer support groups, and recess game clubs are just some of the interventions that you can suggest to your child's school to help further promote social development. The best part is that these groups do not cost the school any money to implement.
- Handwriting is an area where quirky students may struggle. Often this can be due to fine motor coordination issues. Consultation and assessment by an occupational therapist would be indicated if you are concerned about a child's ability to write properly. However, handwriting challenges can also occur beyond fine motor delays and instead involve the ability to generate ideas and get those ideas onto paper.
- Please remember to emphasize to your quirky child that having one bad moment in a day does not ruin the entire day. I often encourage students to visually represent a reset button in their brain to help them understand that they can have a mistake or experience an "oops" or "uh oh" moment and still recover.

Teaching them to anticipate mistakes as a normal and expected part of development helps to alleviate the stress and anxiety they often experience from making a mistake.

- If you anticipate that your child is going to have challenges regarding the execution of homework, then it is strongly encouraged that you begin to establish scheduled blocks of time, preferably beginning in the third or fourth grade, in which homework is to be completed each evening.

UNDERSTAND DIAGNOSTIC CRITERIA AND TREATMENT

If you are a parent, there will inevitably be a time in your child's development when you question whether something is wrong. This could be a toddler who is not talking enough, an elementary school student who does not seem to be learning at the same pace as the others his age, or a teenager who is moody and isolating herself from the family. Most people have a quirk or two that makes them unique. For example, a nine-year-old child who loves to learn about the *Titanic* is not going to set off any alarm bells of concern. However, if this interest becomes so pronounced that most people who know the child are forced to listen him discuss this subject at length, we begin to question whether there is a need to investigate his profile further. Furthermore, if the child begins to develop a variety of behaviors that seem outside the norm, you would need to tune in accordingly.

I recommend using a combination of what I call the frequency formula, in addition to a review of the Four D's of pathology (originally presented in the Introduction) when trying to determine if professional evaluation or treatment is indicated. The frequency formula is as follows: one occurrence is a fluke, two occurrences are a coincidence, three occurrences are a trend, and four occurrences are a pattern. This formula tells you nothing about whether a behavior is in the normative, quirky, or pathology category. It simply helps you understand frequency. Many people use it in sports, such as when a team unexpectedly wins a championship

NORMATIVE	QUIRKY	PATHOLOGY
Meeting Developmental Milestones	S: Social Challenges	Deviance
Curious About New Things/ People	T: Transitional Stress	Distress
Comfortable with People	R: Regulatory Difficulties	Dysfunction
Approachable (Even when Shy)	E: Executive Dysfunction	Danger
Variety of Interests	S: Sensory Sensitivity	
Understands/Uses Humor	S: Smart/Social imbalance	
Flexible Thinker	E: Emotional Reactivity	
Adaptable to Change	D: Depth Seeker/ Disinterest in Imaginative Play	
Can Self-Regulate (Emotion and Behavior)		
Affect Appropriate to Context		
Awareness of Surroundings		
Effective Two-Way Communication		

FREQUENCY FORMULA
(1 = Fluke, 2 = Coincidence, 3 = Trend, 4 = Pattern)

game and some call it a fluke. If the team continues to win in future years, perhaps they have talent. The same frequency formula applies when a child demonstrates a behavioral challenge. If a young child who is generally well behaved has a bad day and screams at his teacher, we would call that event a fluke. If he continues to engage in this behavior going forward, then a trend or pattern emerges and we must investigate further.

The Four D's model helps us continue to investigate any concerns. The model looks beyond frequency of an event occurring and helps determine whether a symptom or cluster of symptoms warrants professional evaluation and treatment. The Four D's are: deviance, distress, dysfunction, and danger.

Imagine you have a nine-year-old son who still loves playing with trains. Using the frequency formula, playing with trains at an older than expected age is the one concern about the child, so it falls under the "fluke" definition. However, you remain concerned because he plays with trains at the expense of other interactions, so you begin to apply the Four D's model. At nine years old, most other children are no longer interested in trains. Thus, you think that there is some deviance from what is normative, resulting from the interest. It is unlikely that the child is experiencing distress over the interest in trains, but distress may result if the peer group begins to criticize him for enjoying this topic or if he is so insistent about discussing trains and begins to receive feedback from others to stop talking about it. Your son talks about lots of different things, even though he would love to talk about trains most of the time. The dysfunction criteria would not be met unless that child becomes so absorbed by this interest that it makes transitions or completion of activities difficult (e.g., difficulty stopping playing with trains to come to dinner or leave the house to go to school, or extreme tantrum/meltdown when told to transition away from the trains). Your child does not have any issues when asked to stop playing with trains.

So if you were the parent of this boy, here's how you would use the model of quirky versus pathology. Once you have identified a quirky behavior, in this case interest in trains that seems inappropriate or immature for the child's age, you would begin to ask yourself the questions about the items in the normative column presented in the Introduction. Remember that no person is expected to achieve all of the normative characteristics all of the time. The child's age and stage of development needs to be considered. You determine that your child is meeting most of the normative criteria, so you can rest easy that he has a unique interest in trains that is uncommon among most other nine-year-olds (i.e., meets the deviance criteria of pathology), but there are no other criteria met when you examine the quirky criteria or the pathology criteria, so you have just determined that the child really likes trains and that's as much as you need to know.

In the event that you determined that the child was demonstrating a pattern using the frequency formula, and the pattern resulted in the Four D's mostly being met, then the child is entering into the pathology category. This chapter provides information about neurodevelopmental diagnoses that can develop from both a normative and a quirky profile. In the event that you are concerned and want to seek a professional evaluation of your child, this chapter helps you navigate that process and understand the steps to take along the way and introduces you to some of the specialists you may come into contact with.

A Pop Culture Impression of Quirky

For many years, Hollywood has incorporated quirky characters into television shows and movies. Audiences tend to find humor in the things these characters say and do. A notable quirky character is recent years is Sheldon Cooper from the television show *Big Bang Theory*. Sheldon is a highly intelligent physicist who demonstrates the high IQ/low EQ discrepancy described in Key 2 in the smart/social imbalance category of the STRESSED model.

Sheldon has poorly developed social skills, adheres to a strict routine while interacting with his environment, and often comes across as narcissistic or relating to others as intellectually inferior. In real life, such a person may be difficult to tolerate and would probably have challenges connecting with the world around him. Even the other characters on the *Big Bang Theory* have a difficult time coping with Sheldon's eccentric behaviors and his mental rigidity and apparent lack of empathy toward others.

Sheldon is extremely uncomfortable with physical contact such as hugs, he becomes irritated and stressed when he is interrupted or hears others arguing with each other, and he has a very difficult time keeping a secret (he lacks an interpersonal "filter"). However, add a laugh track and remove yourself one step by watching it happen on television rather than have it happen to you in real life, and all of these behaviors become amusing and even tolerable.

Perhaps Sheldon has an excuse for these quirks. After all, he is highly intelligent. He tells his friends, when they are critical of him, "I'm not crazy, my mother had me tested." In many ways, Sheldon does what he likes. He loves comics, role-playing games, fantasy fiction, video games, and action figures. He may be perceived by others as a geek or a nerd, and certainly he is quirky. Do Sheldon's quirks necessitate a clinical diagnosis? If he were to receive a formal diagnosis, how would this help him? After all, he is a brilliant physicist.

Is There *Really* a Problem?

Questions regarding diagnosis may not be as important for an individual at Sheldon's stage of life. He has made it through elementary school, high school, college, and even graduate school! He has a doctorate, a job, and roommates. He even has a romantic interest. Adults who are quirky and have accomplished some success in life are typically not motivated to seek out diagnostic clarification when nothing seems to be interfering with their functioning, especially from their own perspective. Typically, it is a request or recommendation from a loved one, family member, or employer that results in an adult seeking an evaluation of their social, emotional, and behavioral profile.

Children are much the same. They are typically oblivious to many of their quirks and may only begin to experience ancillary symptoms such as anxiety and depression during adolescence when the peer group outwardly rejects them for something they had been oblivious about until that time. Imagine that realization for a moment.

A child can grow up with quirky behaviors and lack insight into their behaviors, and his family may either explain it away (as something they once did or that all kids do) or decide they did not want their child labeled. The child is living life as if all is well, and suddenly he is in junior high and the peer group is giving him very different feedback. During a period of development in which the social stakes couldn't be higher and the slightest differences make you an outcast, this child is now experiencing an identity crisis of epic proportions. Cue anxiety and mood symptoms, and add the influx of hormone production associated with puberty and you can imagine what begins to occur.

This is why the question of pathology is so tricky when evaluating children because a child can be experiencing a variety of pathology symptoms but not yet experience distress or be aware of dysfunction. For younger children, it may be the adults such as parents, day care staff, or teachers as well as other children who are the ones experiencing distress and noting dysfunction or danger due to the child's profile.

Many quirky children experience their greatest level of difficulties during the transition into and progression through adolescence, in large part because of a newly developed ability to be self- and other-aware or notice the differences that are causing challenges during daily interactions. One major contributing variable to the increase in stress experiences is the fact that the social demands are increasing at such intensity that the social and emotional gap widens between the child and his peer group. Even those who have received support and counseling prior to this time can begin to experience new, heightened levels of distress.

Not all will suffer. Those who are more oblivious to the perceptions of those around them can remain fairly insulated from stress and the resulting anxiety and mood symptoms. This is a powerful catch-22 for quirky individuals with social challenges. Many lack the insight and self-awareness to seek change or assistance. Although this may insulate them from distress, it also prevents them from making the necessary adjustments and seeking assistance to improve their social profile.

Sheldon Cooper is like this in many ways. He is often confused by the adverse reactions of others regarding his interpersonal style. Due to his challenges with perspective taking, he remains matter-of-fact about the agitated responses from others as if it has more to do with them rather than anything he did wrong. This creates more distance socially, although Sheldon's self-esteem remains intact with this style of response.

In many ways, treatment can become a catch-22 as well. Although the goal may be to increase insight so that the individual can make the necessary changes, as that insight improves it leaves him increasingly vulnerable as awareness to the negative reactions of others is heightened.

To Evaluate or Not to Evaluate

The decision to seek a developmental evaluation to assess a child's profile is not one that any parent or guardian takes lightly. Some families are eager to understand their child and provide them with the best possible outcomes. Others are resistant to the idea of a label or something that may be "wrong" with their child. These parents may wait with the hope that it goes away on its own or the child grows out of it.

Most parents want to fully understand their child's profile and learn how to respond to it in a manner that will produce desired outcomes. Many would prefer to acquire this information without the need to label the child, especially if it is a term that may follow him or her later in life and perhaps even affect their ability to receive admission into schools, employment, and so on. So what is a parent to do?

Many eccentric or quirky children possess qualities and attributes that can be celebrated and nurtured. These are the characteristics that make the child unique and special. I only offer guidance to the families who are concerned that a child's quirky profile is creating stress or adversely affecting the child, family members, peers, or school personnel in a significant way. The following section provides an overview of what to expect if you find yourself considering a formal evaluation of your child's unique profile.

The Evaluation Timeline

The decision to seek a developmental and behavioral evaluation may be a personal one or it may be at the recommendation of an educator such as the child's teacher or a medical professional such as a pediatrician. I see many families who are comfortable discussing their child's quirks with family members and friends, and my name as a specialist is often passed along via word of mouth. Other referrals are made when a school reports concerns or a pediatrician may recommend an evaluation. Typically pediatricians may observe something in their office during a routine health exam or the family may report stress or concerns to the pediatrician or other health professional that warrant further evaluation.

Should I Be Concerned?

Depending on the nature of the child's profile, parents may or may not have serious concerns. Typically, aggressive or hyperactive behaviors as well as speech delays, sensory concerns, and repetitive behaviors result in earlier referrals for evaluation, especially if they are frequently occurring (see the frequency formula) and meeting criteria for any of the Four D's described in the Introduction and the beginning of this chapter. Symptoms of various neurodevelopmental diagnoses that often overlap with a quirky profile (STRESSED characteristics) are described later in this chapter. For any other behaviors, it may require a consultation with your primary health care provider, knowledge of child development and what is typical or abnormal, or simply following your instincts (e.g., "Something just isn't right"), which I often find to be accurate when working with families. Obviously issues such as depression and anxiety should always result in concern, especially if they occur at a level that interferes with a child's daily functioning.

I am not referring to your child specifically in any of the examples I have provided in this book. Thus, you must attempt to apply the information to your specific situation. This book provides a model to help you evaluate the need for additional services. In addition to anything clinical as far as when to be concerned, I always trust parental instinct. The best rule of thumb when tuning into your instincts is: when in doubt, check it out.

A few other things to consider when determining whether to arrange an evaluation for your child include a recommendation from a child specialist such as a pediatrician or educator, a persistent display of the behavior(s) of concern for two months or more (child development does have a way of working things out in some cases, but persistent quirky behaviors should be checked), or a pattern of behavior or symptoms that have caused disruption in a child's ability to function or interact with others in more than one environment. For the latter rule, a school-age child would most likely demonstrate the symptoms at home and school at a level that result in disruption in daily functioning.

The Blind Spot

There are some children who are experiencing developmental challenges but who fall into the blind spot of parents, teachers, or health providers. Parents are forced to follow their instincts with these children when seeking an evaluation because they may have a child who is quiet, yet distant and disengaged. The child in the blind spot may not cause any disruption in their environment but instead fade into the background and keep to himself. "He's just quiet" or "She's shy" may be explanations used by the adults who know the child best to explain this pattern of behavior. This is true; many children are simply shy, but you should be careful when applying these descriptors in social contexts because it could inadvertently perpetuate the behavior you are trying to address.

Children learn that if they don't respond to others, their parent will excuse the behavior, and the cycle becomes reinforced. I tell families that even shy children can say "hello." In fact, most do this by standing close to their parent and looking away, but they will say "hello" in a reciprocal manner. Many shy children will smile and close their eyes, but those who may be experiencing some true social challenges will respond in a much less socially acceptable fashion. Beyond the age of five years, any greeting shyness of others should begin to fade away, even for children who are somewhat shy. When you cannot get a child to even reference you in some fashion, even nonverbally, there should be cause for concern.

The old adage "The squeaky wheel gets the grease" is often painfully true for children who could benefit from additional support services in school but do not cause enough of a disruption. Indeed, a child who is sweet, polite, and well behaved but only wants to talk about specific models of automobiles with other children is not likely to raise enough concerns in school to receive any additional services. The painful reality here is that families often have to seek outside help when a child demonstrates this blind spot presentation. Many girls with attention deficits or anxiety also fall into this blind spot. Others view girls with attention or anxiety challenges as "daydreamers" or "shy" and "quiet." These girls may miss out on important academic material due to their attention controls, or they miss out on social exchanges due to their nervousness. When I am able to meet with these girls, they describe a longing to connect with others around them, and also cite extreme fear and hesitation. These girls stay under the radar so that school won't intervene, and thus families bring them to work with someone like me.

What to Expect on Your Evaluation Journey

When a developmental evaluation is recommended, you may be fortunate enough to receive the name and contact information of a highly regarded developmental specialist who regularly works with children and their families on the issues described throughout this book. If such a person is not available or well known in your area, you may receive a list of providers or need to research some in your area. If you want your insurance to help with the cost, you will most likely need to choose a provider from your insurance company's list of approved providers. Any names you have been provided by a referral source (such as a pediatrician) may not appear on that list. This is because many specialists opt out of insurance panels because their area of emphasis is so specialized they have difficulty getting reimbursement from insurance. This has everything to do with laws and politics and should not reflect poorly on a treatment provider.

Insurance versus Self-Pay

If you have insurance, especially a policy that you pay for, you probably want to use it when it comes to receiving any form of health care. Your insurance provider typically requires that you obtain services from a professional in their network. There are certainly highly skilled providers available for general developmental concerns who are part of your network. However, many highly specialized providers elect to remain a fee-for-service provider, meaning that they bill you directly at the time of service and then provide you with the billing codes and receipt so you can get reimbursement from your insurance.

The reasons providers elect to opt out of insurance panels are varied but generally involve the amount of time and resources required to receive reimbursement as well as the reimbursement rate, which is usually set at a specific amount regardless of the degree of specialization the provider possesses. Families that insist on using their insurance benefit at the time of service must do their research to be sure the provider they choose has the necessary qualifications to adequately and accurately evaluate the child.

Families must keep in mind that services are often reimbursed based on a diagnostic code. Some developmental diagnoses are still not covered by insurance companies despite the impact they have on the child's life. Issues also arise with the diagnostic code requirement when families want to protect their health information. If they choose a fee-for-service provider who does not interact directly with insurance, their information is protected and only released to the family and anyone the family authorizes to receive the information.

When working with insurance, the child's diagnostic code is stored in a database with a possibility to be accessed in future years. This information can presumably be accessed at a much later date such as when a person seeks employment, life insurance, or a career in the military. You should always check with your provider or directly with the insurance company if you are concerned about how your information will be stored, accessed, shared, and used in the future.

Another consideration is that quirky kids often don't fit neatly into a specific diagnostic category, and thus even if the family uses their insurance they may not receive full or even partial reimbursement because a diagnostic code was not determined. Furthermore, if the quirky profile is consistent with an autism spectrum diagnosis, your state may subscribe to laws that deny reimbursement for individuals with this classification. Regardless of whether you choose to work with your insurance for an evaluation, do your research and know whom you are going to see. The section that follows describes professionals who may be able to help you better understand your quirky child.

Potential Evaluators

Child/Pediatric Psychologist

A psychologist is a health provider who has completed extensive training in human development and behavior. There are many different types of psychologists, but it is unlikely that one who sees adults can also be truly specialized in children and teens. I would suggest that you try to work with a psychologist who has completed their doctorate (Ph.D. or Psy.D.) in psychology with specific emphasis in child development. This can be a developmental psychologist, a child psychologist, a pediatric neuropsychologist, or a pediatric psychologist (I am a pediatric psychologist). Furthermore, if possible, be sure that this individual has experience working with children with social interaction challenges and ideally neurodevelopmental disorders.

A psychologist who specializes in child development will spend at least two hours with the child and parent(s) to gather relevant history, observe the child as he or she interacts with the items and people in the evaluation room, ask the parent to complete developmental questionnaires, and may even conduct some standardized testing and evaluation procedures. The evaluation should be fun for the child and involve playing with toys and other items.

Some children become tense and nervous at a young age when going to visit a doctor. Their early recollection of what happens in a doctor's office usually involves shots, and you should reassure the child that they are there to play and talk at this appointment. Some psychologists have pictures of their office on their website to show the child so that they see it is a fun office with no exam table or white lab coats. If parents are nervous about what to say or when to say it, these concerns should be discussed with the provider's office prior to arriving at the appointment so all of the necessary information can be obtained to comfort all involved.

You are encouraged to bring to the appointment any documents or records that may be relevant to the evaluation, such as school reports, education plans, and evaluations from outside sources.

Developmental and Behavioral Pediatrician

A developmental and behavioral pediatrician is a health provider who may be difficult to locate depending on your geographic area. As a result they are often highly sought after and can have lengthy waiting lists. They are able to prescribe medications and can also help rule out any physical or organic causes for the child's behaviors.

An evaluation with a developmental and behavioral pediatrician may also include a physical examination to assess for any physical malformations that would warrant a genetics screening. This includes looking at facial features and the symmetry of the face as well as the hands, fingers, feet, and toes. You may also be asked if the child has any birthmarks or other notable bodily characteristics or markings, and the doctor can examine these at the time of the appointment. The child may be weighed at this appointment, especially if there are concerns about growth or medications are being discussed. Medical history, if available, can be reviewed.

If the developmental and behavioral pediatrician operates in a medical clinic, there may be the standard exam table and tools such as stethoscope and otoscope in the room. If the provider is in private practice, the room may look more like an office with toys, and any medical equipment is typically kept out of view unless it needs to be used. Developmental and behavioral pediatricians can be quite skilled at disguising a physical exam as a form of physical play, such as pretending to count the child's fingers in a silly way while inspecting them for anything notable.

Neurologist

A neurologist is a health provider who is able to assess neurological conditions. I often refer families to neurology if I am concerned about possible absence seizure activity. This condition involves a child who seems to go into a trance or stare blankly at times throughout the day. The neurologist can ask the child to engage in an activity such as blowing repeatedly on a pinwheel toy to see if the child experiences this trance in the office. He or she can also order any additional testing, scans, or evaluations that may help further understand the child's overall profile. Although bedside manner varies dramatically among health care providers, neurologists tend to use more of a medical model of evaluation, and thus the appointment may remain focused on evaluation and not resemble play.

Center-Based Evaluation

Depending on where you reside, you may choose to visit or be referred to a child developmental center or children's hospital where you will spend considerable time visiting with a variety of specialists. This may take place over the course of one or several days. A center-based developmental evaluation may include visiting with a speech therapist, physician, psychologist, occupational therapist, and possibly a physical therapist. A genetics screening may also take place. Developmental evaluations are approached differently depending on the provider but generally contain consistent elements. Thus, a good evaluation should yield similar results across treatment providers. Keep in mind that many developmental diagnoses remain subjective meaning that they are based on history gathering, observation, and some type of formalized testing such as a developmental screening tool or parent-teacher rating form.

An important principle to consider during an evaluation is that no conclusion can be reached about your child based on one piece of an evaluation. The assessment or observation must include history, parent interview, observation, and interaction with the child at the very least. Because some children only demonstrate certain behaviors in one context, the clinician may consider going to that location to complete an observation of the child in that environment, such as a school observation. Keep in mind that most clinical/developmental diagnoses require that a child demonstrate delays or problematic behaviors in at least two settings (school and home) consistently.

Treatment

After you have met with a developmental specialist, that professional should provide you with a clinical impression of the child or diagnosis, as applicable. You should then spend some time discussing the child's profile and a plan for treatment.

If medication is recommended, the provider may prescribe it or coordinate care with your pediatrician to manage medications. It is a good idea to allow any developmental specialist who is working with your child to coordinate with your pediatrician to ensure continuity of care. Your pediatrician may have made the referral in the first place, and they should be included in any reports or documentation of the child's developmental evaluation.

The professional who evaluated your child will often refer you to other specialists or treatment programs such as those described in the next section.

Speech and Language Therapy

If your child is experiencing speech or language issues, then a speech language therapist will be recommended to further evaluate and treat the child accordingly. Speech disorders include articulation disorder (i.e., difficulties producing sounds to an extend that others cannot understand the child), fluency disorder (e.g., stuttering), prosody challenges (i.e., rate, pitch, volume, or quality of speech), and dysphagia or feeding disorder (i.e., challenges eating, swallowing, or problems with drooling). Language disorders typically involve problems with expressive and/or receptive speech, such as not understanding or comprehending speech or not speaking at the expected rate for the child's age.

Occupational Therapy

Occupational therapists help people across the life span participate in the things they want and need to do through the therapeutic use of everyday activities (occupations). Common occupational therapy interventions include helping children with disabilities to participate fully in school and social situations (e.g., helping a child learn to regulate the movement of his body through space, helping a child with a weak handwriting grasp hold a pencil more effectively), and helping people recovering from injury to regain skills. Occupational therapists often work with children who experience too much or too little stimulation through their senses and have trouble integrating information. As a result, it's difficult (if not impossible) for these children to feel comfortable and secure, function effectively, and remain open to learning and socialization.

Occupational therapists (OTs) are often employed by a school district and can also be located in private clinics and hospitals.

The OT may recommend follow-up treatment in a clinic, which is often fun for the child and full of toys and play equipment. The OT may also provide you with strategies to use in the home to help address your child's unique sensory profile.

Early Childhood Services

If your child is between the ages of 18 months and 5 years old, one of the first referral sources you may hear about is your school district. Your pediatrician may provide the necessary contact information, or you can look up early childhood services in your school district and call directly. When you call to inquire about services, you will be asked to describe your child's development and any concerns you or your health provider may have. These evaluations are provided to you at no direct cost as they are covered by tax dollars. Depending on your school district, the evaluation may involve one or more specialists visiting with you and your child in your family home, or you may be asked to meet with specialists in a school or district office.

The most common reason for an early childhood evaluation through the school district is a speech delay. Some families may already have a diagnosis such as Down syndrome or autism and can call their district to inquire about additional school evaluations and services. Be aware that schools do not provide clinical diagnoses. Instead, they evaluate the child to determine if there is a developmental delay that would interfere with his or her successful transition into a general education environment. Thus, if a child is not yet speaking at three years old, the school will want to begin providing speech services. A developmental preschool may be available through the school district that allows the child to work directly with specialists, such as speech pathologists and occupational therapists, while becoming accustomed to the school experience of morning meeting/circle time, centers, and other activities.

While it's always a plus to have your tax dollars go to work for you and not incur any expenses for therapy, keep in mind that many school districts are overwhelmed with families seeking services, and there may only be a few specialists available to provide services. Thus, children under the age of two who qualify for services may only receive 20 minutes to an hour of therapy each week. Depending on your child's needs, this may or may not be sufficient, and thus you would need to decide if additional private therapies, at your expense or by using your insurance, would be needed. The good news here is that typically when a child approaches the third year of life, a comprehensive program often becomes available in the school district, allowing for the child to attend a developmental preschool four to five days per week for approximately three hours a day. This significantly increases the intensity of services.

Social Skills Groups

Social skills groups are often available within the context of your child's school day, and children can sometimes be allowed to participate in these even if they do not have a specific educational support plan. Social groups are also likely to be available in your community and can often be located with an online search or through word-of-mouth from other parents.

I offer social groups throughout the year in my clinic, with a specific focus on children who are quirky. Many social groups are geared toward children on the autism spectrum, and thus you need to assess the goodness of fit for your child participating in the group if other members have dramatically different needs. In my groups, for example, we do not focus on a child's diagnosis or lack thereof. The groups help members build confidence, practice new ways of relating to and communicating with each other, and provide the children with a safe, comfortable environment to connect with others who are similar. Many children experience a sense that they are so different from others that no one will ever understand them or want to connect with them. The moment they enter the room in my groups, they realize "there are other people like me" and they use this corrective emotional experience as a foundation to build confidence and share ideas and strategies that they will use when trying to connect more with the children they typically spend time with in their daily lives.

Timing

As described in Key 3, the opportunity to maximize growth and learning for foundational developmental milestone such as speech, coordination, and play occurs in the first six years of life. This should not cause panic if you are reading this book with the hope of assisting a child who is older than six. Instead, it means that the results may just not come as quickly or easily, but they will still come. For some children, differences in development will not be apparent until the social demands outweigh the child's ability to keep up with the peer group. This noticeable difference may not occur until third grade and beyond, even into the junior high or high school years. Even for families who are determined to provide intervention for their child's specific challenges, the child may not yet be fully receptive to the intervention for a variety of reasons. This is why consultation and evaluation by a developmental specialist is so important. There are many factors that go into answering the question of what to do and when to do it. It is a highly individualized process to determine who needs what and when. This is the very reason I caution parents to avoid following suggestions from other parents or online. These individuals or websites do not possess the necessary knowledge of your child's developmental profile to be able to accurately make recommendations. What may have worked for them is simply that: something that worked for *them*.

Genetics

Many parents may be concerned if a developmental specialist recommends a genetic evaluation. The purpose of this would be to rule out a possible identified genetic anomaly that explains a child's developmental profile. Mother nature is a mad scientist, and genetic specialists are often learning as they go as many anomalies begin to show up but have not yet been observed in a large enough subset of the population to warrant a specific genetic classification.

I do not take referrals to genetics lightly. As a psychologist, I always consider the impact on a family when I ask them to pursue a genetics evaluation. There are genetic syndromes that are carries solely on the mother's side and others on the father's side. Mother's age at the time of pregnancy and other factors such as substance use and family history can all play a role in the occurrence of genetic anomalies. Evaluation alone can be stressful to families, and I certainly don't want to add insult to injury. A good genetics evaluation will include genetics counseling and referrals for support if necessary. I can only imagine what it feels like to learn that your child has a problem with their genetic code and it was caused by your genes or something passed along from your side of the family. If parents are together at the time of such findings, I can only imagine how this may create stress, tension, and guilt depending on the nature of their relationship and way of coping. In many cases, nothing is detected, and the parents receive peace of mind that the child is not carrying any traits that need to be addressed beyond those observed during the developmental evaluation. In these cases, the family can move forward using the recommendations from the evaluation. If there is a genetic explanation, the family may need to take some time to process it but will now possess some powerful information that can guide their response to the child from this point forward.

Diagnosis

I often meet children as they enter the elementary school years who have been diagnosed with a variety of things that include obsessive compulsive disorder, attention deficit disorder, oppositional defiant disorder, and even in some extreme cases bipolar disorder. Not to be negative toward any clinicians who interacted with these children prior to their arrival in my office, but diagnoses such as bipolar disorder and obsessive compulsive disorder are so rare in children under the age of 13 years that it is highly unlikely that a child's symptom pattern is the result of such a diagnosis.

Behavior doesn't explain causes. When I see such a variety of diagnostic labels applied to a young child, I begin to tune into more social thinking challenges, which typically arise in categories reserved for children with autism spectrum disorder or nonverbal learning disorder (described in the next section). When evaluating a child prior to their entrance into kindergarten or elementary school, I understand that diagnosis can be a challenge because the child may not have yet experienced the social demands necessary to fully observe and understand their true diagnostic profile.

Many of these children prior to the age of six may present simply as quirky or as fairly dysregulated. I use a diagnostic term referred to as a regulatory/sensory processing disorder as a way of tracking and monitoring this symptom profile. At this stage I can only say that this child may be at risk for an attention deficit disorder but may also have an underlying autism spectrum profile, such as that found among children with Asperger's syndrome. As frustrating as that may be for families who want a clear definition of the issue, we need to be careful to not rush to label children given that this shifts the course of parenting and the overall approach to the child socially, academically, emotionally, and behaviorally.

What I propose that clinicians do instead is to begin to give tools to the family to start to chip away at the child's profile in terms of things they need for school readiness and wait and see once they enter the structured, persistent social environment that school provides to see exactly how they are relating to the environment around them. I urge families to allow for the child to get through the honeymoon phase (usually the first few weeks of school), and typically I begin receiving phone calls in October or November, allowing teachers enough time to observe patterns of behavior.

The following sections describes some of the diagnoses that overlap with a quirky profile.

Autism Spectrum Disorder

Autism spectrum disorder (ASD) is a developmental disability that can cause significant social, communication, and behavioral challenges. There is often nothing about how people with ASD look that sets them apart from other people, but they may communicate, interact, behave, and learn in ways that are different. The learning, thinking, and problem-solving abilities of people with ASD can range from gifted to severely challenged. Some people with ASD need consistent guidance and monitoring in their daily lives; others need less.

A diagnosis of ASD now includes several conditions that were previously diagnosed as separate entities: autistic disorder, pervasive developmental disorder not otherwise specified, and Asperger's syndrome. These conditions are now all contained within an umbrella diagnosis of ASD.

Individuals with ASD often have problems with social, emotional, and communication skills. They might repeat certain behaviors and might not want change in their daily activities. Many individuals with ASD also have different ways of learning and struggle with attention, initiation (i.e., showing/sharing interests or objects, approaching others to interact), and engagement (i.e., connection with others). Signs of ASD begin during early childhood and typically last throughout a person's life.

Children or adults with ASD might:

- not point at objects to show interest (for example, not point at an airplane flying over)
- not look at objects when another person points at them
- have trouble relating to others or not have interest in other people at all
- avoid eye contact
- prefer to be alone and keep their world or environment the same

- have trouble understanding other people's feelings or talking about their own feelings
- prefer not to be held or cuddled, or might cuddle only when they want to
- appear to be unaware when people talk to them, but respond to other sounds
- be very interested in people, but not know how to talk, play, or relate to them
- repeat or echo words or phrases said to them, or repeat words or phrases in place of normal language
- have trouble expressing their needs using typical words or motions
- not play pretend games (for example, not pretend to feed a doll)
- repeat actions over and over again
- have trouble adapting when a routine changes
- have unusual reactions to the way things smell, taste, look, feel, or sound
- lose skills they once had (for example, stop saying words they were using).

Diagnosing ASD can be difficult because there is no medical test, like a blood test, to confirm the disorder. Developmental specialists look at the child's behavior and development to make a diagnosis. ASD can sometimes be detected at 18 months or younger. By age two, a diagnosis by an experienced professional can be considered very reliable. However, many children do not receive a final diagnosis until they are older. This delay means that children with ASD might not get the early help they need.

There is no cure for ASD. However, research shows that early intervention treatment services can improve a child's development. Early intervention services help children from birth to six years old learn important skills. Services can include therapy to help the child talk and interact with others. Therefore, it is important to talk to your pediatrician as soon as possible if you think your child has ASD or another developmental delay. In addition, treatment for particular symptoms, such as speech therapy for language delays, often does not need to wait for a formal ASD diagnosis.

Asperger's Syndrome

Asperger's syndrome is an ASD considered to be on the "high functioning" end of the spectrum. As indicated in the preceding section on ASD, the term *Asperger's* is now considered to be a part of a broader umbrella diagnosis of ASD. Individuals who were historically diagnosed with Asperger's syndrome can continue to understand themselves within the Asperger's classification. Many clinicians will classify an individual with Asperger's syndrome with ASD per the current diagnostic guideline, and educate the child and the family about Asperger's syndrome given the vast amounts of information that already exist about Asperger's and the clinical differences in presentation that require specialized approaches.

Children with Asperger's syndrome have difficulty with social interactions and exhibit a restricted range of interests and/or repetitive behaviors. Motor development may be delayed, leading to clumsiness or uncoordinated motor movements. Compared with those affected by other forms of ASD, however, those with a historical diagnosis of Asperger's syndrome did not have significant delays or difficulties in language or cognitive development

The following behaviors are often associated with Asperger's syndrome. However, they are seldom all present in any one individual and vary widely in degree:

- limited or inappropriate social interactions
- "robotic" or repetitive speech
- challenges with nonverbal communication (gestures, facial expression, etc.) coupled with average to above average verbal skills
- tendency to discuss self rather than others
- inability to understand social/emotional issues or nonliteral phrases
- lack of eye contact or reciprocal conversation
- obsession with specific, often unusual topics
- one-sided conversations
- awkward movements and/or mannerisms

Nonverbal Learning Disorder

Nonverbal learning disorder (NLD, sometimes NVLD) is a developmental disability that is often misdiagnosed or undiagnosed. Children with NLD possess strong verbal intelligence abilities and have their greatest challenges in the nonverbal domain of intelligence. These children are bright and often possess a strong vocabulary and even a love for reading. However, they struggle with social interactions, activities of daily living, and gross motor and fine motor coordination and can experience challenges in mathematics. Sometime the math difficulties are the result of visual-spatial challenges, such as not lining up the columns of math problems correctly, confusing the order of operations, or adding when they should subtract.

Children with NLD struggle with executive functions and can forget or misplace homework. They have difficulty gleaning meaning or "reading between the lines" in social contexts, and this can cause challenges in the academic context as well. They may be characterized as lazy or unmotivated when they are actually very motivated and hard-working.

Evaluation for NLD will involve a neuropsychological or psychoeducational evaluation of the child's intellectual or cognitive abilities as well as their academic abilities. Furthermore, the evaluation will assess coordination, fine motor control, and social/emotional/behavioral development. Consultation with the school is indicated to assess the child's academic and social competence in school. If you think your child may have NLD, you should consult with a pediatric psychologist or neuropsychologist in your area who is familiar with NLD.

Social (Pragmatic) Communication Disorder

A social (pragmatic) communication disorder (DSM-5; American Psychiatric Association, 2013) involves persistent difficulties in the social use of verbal and nonverbal communication as manifested by *all* of the following:

- Deficits in using communication for social purposes, such as greeting and sharing information, in a manner that is appropriate for the social context.
- Impairment of the ability to change communication to match context or the needs of the listener, such as speaking differently in a classroom than on a playground, talking differently to a child than to an adult, and avoiding use of overly formal language.
- Difficulties following rules for conversation and storytelling, such as taking turns in conversation, rephrasing when misunderstood, and knowing how to use verbal and nonverbal signals to regulate interaction.
- Difficulty understanding what is not explicitly stated (e.g., making inferences) and nonliteral or ambiguous meaning of language (e.g., idioms, humor, metaphors, multiple meanings that depend on the context for interpretation).

The symptoms of social (pragmatic) communication disorder should not be better accounted for by another psychiatric disorder (e.g., ASD). If so, then another diagnosis results. Social (pragmatic) communication disorder results in the child having a difficult time communicating effectively with others and participating in a socially appropriate manner with others, and can even adversely affect academic performance.

Sensory Processing Disorder

Children with sensory processing disorder have difficulty processing information from the senses (touch, movement, smell, taste, vision, and hearing) and responding appropriately to that information. These children typically have one or more senses that either over- or underreact to stimulation. Sensory processing disorder can cause problems with a child's development and behavior.

Children with autism and other developmental disabilities often have sensory processing disorder. This disorder can also be associated with premature birth, brain injury, learning disorders, and other conditions.

The exact cause of sensory processing disorder is not known. It is commonly seen in people with autism, Asperger's syndrome, and other developmental disabilities. Most research suggests that people with autism have irregular brain function. More study is needed to determine the cause of these irregularities, but current research indicates they may be inherited.

Children with sensory processing disorder cannot properly process sensory stimulation from the outside world. Your child may:

- either be in constant motion or fatigue easily or go back and forth between the two.
- withdraw when touched.
- refuse to eat certain foods because of how the foods feel when chewed.
- be oversensitive to odors.
- be hypersensitive to certain fabrics and only wear clothes that are soft or that they find pleasing.
- dislike getting his or her hands dirty.
- be uncomfortable with some movements, such as swinging, sliding, or going down ramps or other inclines. Your young child may have trouble learning to climb, go down stairs, or ride an escalator.
- have difficulty calming him- or herself after exercise or after becoming upset.
- appear clumsy, trip easily, or have poor balance.
- have odd posture.
- have difficulty handling small objects such as buttons or snaps.
- be overly sensitive to sound. Vacuum cleaners, lawn mowers, hair dryers, leaf blowers, or sirens may be upsetting.

A health professional, often an occupational or physical therapist, will evaluate your child by observing his or her responses to sensory stimulation, posture, balance, coordination, and eye movements. Although many children have a few of the symptoms just described, your health professional will look for a pattern of behavior when diagnosing sensory processing disorder.

Sensory integration therapy, usually conducted by an occupational or physical therapist, is often recommended for children who have sensory processing disorder. It focuses on activities that challenge the child with sensory input. The therapist then helps the child respond appropriately to the sensory stimulus.

Therapy might include applying deep touch pressure to a child's skin with the goal of allowing him or her to become more used to and process being touched. Also, play such as tug-of-war or with heavy objects, such as a medicine ball, can help increase a child's awareness of her or his own body in space and how it relates to other people.

Attention Deficit/Hyperactivity Disorder

Attention deficit/hyperactivity disorder (ADHD) is one of the most common childhood brain disorders and can continue through adolescence and adulthood. Symptoms include difficulty staying focused and paying attention, difficulty controlling behavior, and hyperactivity (overactivity). These symptoms can make it difficult for a child with ADHD to succeed in school, get along with other children or adults, or finish tasks at home.

Inattention, hyperactivity, and impulsivity are the key behaviors of ADHD. It is normal for all children to be inattentive, hyperactive, or impulsive sometimes, but for children with ADHD, these behaviors are more severe and occur more often. To be diagnosed with the disorder, a child must have symptoms for six months or longer and to a degree that is greater than other children of the same age.

Children who have symptoms of inattention may:

- be easily distracted, miss details, forget things, and frequently switch from one activity to another.
- have difficulty focusing on one thing.
- become bored with a task after only a few minutes, unless they are doing something enjoyable.

- have difficulty focusing attention on organizing and completing a task or learning something new.
- have trouble completing or turning in homework assignments, often losing things (pencils, toys, assignments) needed to complete tasks or activities.
- not seem to listen when spoken to.
- daydream, become easily confused, and move slowly.
- have difficulty processing information as quickly and accurately as others.
- struggle to follow instructions.

Children who have symptoms of hyperactivity may:

- fidget and squirm in their seats.
- talk nonstop.
- dash around, touching or playing with anything and everything in sight.
- have trouble sitting still during dinner, school, and story time.
- be constantly in motion.
- have difficulty doing quiet tasks or activities.

Children who have symptoms of impulsivity may:

- be very impatient.
- blurt out inappropriate comments, show their emotions without restraint, and act without regard for consequences.
- have difficulty waiting for things they want or waiting their turns in games.
- often interrupt conversations or others' activities.

Parents and teachers can miss the fact that children with symptoms of inattention have ADHD because they are often quiet and less likely to act out. They may sit quietly, seeming to work, but they are not paying attention to what they are doing. They may get along well with other children, whereas children who have more symptoms of hyperactivity or impulsivity tend to have social problems. Children with the inattentive kind of ADHD are not the only ones whose disorders can be missed. For example, adults may think that children with the hyperactive and impulsive symptoms just have disciplinary problems.

Tourette Syndrome/Transient Tic Disorder

Tourette syndrome is a neurological disorder characterized by repetitive, stereotyped, involuntary movements and vocalizations called *tics*. Tics are classified as either simple or complex.

Simple motor tics are sudden, brief, repetitive movements that involve a limited number of muscle groups. Some of the more common simple tics include eye blinking and other vision irregularities, facial grimacing, shoulder shrugging, and head or shoulder jerking. Simple vocalizations might include repetitive throat clearing, sniffing, or grunting sounds.

Complex tics are distinct, coordinated patterns of movements involving several muscle groups. Complex motor tics might include facial grimacing combined with a head twist and a shoulder shrug. Other complex motor tics may actually appear purposeful, including sniffing or touching objects, hopping, jumping, bending, or twisting. Complex vocal tics include words or phrases.

Perhaps the most dramatic and disabling tics include motor movements that result in self-harm, such as punching oneself in the face, or vocal tics including coprolalia (uttering swear words) or echolalia (repeating the words or phrases of others). Some tics are preceded by an urge or sensation in the affected muscle group, commonly called a premonitory urge.

Some individuals with Tourette syndrome will describe a need to complete a tic in a certain way or a certain number of times to relieve the urge or decrease the sensation.

Tics are often worse with excitement or anxiety and better during calm, focused activities. Certain physical experiences can trigger or worsen tics, for example tight collars may trigger neck tics, or hearing another person sniff or clear their throat may trigger similar sounds. Tics do not go away during sleep but are often significantly diminished.

Take-home points:

- Typically, aggressive or hyperactive behaviors as well as speech delays, sensory concerns, and repetitive behaviors result in earlier referrals for evaluation, especially if they are frequently occurring (see the frequency formula) and meeting criteria for any of the Four D's described in the Introduction and the beginning of this chapter. Symptoms of various neurodevelopmental diagnoses that often overlap with a quirky profile (STRESSED characteristics) were described in this chapter. For any other behaviors, it may require a consultation with your primary health care provider, knowledge of child development and what is typical or abnormal, or simply following your instincts (e.g., "Something just isn't right"), which I often find to be accurate when working with families.

- The child in the blind spot may not cause any disruption in their environment but instead fade into the background and keep to himself. "He's just quiet" or "She's shy" may be explanations used by the adults who know the child best to explain this pattern of behavior. This is true; many children are simply shy, but you should be careful when applying these descriptors in social contexts because it could inadvertently perpetuate the behavior you are trying to address. The old adage "The squeaky wheel gets the grease" is often painfully true for children in the blind spot who could benefit from additional support services in school but do not cause enough of a disruption or who are doing well enough academically to not warrant any concern.

- The opportunity to maximize growth and learning for foundational developmental milestones such as speech, coordination, and play occurs in the first six years of life. This should not cause panic if you are reading this book with the hope of assisting a child who is older than six years. Instead, it means that the results may just not come as quickly or easily, but they will still come.

- Various developmental specialists may be asked to evaluate your child. These include psychologists, pediatricians, neurologists, speech pathologists, occupational therapists, and physical therapists.

- A variety of diagnoses overlap with a quirky profile. These include autism spectrum disorder, nonverbal learning disorder, sensory processing disorder, attention-deficit/hyperactivity disorder, and Tourette syndrome.

KEY 8

MANAGE CHALLENGES
AT HOME

Take a moment to reflect on when you first learned you were expecting your child. If your child was adopted, think back to when you were accepted for adoption or met the child for the first time. These are the moments of extreme joy and also when we begin wonder and fantasize. Will it be a boy or a girl? What will she be like when she's older? For a second or later child, many parents wonder, "Will I be able to love the child as much as the first?" We all wish for our children to be happy, safe, and successful. The moment something interferes with one of these goals, we work to try and fix it. When we try approaches that don't seem to be helping, we become frustrated and our decision making and judgment suffers. We may try to force the issue or punish behaviors until things improve. When this does not work, we feel dejected and frustrated, and this can begin to erode the parent–child relationship.

The purpose of this chapter, and really this whole book, is to help you fully understand and support your child. There is no difference in the love a parent feels for a child within the normative category of development versus one within the quirky or pathology categories. The main difference is that parents of children within the quirky/pathology categories tend to experience more stress because of the persistence and intensity of the child's challenges. I wrote this book because I fear that there are many parents who are very stressed due to their difficulty understanding their child's unique way of relating to the world around them. These parents have many questions and may be struggling to find to answers. The purpose of this chapter is to explore strategies that can bring peace and comfort to your home environment.

Humor, Affect, and Levity

When a family has been working to support a child who is experiencing various developmental challenges, all involved can experience stress, including siblings. When I am meeting with a family who has been working toward developmental progress for some time and they have not experienced the gains they were hoping for, hope is not lost, but it exists at dangerously low levels. Given that many quirky children experience challenges when it comes to the use and/or interpretation of humor, I work with families to incorporate fun and levity into their interactions with one another. I ask parents to approach challenging situations effectively and consistently, but also with some humor when appropriate. This approach can serve two important purposes. (1) It allows parents to model the appropriate use of humor to further promote the child's social development. (2) It allows all involved to relax and alleviate stress, making problem solving easier while improving family relationships.

When parents can shift their focus away from frustration regarding an ongoing concern that does not appear to be improving and onto each challenging situation as an opportunity to teach their child, the momentum shifts in the direction of positive change. When faced with a difficult situation involving the child, instead of saying, "Here we go again," you can begin to say, "Here's my chance to change this." Any existing frustration is usually the result of a parent attempting either the wrong approach or the correct approach at the wrong time. Thus, parents lose hope and run the risk of losing the fun in providing their child with the necessary learning opportunities.

Panic and Pounce

When parents are at a loss for what to do to effectively address an unwanted behavior or promote a desired behavior, they often panic. This feeling of panic creates a sense of urgency, and when emotions are elevated, logic declines. Let's say that your child has been whining for 15 minutes about not getting her way. You did your best to empathize and redirect their emotions and attention onto something else, but the whining continues. In a moment of panic that your child can't calm down, you begin to yell, "I am so sick of this! You are acting like a spoiled brat!" Granted, many would agree with your characterization of this child's reaction, but you have just pounced on the child with more emotion, which only escalates the situation.

If escalation of emotion is a recurrent pattern in your home, then the sense of helplessness and panic about effectively addressing the behavior only grows. Try the following demonstration for a moment. Place both hands in front of you, palms down. Your right hand represents logic (as controlled by the left side of your brain) and your left hand represents emotion (controlled by the right side of your brain). As you slowly lift one hand up (keeping the palm flat), lower the other hand down. As you do this up and down motion, you are visually representing that for logic to be up, emotion must be down. The reverse is also true: when emotions are high, logic is low. This is how the human brain operates, and you should remember this principle from this point forward.

This simple exercise can guide you so much in terms of your approach to parenting as well as your child's reactions to situations. If you don't believe me, try to solve a problem with your child when he is in the midst of a tantrum or crying episode and see how successful you both are. Better yet, try to work on your taxes after you have just argued with your spouse, or better yet *while* you're arguing with your spouse! You must allow for time to calm down and regulate your emotions before you can be an effective and logical problem solver.

Video Games

Video games have been referenced throughout this book as examples of depth-seeking interests that create significant challenges for quirky children and their families. As much as children enjoy these games, this enjoyment often comes at a cost beyond the expense of the console or the games. Although many children in the normative range of development can balance their interest in video games with family life, social relationships, school work, and other activities and interests, other children become consumed with the games and begin to neglect or struggle with all of the aforementioned areas of their lives. Children within the quirky category of development are especially at risk for obsession and even addiction to video games as a depth-seeking activity.

In the book *Cyber Junkie: Escape the Gaming and Internet Trap* (Roberts, 2010), the author examines video game addictions that many individuals experience. Although not yet recognized as a distinct entity in the *Diagnostic and Statistical Manual of Psychiatric Disorders*, video game addiction was a classification that the diagnostic selection committee had been considering in the most recent revision of the manual (DSM-5; American Psychiatric Association, 2013). One important consideration for a diagnosis in this area would be an examination of the differences between obsession and addiction. In my clinical work, a good majority of the quirky children and teens that I treat experience some sort of video game obsession at one point or another in their development, and many will go on to develop what may one day be referred to as a video game addiction.

When a child spends a majority of his waking moments that he is not playing video games either thinking about or discussing video games, watching Internet videos of others playing video games, or asking to play them and wondering when he can get to them next, he has at least entered into an obsession, and it will be important in the immediate future to help him address his need to interact with these games so often.

A highly popular video game in the recent past is World of

Warcraft, which is often cited for its addictive properties of keeping game players engaged through the ability to personalize character development and exhance game play with expansion packs. There has even been a website support group, Warcraft Widows, created in response to the game. This site chronicles the trials and tribulations of families who have essentially "lost" a loved one (not necessarily a spouse) because of this game and its addictive properties.

This is not to say that the game itself is to blame. Many individuals who play it lose interest entirely or can monitor and set appropriate limits around how often or for how long they play. However, if you are the parent or a loved one of a quirky child, you should be on high alert that electronics and video games like World of Warcraft (or other massive multiplayer online role–playing game [MMPORG] or open world/"sandbox" games such as Minecraft, where a player has the freedom to roam and set up a virtual world as they please) are high-risk territory for these individuals in terms of developing obsessive and addictive tendencies in response to playing them. This is due in large part to the child's difficulties effectively interacting with the real world.

I caution parents about these games and encourage containment or restrictions regarding the amount of access a child has to them because of the risk of obsession or addiction. In Key 3, you learned about the role of dopamine in the reward or pleasure center of the brain and how depth-seeking activities like video games activate this brain region. You have also learned that children who struggle with social connection and engagement can blur the lines between reality and fantasy. If we want a child to be successful in real-world interactions, the only way to learn the necessary skills is to participate in real-world interactions. Online gaming is not a real-world interaction. As much as children enjoy these games and relieve stress while playing them, secondary to the dopamine release, they will eventually need more access to the game to continue to achieve the desired result, further blurring their fantasy and real lives and creating more social isolation and challenges.

Boredom and Technology

Boredom is an area which many of today's youth have challenges dealing with. At the risk of sounding like the know-it-all, grumpy old-timer who lectures the youth about what it was like to walk two miles uphill to school in the snow with bare feet, there definitely are trends occurring among today's youth that indicate they struggle more than any other generation before them when it comes to tolerating boredom.

Some have speculated (and I tend to agree) that the advances in technology have made it almost impossible for the today's youth to experience and desensitize themselves to boredom long enough to be able to tolerate it. Indeed, it seems that the moment a young person, who often has an electronic smart phone or other electronic device on hand, begins to feel the discomfort associated with boredom, they immediately access this device and the feeling goes away. This boredom buster may be contributing in part to some individuals becoming increasingly obsessive about the use of these devices (recall the dopamine agonist hypothesis from Key 3). Indeed, the experience of boredom is so uncomfortable, and the tolerance for that feeling is so low, that the person relies heavily on access to electronic media to occupy that window and relieve the uncomfortable feeling.

A problem develops when the individual is not allowed to access the device. This is usually only for a brief period of time, such as during class periods at school. Even then, many students can't handle it and sneak the phone out under their desk, away from the teacher's line of sight. Even adults can't seem to drive in cars without interacting with their devices. Our attention spans, tolerance for boredom, and ability to delay gratification and thus be patient to receive things (e.g., food in a drive-through lane that takes more than a few minutes to arrive) are all declining.

We want to be connected at all times, and we want it to happen quickly. Remember dial-up Internet? Nowadays, people think someone is mad at them or does not like them if they don't receive a reply to their text message within a few minutes (or seconds).

Email is now something that mostly "older people" use. Schools adhere to strict electronics policies for phones and other devices, and companies realize the amount of productivity lost from employees checking their phones or social media while on the job. We cannot seem to sit and stay focused without checking in, and if we have to wait for something, it upsets us.

Whether these changes in our attention and tolerance for boredom are solely to blame on electronics is not to be decided here, but the difficulty that many young people, especially quirky children, have tolerating boredom is creating significant hurdles for them socially, emotionally, and academically.

Many of the behavioral problems that I regularly treat are the by-product of boredom, frustration, and the child's inability to occupy himself productively. Parents with whom I consult often remark how their quirky child frequently exclaims how "bored" he is, despite dozens of suggestions and recommendations of things to do to pass the time. I get it, these electronic devices do amazing things and allow us to connect with each other and gather information faster and more efficiently. If you are trying to support a quirky child, however, these advantages are easily negated by the difficulties that regular use of technology create, especially for children more likely to experience social challenges.

Returning to the generation argument, consider previous generations' lack of contact with such devices and the need to explore one's environment to pass the time and alleviate boredom. This exploration was often done in a community where everyone else shared be same goal, which was to create or explore something, and it was often accomplished as a group. The use of media and screen interactions, such as online gaming, texting, or chat rooms, remove the need to be in the room with one another, and this can exacerbate any underlying social quirks. Similar to a muscle in the body experiencing atrophy due to underuse, fewer in-person interactions with people in real time and in the real world will only lessen the strength of this already deprived skill set.

I spend considerable time in my private practice helping children address the behavioral challenges that accompany boredom intolerance. Learning to deal with boredom is related to the dopamine agonist hypothesis (introduced in Key 3), which states that people who are experiencing addiction-like withdrawals go through a process in which the brain needs more and more stimulation. The removal of what had previously stimulated that brain (an electronic device) only serves to cause a cyclical reaction of events that brings the person right back to it unless they can get away from it long enough to find stimulation in other activities.

It is unlikely that a child who is obsessed with technology and has this stimulation removed will be able to find anything else as stimulating, at least not in the short term. This is why he continues wanting to get more of it or go back to it. We now know interaction with technology releases dopamine into the brain and it is the neurotransmitter that is associated with pleasure and reward. (More information about dopamine's role in the quirky brain was presented in Key 3).

We may justify the use of electronics because they are effective at keeping the peace on long trips and help buy us some time when we need to get some things done around the house. We may also justify the allowance of electronics because the child communicates with others while on the device such as during online gaming, or "all the other kids have devices." The brain that struggles to generate its own entertainment, however, will have enough of an exposure during such times that the duration of their day can become a persistent quest to obtain more of the desired dopamine release. I urge parents to remember the following when contemplating video game restrictions for a child: When the games are away, the child will play. You may need to teach him how, but he can learn and be successful.

Screen Time Recommendations

The American Academy of Pediatrics guidelines recommend that parents limit a child's screen time (video games, computer, television) to one to two hours per day *at most*. This recommendation is for children ages two years and older, as well as teens. Children under the age of two should avoid any screen access due to the need to interact with people, which facilitates brain and language development.

An alternative that I have often recommended to families I work with is to limit screen time to one hour on school nights and two hours a day on weekends and holidays. My intention is not to make the child's life miserable (which they often accuse me of trying to do), but to create opportunities for relationships with people. Restricted screen time is recommended and intended to limit noneducational use of screens. Thus, watching movies, television, or playing video games would fall under the restriction guidelines of one to two hours per day. However, using the computer to research a report, reading an e-book on a portable device, or doing math drills online would not count toward the restricted time.

Video games are not social. Even if your child plays with a friend in the same room or online, this is not a spontaneous and reciprocal social interaction. Indeed, if you turned off the video game and asked two children within the quirky category of development to get a conversation going for more than a few minutes, they would inevitably become uncomfortable and want to discuss or return to playing the video game. Please don't misinterpret what I'm saying here. I think that some exposure to video games is a good thing, especially from a social skills framework because many children, especially boys, love video games and thus talk about them with each other at school. Not knowing anything about these games can leave a person feeling left out. My concern with games is that many children cannot limit the time they spend playing them, and this can create considerable conflict between parents and children. It can also become a solitary (and sedentary) depth-seeking activity for the child that significantly interferes with social opportunities, and the development of social skills.

The strategies for how to wean a child from excessive video game usage vary from family to family, but a few points of advice may provide a good start:

- Make conversation a priority in your home.
- Read to and with your children.
- Play with your children.
- Encourage active recreation and engage the child in it.
- Get the TV sets, computers, tablets, and video game systems out of your children's bedrooms. It is not a good idea to have TVs and computers in bedrooms at any age, even if the child is younger and you think that it is harmless because they only look at children's websites, or you have an Internet filter set up. The fact is, you are training their brain to want and need this technology available in their room, which will affect sleep habits as well as social interactions, especially with family members.

Children who excessively play video games or watch television tend to do so for a reason. Whether it is loneliness, social skills difficulties, anxiety, or depression, the use of video games and television viewing becomes self-medicating and a means to quickly pass the otherwise painful time spent thinking about reality. The strategies mentioned here are only the start if your child is experiencing social or emotional difficulties and is using video games to cope.

If you are fortunate enough to be reading this while your child is still young, the best form of intervention is prevention. Start early and set limits now while encouraging appropriate uses of your child's time. Get him involved in fun activities out of the home to keep him interested and active. If your child is already hooked on video games for excessive amounts of time, it may be worthwhile to seek a professional consultation to begin breaking addiction or obsession and develop a schedule to reduce playing time and replace it with more productive activities.

Children often play on their electronic devices during car rides. Whatever happened to good old-fashioned conversation while on car trips or a game of I Spy? Perhaps Mom or Dad are too busy on their phones or devices to have a dialogue with the child. This is one of my pet peeves, especially when I see a parent pick a child up from school after not seeing them all day and they are on the phone instead of greeting the child and catching up on the day! It is essential to create a positive experience in the car with your kids by talking, playing games, and even listening to music and singing together. It is equally important to practice what you preach and limit your own screen time (e.g., how often you check your email or text on your phone in front of the child) if you are to limit the child's time. It's very important to remember that modeling is a powerful force in the life of a child, and when they see you worshiping your phone and ignoring their requests for attention, you are headed for trouble.

Tantrums

During the early years of life, especially during the toddler phase, children throw tantrums almost as an everyday occurrence. In many ways this has much to do with fast and furious brain development, which makes emotional control very difficult, as well as children's status in life, which is essentially that of someone who wants things their way, right away, but has very little access and control over obtaining the things that they want.

We often see toddlers in the middle of a store crying, whining, kicking, and screaming because their parents refuse to buy them a toy or get them a treat. Almost as a cruel joke or obstacle course for parents of toddlers, most stores place candy and other kid–friendly, appealing items right at the checkout counter, which allows children plenty of time to study all of these items as they wait in line. Children often try to exploit the opportunity of being in a public setting and frequently succeed in getting their parents to give in to buy them what they want to avoid an emotional outburst in public. Parents who are able to stand strong and avoid the public embarrassment are often able to extinguish the tantrum behaviors quickly, especially if they practice what they preach with the mantra, "You get what you get, and you don't throw a fit."

As children within the normative category of development approach kindergarten (recall Key 5), their brains are better able to tolerate frustration and cope with disappointment and unmet expectations, and although they may still have some emotional reactivity, we can generally expect their tantrums to occur with less intensity and frequency. Children who have emotional outbursts at school can begin to frustrate the peer group, although those who cry or are otherwise emotional during preschool and kindergarten are unlikely to draw too much unnecessary attention given that such reactions are still fairly typical at this age. However, one can easily imagine that once a child is in second grade and beyond, continuing to react to situations in this way begins to wear out other children as well as adults. As a result, the peer group may begin to view these types of reactions as disruptive and may refer to the child as "acting like a baby."

What may have begun during the toddler years as an attempt to obtain attention and get what they want eventually represents significant challenges for the older child in regulating emotions and dealing with disappointment or delays of gratification. A quirky child may be at higher risk for tantrums and meltdowns when he is told "no," told to stop doing something (especially if what he was doing was enjoyable), or when his expectations are unmet, such as when there has been a change in plans or schedule.

There are numerous methods to deal with meltdowns and tantrums, although the tried-and-true approach is to remain consistent with your response regardless of what the outburst is. Be very careful to not inadvertently reinforce the behavior by paying attention to it or trying to wait it out and then eventually giving in, which is the most powerful mechanism of reinforcing the behavior. I tell parents that tantrums get old very quickly if there is no audience available, and thus a child who is screaming and throwing a fit is more likely to continue to engage in this behavior if someone is standing around talking to them and trying to get them to calm down.

If you have ever ignored a toddler's tantrum, you can see how the child will quickly realize that no one is paying any attention and almost immediately reset their behaviors. However, some quirky children can become so upset that they forget what they were upset about in the first place and eventually just become emotional about the fact that they are feeling very strong emotions. If this is the case, use the antecedent approach from Key 5 whenever possible to keep the tantrum from happening in the first place, especially if the tantrum regularly occurs following a specific request or in a specific environment. One such approach is explained in the next section.

The Public Outing Escape Plan

If you can't beat 'em, join 'em. This is the approach that many families wisely choose when dealing with a child who struggles to complete activities in a public environment. In the event that you are dealing with a child who acts out or experiences sensory overload in public situations (birthday parties, grocery stores, shopping malls, restaurants), the escape plan procedure can be helpful. The anxiety a child experiences about a particular situation can result in behavioral escalation. If you can anticipate the social or sensory stress the child experiences and provide an acceptable out, you can often avoid the tantrum or meltdown. The escape plan involves determining an acceptable location where the child can retreat if they are overwhelmed. Depending on the age of the child and the specific situation, you will may need to "join 'em" in the escape. The important aspect to this plan is that reintegration is expected. Thus, if the child is feeling overwhelmed, he can retreat and relax but is expected to return to the situation within a reasonable period of time. The best thing for you to do when following this plan is to monitor the child's stress levels in a particular situation and offer the escape when indicated. If you intervene soon enough in the emotional escalation, you can join your child by walking away to calm down and help her reintegrate.

Some children will refuse the escape plan or escalate their behavioral response and affect so much that the parent is left with no option other but to excuse themselves from the situation completely. Although this may provide the child with a sense of relief, it also reinforces an avoidance mentality. Thus, the child learns that as long as he escalates his behavior and affect enough, he will be allowed to leave. If you are forced into this situation as a parent, then your response helps prevent reinforcing escape behaviors in the future.

Additional information about how to respond to a child who acts up during an outing was described in Key 5. The best thing you can do if your child needs to be removed completely from a situation is to remain quiet and calm, regardless of how upset you or the child may be. This takes practice, and anyone involved with the child during this interaction needs to abide by this requirement. Remain calm and quiet, and sit next to rather than face-to-face with the child because this latter physical approach often results in the child feeling as if she is being interrogated, which can heighten their emotional experience. Another note is to never videorecord a child having a tantrum with the hope of later showing him how poorly he behaved. You are throwing gas on a flame if you try to teach a child in this manner.

Activities of Daily Living

Hygiene

Hygiene is an activity of daily living that presents challenges, most notably during the preteen and adolescent years and is still problematic for children in the younger years when it comes to bathing, brushing teeth, and getting dressed in the morning or evening. What is it about children that they seem genetically predisposed to struggle completing these activities during the times of day in which parents are the most tired? Perhaps the reason they struggle so much is the same reason adults become so upset that the child is struggling: they are just as tired and in need of sleep as the adults requesting that children complete these activities.

Hygiene is an area in which parents frequently question how to get the child to independently complete their tasks or activities of daily living. To understand how to best approach a child who is having challenges completing hygiene tasks, I urge you to consider the developmental age of the child. This developmental age assessment helps many parents understand that although their child has reached a certain chronological age, they are operating more like a younger child would. While we would expect most eight-year-olds to be able to independently brush their teeth and get dressed, we may have to stay close to the child and offer periodic assistance or hand-over-hand help as if he were a six-year-old.

Many parents become exasperated or frustrated because of the challenge a quirky child experiences being able to complete things at an age-appropriate level. For children who take a shower (instead of a bath), but do not soap up or rinse off appropriately, the parents may need to stand by as they complete such tasks. If there are concerns about personal boundaries, such as a parent who needs to be in the bathroom or peek into the shower to assess that the task is completed properly, the child may have to complete a shower with a bathing suit on so that a parents or caregivers can stand by comfortably and not shame or embarrass the child or feel uncomfortable themselves. Parents may also consider installing a shower mirror so that the child can self-monitor the lathering or rinsing process. Some children may not be able to "feel" that they have missed a portion of their hair while shampooing or rinsing, and the mirror removes any guesswork.

Some children do not understand the concept of time in terms of how long it should take to complete a task or activity. Instead of using a clock or timer to measure this, I have found that using music can be beneficial. Indeed, for many children and even adolescents, setting up a playlist on an electronic device that contains three to five songs can be helpful. The child is required to complete the hygiene activities during that playlist, which helps him monitor the time completing the task. For example, a shower may require ten minutes of music. If the shower ends before the music stops, then it's not a long enough shower. If the child is still showering after the music stops, they need to finish up and end the shower (for children who stay in too long). Perhaps the child is instructed to shampoo and wash his body during the first song, rinse off during the second song, and wash his face/apply conditioner during the third song. This is similar to the approach many health clinics use that teaches young children to sing or hum the alphabet song one or two times while soaping up their hands after using the bathroom.

Brushing teeth would require the child to select one song to play that is approximately two minutes in length. The child should not complete the tooth brushing routine until the song has stopped playing. She can even brush to the rhythm of the song!

For some morning routines, the approach can be as simple as looking at the layout of the home and realizing that the child must walk some distance between where they completed the previous activity and where they need to finish the next activity, such as brushing teeth. This can be alleviated by simply moving the tooth brushing materials into the kitchen. For example, once breakfast is completed, the child can brush her teeth after she puts her plate in the sink.

There may be other variables that need to be considered when it comes to morning hygiene, such as the child resisting going to school because of negative experiences. Thus, if the child realizes that the sooner she gets her teeth brushed the sooner she has to go to school where she is bullied or experiences embarrassment in the form of academic failure, she may stall the completion of tooth brushing as a means of delaying the onset of these negative feelings. If this is the case, more planning must take place within the school to alleviate the stress and tension resulting from the transition into the building.

For some children, getting their mind onto something positive while entering school can be beneficial, such as having an early morning job or responsibility (e.g., helping the teacher take chairs off the desks, making copies) that they look forward to as a means of getting them into the school building with confidence and self-esteem. You will be surprised how eager your child may become to get to school in the morning. They may even accuse you of running late!

Some parents reward completing activities of daily living quickly in the morning by allowing the child additional time to view a favorite television program or play a game provided they have completed all the activities within a reasonable time period. This is only recommended provided that the child can transition away from these activities and get into the family car or out of the home for the school bus on time without problems.

As frustrating as it may be for kids to complete these activities of daily living, my experience tells me that adults need to be patient and take the time to establish the sequence and do these activities more with their children. Parents who have their own organizational challenges may need to restructure their morning routine as well to be able to offer the necessary support and assistance to the child. Indeed, much of the stress that results from the morning routine is the result of parents trying to get ready themselves and not having enough time to support their child during the morning routine.

The way a parent gives directions to the child also plays a critical role in the completion of routines. We become too complacent when it comes to giving directions from a distance. Instead, you may need to take the time to go through the motions with your child. Thus, instead of calling out to your child to hurry up and brush her teeth, you may need to do it alongside her and share the morning routine. If your child struggles with the sequence of a task or activity, you may need to go through it and break it down into manageable parts so that the child understands the steps required. For example, brushing one's teeth requires putting the toothbrush under the water, applying the toothpaste, brushing one's teeth for approximately one to two minutes, rinsing, and putting away the toothbrush.

If your child is stuck, follow this model: do it for them (e.g., apply the toothpaste and move the brush around in his mouth), do it with him (e.g., set aside time to brush your teeth together in the kitchen each morning after breakfast), and then have them do it while you supervise/observe and praise his success and troubleshoot as needed. When dealing with a child who struggles with morning or bedtime routines, remember this: the closer you are in physical proximity to the child when you need him to begin and complete the task and the longer you stick around while the child completes the task, the greater your likelihood of success.

Morning Waking

The lion in the zoo quickly learns that it doesn't have to hunt for its food. As a result, the lion lies in his synthetic den with comfort and confidence that his needs will be met. As your child grows older, you may be caught in the trap that if you do not wake your child up in the morning, he will not be ready to get to school on time. The child becomes the lion in the zoo because he learns that no matter how much he sleeps in, someone will enter his room and make sure that he is up and ready on time.

Take a moment to reflect on your life and try to recall a time in which you overslept. Do you remember how you felt the moment you looked at the clock and realized that you were late? If you're anything like me, when this happened to me in high school and my parents refused to play the role of zoo keeper, you freaked out and, in a mixed state of awakening and panic, hurried to get yourself together and out the door. By virtue of this experience, you learned that you did not like this feeling, and thus you changed your behaviors to ensure that this feeling and experience did not reoccur (e.g., double-check alarm clock volume, purchase battery backup alarm, set a second alarm clock, set alarm 20 minutes earlier). The point here is that once a child is old enough and capable to wake himself up, don't be the zoo keeper. Allow your child the opportunity to experience the natural consequence of oversleeping so that he does not become the lion in the zoo.

Morning and Evening Routines

The morning and evening daily routines can be some of the most trying times in the home of a quirky child, especially if the child has significant transition stress as described in the STRESSED model in Key 1. Transition stress peaks either at the beginning of the day when the family is rushed to get out of the house to be somewhere on time, or at the end of the day when parents are tired and ready to recharge their batteries with some relaxing alone time.

Quirky children may struggle during these times because they are fixated on a particular area of interest. These children will not necessarily understand how important it is for you to be on time in the morning or finish the bedtime routine, even if you explain it to them every day. The main reason they don't understand is difficulty with perspective taking or self/other awareness. Furthermore, if the child experiences any attention or concentration challenges, it can be difficult to complete the necessary steps to be ready to go at a certain time despite knowing what the routine is and being reminded of it.

At some point during a quirky child's upbringing, families may be forced to decide whether they are going to allow their child to be late and suffer the natural consequences of this, such as going to school in their pajamas, as is often recommended in approaches discussed in *Parenting with Love and Logic* (Cline and Fay, 2006) or *Positive Discipline* (Nelson, 2006).

Recall the A-B-C's of behavior described in Key 5and keep in mind that persistent reminders, which result in frustration and upset are not going to address the problem in the long term, although reminders or prompts to "hurry up" may help the child to get it into gear for the time being. However, parents are repeatedly frustrated, especially if their child is older, that they have to follow them around and remind them—especially when parents are trying to get ready themselves.

Recall from Key 5 that an example of an antecedent approach to difficulties with the morning routine would be to figure out how much additional time it takes this child to get ready and begin waking him up earlier. Parents often struggle with this recommendation because they want their child to get enough sleep and don't like the idea of waking a child up earlier. The solution is simple: the child has to go to bed earlier the night before.

Whenever possible, you want the child's difficulties getting himself together to become *his* problem and remove yourself from becoming caught up in it.

There are clearly some children who are so out of focus in the morning that completion of morning activities independently is nearly impossible, such as the child who takes prescription medications to address attention deficit symptoms but the medication has not reached its therapeutic level soon enough to be of use early in the morning. In these scenarios, I again work on the antecedent approach and structure the home environment in such a way that makes it as easy as possible to complete tasks, such as having clothes laid out in a central location and allowing things like brushing teeth to take place at the kitchen sink, if necessary, to eliminate too many steps between rooms that would allow for more distraction.

If your child has distractibility challenges, you want to minimize the distance. First, the distance between where you are and the child is when you are giving him a direction needs to be short. The closer you are in proximity, the better. For some children, you need to go to them, get on their eye level to get their attention, give them the direction, and then stay with them as they follow through. Second, the distance in which a child must travel to accomplish a task needs to be kept as short as possible. If you live in a two-story house and the child needs to walk from the kitchen downstairs to their room upstairs, you are increasing the likelihood that he or she will become distracted by everything along that route, and decreasing the likelihood that they will successfully complete this task. The fewer the steps, the greater the success.

Broken Expectations

Quirky children often adhere to an internal agenda or plan that others around them may not be aware of. This is one of the primary reasons transitions are often difficult for a quirky child. The child may decide, in his mind, that he will be able to complete a particular task, such as finishing a book chapter, completing a Lego project, constructing a toy train setup, or finishing a level on a video game. Parents and other adults have no way of knowing that this plan has been established by the child. When the parent calls out to the child that he needs to stop, the request is met with strong emotion, almost retaliation, to the direction that this plan needs to be terminated.

Behaviorally, teachers and parents tend to perceive these events as temper tantrums and difficulty with transitions. They are correct. However, adults must begin to understand that the child will continue to operate based on their internal agenda regardless of consequences to any resulting tantrums or emotional outbursts. Thus I strongly encourage adults to check in with children about their plans either before an activity begins or before a transition will occur.

Ask the child, "What is your plan?" when you are about to begin a transition. This does not mean that the child will get to follow his plan. We are simply trying to find out what he's thinking. What happens next requires some flexible thinking and skill because life happens and the child cannot always complete his plan. Children will benefit from repeated exposures to transitions in which their plan cannot be completed, and adults must be skilled in how to work the child through this stress and frustration.

I am a strong proponent of Dr. John Gottman's emotion coaching approach in these situations. To become skilled in this approach, you are encouraged to review his book, *Raising an Emotionally Intelligent Child* (Gottman, 1998). A brief overview of Gottman's approach is presented here.

Step One: Label and Validate the Child's Feelings

Before we can accurately label and then validate our children's feelings, we need to empathize with them—first to understand what they are feeling, and then to communicate what we understand them. For example, when your child is upset with you about having to stop what he's doing, this would be the opportunity to say, "I can see that you are very angry and frustrated. Is there anything else that you are feeling?" Allow the child to process their emotions. As long as they are discussing things with you instead of acting on those feelings, you can continue to process with the child. The emotion coaching approach states that feelings are always okay, but destructive behaviors are never tolerated.

Step Two: Deal with the Bad Behavior (If Applicable)

If the child is demonstrating an aggressive behavior, it is very important to set limits so that kids learn how to behave well even in the face of strong, negative emotions. Direct the child to a time out (recall the approach from Key 5), and make it clear that these behaviors are not okay: "It is okay to feel angry and frustrated, but it is never okay to hit others." Once the time out is complete, it's time for step three.

Step Three: Problem Solve

Now is the time to dig a little deeper and help the child figure out how to handle the situation better in the future. After you have labeled and validated the emotions arising out of the problem, you can focus on the problem itself: "Were you hoping to be able to complete your Lego project when I told you it was time to stop?" Try to relate to the child's experience and give examples from your life when you felt similarly ("It's also hard for me to stop doing something that I enjoy"). Do *not* tell the child how he ought to feel, because that would make him distrust what he did feel (i.e., perhaps the aggressive act that resulted in a time out felt good). The goal is to put him in touch with his emotions, regardless of whether they are good or bad.

Next, you and the child can brainstorm possible ways to solve a problem or prevent it from happening again. The more parents can coach, instead of direct, and allow kids come up with their own solutions, the better. Ask the child, "What would make it easier for you the next time you have to stop working on a Lego project?" You could then say, "I know what helps me is to ask for a few extra minutes and then to make sure I stop when that time is up."

In sum, the steps of the emotion coaching approach are: first, label and validate the emotions you see. Second, deal with misbehavior if you need to. Finally, help your child solve the problem.

Often, quirky children become upset because the task they are being asked to stop or walk away from has significance for them. They don't think about how they can return to it later or do it over again; they think that their fun or their project is being destroyed. When children are having fun playing in my office and it's time to leave, many have challenges doing this calmly. I like to ask the parent who is with the child if they have a camera on their phone. (In this day and age, most do. If not, then I use my iPad.) We photograph the scene at the time of the transition and save it for kids to view when they return to future sessions. Interestingly, most kids never ask to see the picture, but that's not the point. The point is that the child believes that their work is being preserved or saved, and thus respected. I instruct the parent to photograph the toys that have been set up thus far, and this immediately calms the child and allows him to feel good about cleaning up.

One final approach involves the use of "first/then" or the "what's next?" question. This helps the child begin to shift onto what is about to follow. You would ask "What's next?" to help the child shift his thinking away from what he's doing and into the future. Or you would say, "*First* we need to clean up these toys and *then* we are going to Grandma's house." This is especially useful in situations in which the next activity is something enjoyable. Clearly, telling a child "First we are going to clean up the toy and then we are going to bed" would not help. If the "then" involves something nonpreferred, you are encouraged to use another strategy such as the photograph to move the child onto the next activity.

Parenting Stress

Depending on when I first meet with a family, their concerns about their child's development may be emerging or they may be ongoing. Some families choose to "wait it out," and I may meet with them for the first time when their stress has reached peak levels. Other families may have sought guidance from other professionals but did not find the information helpful or effective. Thus, I often spend the initial stages of my time with families trying to understand any frustration and stress they are experiencing, while also gathering enough history to avoid replicating approaches they did not find particularly useful. In many ways, the approaches previously suggested are generally effective, but they may have been applied at the wrong time. I have to work to assure the family that it was not the approach itself that failed, but the timing.

I often complete a family genogram when working with a family. A *genogram* is a pictorial display of a person's family relationships and medical history. It goes beyond a traditional family tree by allowing the user to visualize hereditary patterns and psychological factors that influence relationships.

Family members profoundly affect each other's thoughts, feelings, and actions. Families solicit one another's attention, approval, and support and react to each other's needs, expectations, and distress. This results in the family functioning in an interdependent manner. Thus, a change in one family member's functioning changes the entire family dynamic. Families differ in terms of how much they influence one another, but some degree of influence among and between family members is always present.

When a family member becomes anxious, the anxiety can spread infectiously to other members. One parent may jump in to buffer the stress by accommodating the child's difficulties. The other parent may refer to this as babying or coddling the child. Although it is not always the mother who jumps in, she is the one who generally spends the most time with the child, and some additional accommodation from her is to be expected.

Unfortunately for the mother (or any family member who is trying to alleviate the child's stress), the one accommodating the child literally begins to "absorb" the child's anxiety and becomes the person most vulnerable to problems such as depression, anxiety, or physical fatigue and even pain. A vicious circle may begin where the mother is fatigued because she is absorbing the anxiety, and as a result she lacks the energy to assist the child in his social, emotional, and behavioral development. If your family is already absorbing the stress of one of its members and it is taking a toll, you might consider consulting with a mental health professional. In addition to helping the family dynamic, this is useful for the child who may be the identified "patient" because it fosters a sense of collaboration among family members and diffuses the stress, so that the child is not left feeling that the family stress is his fault.

Eating Habits

Children are generally picky, quirky eaters. There may be a variety of reasons for children becoming picky eaters. This can include food texture sensitivities, acid reflux, allergies, or the most common reason: parents who give in to their child's picky eating habits. Parents of young children need to remember that children are learning about food flavors and textures for the first time. Like many other situations in a young child's life, eating provides an opportunity to test how much control the child has over the parent. The parent, on the other hand, feels an obligation to feed and nurture the child and can easily become the victim of a child's clever strategy to be able to eat only what she wants. This is more often the case if a child is low weight and/or there are concerns about nutritional intake. Families must work closely with their pediatrician in these cases and are often referred to a dietician or nutritionist as well as a developmental specialist who can address behaviors that interfere with eating.

The parent reading this book needs to keep in mind that if weight is not a concern, kids will often attempt to shape their parents to only provide the foods that they want to eat. I once worked with a family who informed me that their five-year-old daughter would only eat one type of pizza from a particular pizza delivery place, to which I replied, "Who keeps buying her this type of pizza?"

Many quirky children have a strong desire to adhere to rigid routines. They establish patterns and routines or ways of relating to the environment that help them alleviate stress. If we want the child to be able to adapt to the ever-changing landscape of the world, he or she must receive the necessary exposures in the home and beyond that will lead to increased comfort and flexibility in later years. Parents have to be willing to tolerate this initial period of stress when the child objects to what they are served for a meal and experience one of the most powerful natural consequences available, which is hunger.

Yes, hunger creates irritability and stress, but that's part of the parenting role to be able to tolerate these reactions to best promote the child's future development. Actual starvation will not begin to occur until day three of absolutely no food. If your child can wait you out that long, then it is time to consult with a developmental specialist. If you take only one thing away from this section of the book, I hope it is this: a parent's responsibility is to prepare the food and serve it. What the child chooses from that point forward is just that—the child's choice. When the child refuses food so they can leave and play or because they don't like what you served, you can empathize with him when he complains about how hungry he is and remind him that eating what is served will fix this problem next time.

The following are some strategies that can help address your child's picky eating attempts. First, you can provide him with a small amount of what you know he will eat, but not enough to fill him up. This way, we can begin to increase their familiarity with other foods while giving him an opportunity to try new things. Parents should also model good eating behaviors by trying new things and be careful to not eat too selectively themselves. I recommend that a parent verbalize in front of the child, "I'm not sure I will like this, but I won't know until I try." The parent can then take a bite and say, "Well, it's not my favorite thing, but it's not *that* bad!" Incorporating a light-hearted and humorous tone of voice can go a long way.

Young children can often be swayed to eat less familiar or nonpreferred foods if you can form an association of the food with a beloved toy or children's character. You can announce, "We are having a superhero dinner tonight! These are all the foods the Avengers use to build their muscles to fight the bad guys! We have Hulk's broccoli, Iron Man's fruit salad, and Thor's chicken!" Then the parent can eat a piece of broccoli and flex their biceps while asking the child to feel them to see how it's working.

For parents who are stressed about a child's strong will toward eating, you can simply cover their uneaten meal with foil and allow the child to try again later. The reality is that the child will learn to eat when food is served if the parent uses a consistent approach. Once a parent makes an accommodation or becomes a short-order cook, it's over. The child has learned that they have control and some children will narrow their food selection into three to five of the tastiest or safest options. This rigidity only develops for the child if the parent is willing to entertain it.

Remember that kids are learning about the world through trial and error and are looking to the adults around them for guidance and direction. If they try something that works in their favor, then they will keep doing it. If they try something and it does not work, they may become upset and tantrum, but they are looking to the adult to see what the response will be. If we end up preparing the child's preferred food following a tantrum, we have just trained the child that if they protest when they don't get what they want, they will eventually get the adult to cater to them. Thus, if you have difficulties tolerating conflict and believe that it is your obligation to make sure your child eats no matter how particular the selection is, then you are going to have a very picker eater in your home.

An obvious caveat would be serving your child obscure foods and expecting them to eat them, such as octopus or frog legs. Children who don't know any differently grow to love fruits, vegetables, and other healthy foods. Do not bring emotion into the situation. Making threats that they must eat everything on their plate or they won't get dessert only adds to the power struggle. Again, prepare and serve the food and let the child do the rest.

Remain calm and matter-of-fact, and allow the natural consequences to take effect and your child will be expanding their palate in no time.

Also, avoid any bribes to get the child to sit at the table. Don't allow electronics or other items to be used during meals to keep them seated. If they don't sit to eat, then they experience the consequence of hunger. If the child is behaviorally dysregulated, then you might provide a kid-size table to keep them comfortable. Finally, once a child can eat with their fingers or a utensil, you should not have to sit next to them and feed them to get them to eat. I see many children who shape their parents into this behavior, and it does nothing but stall their eating development. If you always allow a child to eat something he likes, he sees no reason to do it any other way.

Sleep

As indicated in the eating section, children look to the adults in their environment for direction. Sleep is an area in which a child's behaviors become shaped and learned based on what they are allowed to do. In many cases, parents are led to believe that a child cannot sleep well unless they sleep with one or both parents. This may be the "lesser of two evils," meaning that the child is able to sleep, but how restful does a parent sleep with a child tossing and turning next to them all night, and what does this do for a couple's relationship when a child is always present in their bed at night?

This section is not an argument against co-sleeping. However, I can tell you that it is developmentally most appropriate and healthy that children sleep in their own beds to develop appropriate sleep habits. The longer a child is allowed to sleep in a parent's room, the more challenging it becomes to correct this behavior. Waiting until the child wants to sleep on his own is not a recommended approach given that this could take years.

You should know that if you need to train a child to be able to sleep independently, it might require some sleepless nights in the early stages of training. Even very young infants can learn to sleep without companionship by using Dr. Richard Ferber's method detailed in his book *Solve Your Child's Sleep Problems* (2006). This method involves increasing the time interval in which you check in on the child by double each time. Thus, when you say goodnight and then close the child's door, you allow them to cry for an interval of one minute. You reenter the room and say goodnight, kiss the child on the head (but don't pick them up), and then leave again. The next time interval is double now, so you wait two minutes before going back into the child's room if he continues to cry. This process is repeated at 4 minutes, 8 minutes, 16 minutes, and so on until the child falls asleep.

You are providing an opportunity for the child to calm down independently while also periodically reassuring him when you use the Ferber method. Some children can calm themselves in shorter intervals while others are more persistent. The point is that the interval needs to be long enough for them to have the chance to calm. If you go in too frequently, you can often make things worse and rob the child of the chance to get himself calm. It's atypical for a child older than an infant to need a parent to get himself asleep.

If your child is needier with you at bedtime, discuss what the plan is in advance. You might read to them next to the bed instead of in the bed. If you don't want to use the Ferber method, then you can use a "successive approximations" approach where you place a chair in the child's room near his bed and read quietly to yourself while the child falls asleep. Do not get into the bed with the child. If they get out of their bed, you simply escort them back and say "goodnight" and return to your chair. No questions should be answered and no conversations should be had. You may have to turn the chair so that you are facing away from the child. After five to ten minutes, you move your chair a few feet away from the child's bed and closer to the door. If the child falls asleep before you have made it to the door, then you exit. If not, you wait until the child falls asleep and then exit.

If the child tries to come in your room in the middle of the night, you simply escort them back and tell them they need to sleep in their own bed and say goodnight. You may need to repeat this process many times until the child learns you are consistent. Some children hold out longer than others. Be patient and be prepared. If you need to save this training for a time where you can lose some sleep, such as a school break or weekend, then do so. If both parents are available, then take shifts and agree on who is responsible for escorting the child back to their room. If you can't stand to hear your child cry and perceive what you're doing as cruel or punishment (and it does not help you enough that I am assuring you there is nothing harmful about these approaches), then you may need to appoint another person in the house to be responsible for the training phase of independent sleep. Good luck, and happy sleeping.

Toileting

Depending on your child's age and developmental profile, toilet training may be a challenge. First and foremost, your child needs to have an interest in using the potty and also must possess the attentional control necessary to be successful. When you believe the time is right, you can begin to introduce the potty in a fun way, such as reading potty books or using mobile apps such as those containing Sesame Street characters. At this stage of training, you are simply introducing the idea; this introduction could go on for weeks.

I recommend using a small, portable plastic training potty first before introducing the actual toilet. You can gradually shape the child's behavior by having him sit on the training potty without any expectation to go, and clap or provide a reward such as a small treat simply for sitting. If you really want to be scientific about the process, you can check the child's diaper/pull-up each hour and keep a log of whether he was wet or soiled the diaper to see if there is a better time of day to begin sitting.

Once you determine that the child is ready, you can begin sitting the child on the training potty for two to four minutes during times they are likely to go. Note: Even though boys urinate while standing, they need to sit to urinate during the early stages of toilet training. After meals is often a good time to encourage sitting, as well as after snacks or liquid consumption and before leaving the home for any reason. If the child has access to liquids throughout the day, try to keep these to scheduled times to keep track of the times the child is most likely to urinate. If the child has been exposed to screens, you can use these strategically such that the child can play an app or watch part of a show while they are seated on the training potty, which can be placed in front of the television. If the child is distracted by the presence of a screen, you may have to mute or pause the screen and "listen" in a fun way to see if you hear anything going in the potty. The child may not have to go, and thus they should not be left on the training potty for an extended period. You will begin to learn the child's cues and can plan your sittings accordingly. The child should receive a prize simply for sitting and trying. If the child goes, you should be prepared with a mystery surprise for the event, which should be something highly desirable, such as a big toy or a trip to a favorite play land or restaurant.

While the aforementioned information is most likely a review of the basics of toilet training, your child may not cooperate or be able to train using a common approach. Some children experience fear of the process or struggle to let go of the ease, comfort, or even the security or familiarity of toileting into a diaper. If this is the case, then a "commando" approach may be warranted. You may want to check with a developmental specialist in your area before beginning this approach, because not all children with toilet training challenges automatically benefit from it.

The commando option is only necessary when the child is developmentally ready to be trained but cannot separate from the use of diapers. What you will need to do is to dedicate a two- to three-day window of time, preferably a week if you can, to remaining close to your family home so that you can carefully monitor your child's toileting behaviors. The commando approach refers to removing the diaper during the child's waking hours and either leaving them with nothing on below the waist or just a pair of underwear. The underwear approach may not work because the child may simply go in their underwear, may not be ready to wear the underwear, or may not like the feel of it. Thus, having nothing on below the waist allows you to know when the child has to go and makes tracking this easier. Be patient and prepared.

The child may go on the floor, and this will require you to clean it up without chastising or scolding. If you become frustrated with the child during toilet training, regardless of the method you are using, he or she will experience setbacks. As frustrating as toilet training may become for you, remember that any towels used to wipe up urine from the floor can easily be washed, and even a carpet cleaner or cleaning service is worth the cost when you consider the importance of toilet training, not to mention the savings that result from not having to purchase any more diapers. With the diaper off during this time, you must make yourself readily available to be near the child whenever possible and inform them that, if they have to go, they need to use the training potty. Follow the child room to room and carry the training potty with you, or purchase multiple potties to keep in various rooms of the home if preferred. Reward the child the same way as described for siting and trying and when they go on the training potty.

For children who are successfully trained for a portion time and then slip back or regress and have accidents, you must first determine if it is a true setback. Accidents following successful toilet training can and will occur and are not usually a cause for concern or for immediately going back to diapers. Again, you cannot become frustrated. This is a big developmental task for the child, and some setbacks are expected. However, you may need to consider shaping the child's behavior if they are having difficulty sitting on the training potty. For some children, it is too much to sit on the potty, especially with the open sensation of having their diaper removed.

If this is the case, try shaping the child to sit on the training potty by allowing him to keep his diaper on while siting on the training potty and allow him to go into the diaper while he is seated. You can do this when training bowel movement voiding by allowing the child to have a diaper/pull-up for bowel movements only, but you would then have them stand in the bathroom while they go. This begins to create the needed association that the bathroom is where the child is expected to go. Gradually the child can be asked to sit on the toilet or training potty (placed on the floor in the bathroom) with their diaper/pull-up on while they go. Once that comfort and routine is established, you can begin to negotiate the removal of the diaper/pull-up (e.g., "We only have five more pull-ups left") until the child is comfortable and confident going in the toilet (or on the training potty placed in the bathroom) each and every time they need to go.

Homework

Homework can be a very stressful time of day for families who are busy with the events of the day and often participate in after-school activities. Whether families have multiple children to attend to, parents are working, or schedules are busy with transportation to activities, homework time can be difficult to come by. Many children experience stress throughout the day and may want down time in the afternoon or early evening hours. Once everyone is fed and beginning their bedtime routines, it's hard to find any time for homework. Add the increasing academic demands being placed on students and it's almost inevitable that stress and conflict begins to occur as parents attempt to fulfill their obligation of helping the child complete homework.

Perhaps it's just easier to sit with the child during homework to increase efficiency. This approach may be effective in the short term, but a quirky child may become conditioned to depend on your presence to complete their work, even as they grow older. For younger children, it is expected that they will require one-on-one support. However, what is a parent to do when the child is in the fifth grade and beyond? How much time should be spent helping a child complete their homework, and who should be responsible to organize the work and pack it away? Many parents report frustration that they send their child to school with a folder full of completed homework only to learn that it is not being turned in.

Over the past 15 years of helping parents address the stress associated with homework, I have developed a protocol that has worked for the majority of families I counsel. Obviously significant learning challenges or behavioral factors could interfere with this generalized approach, and no approach will universally work for all students. If there are significant learning or behavioral challenges present, you are encouraged to consult with a developmental specialist to further tailor this approach. In the meantime, consider using the following approach for students in the third grade and beyond.

Use a calendar to determine a timeframe for Monday through Thursday. One parent should be available during this timeframe, especially at the beginning (to help get started) and end (to answer any questions, check for work completion, and help organize the materials to pack up). Next, determine approximately how much homework comes home each day in terms of time required to complete it. This calculation should be based on actual time to complete the work if the child is focused and persistent. Do not include any time you may spend arguing or negotiating with the child to work.

Younger students in the third and fourth grades may only need a 30-minute window, whereas older students may need a 60- to 90-minute window. If the child receives a packet of work to do throughout the week, you can decide if it can be completed in one day or divide total work time to complete the entire packet into the four to five days of homework time. Breaks should involve no more than two to four minutes to stretch, use the bathroom, or get a drink, and these can be included in the overall homework timeframe. Be sure the child does not have an opportunity to be distracted by a television, computer, tablet, or other engaging activity during a break because this only causes more difficulty returning to the nonpreferred activity of homework.

If other children reside in the home but do not have homework, then consider making this designated homework timeframe a quiet time for the entire family. If you are a parent and you are watching television during this time or engaged in some other enjoyable activity, this can cause stress for the child. Parenting is a sacrifice, and if it is important that your child complete homework, you must sacrifice your fun as well. It sets a good example to model that you are also going to work on something during this time, and this sacrifice promotes a good work ethic for the child, which leads to independent living skills in the future—an outcome most parents tell me they want their child to develop.

Once you have determined the timeframe, it's time to discuss this plan with the child (or all children in the house if indicated). Tell them that you will meet with them at the beginning of the homework time to review their work and help them prepare the necessary materials to complete the assignments. The child is then instructed to begin their work and complete as many problems as they can without help.

Let's assume that Bobby, a third-grader, has 30 minutes of homework each night. Ten minutes of the work involves either math problems or spelling words, and 20 minutes involves reading something of his choice. Bobby would complete the spelling words or math problems, and then be provided with books of interest to look through. Depending on the school's requirements for free reading time, in addition to grade-appropriate books this could include comic books or kid-specific magazines like *National Geographic Kids* or *Time for Kids*.

Toward the end of the 30-minute interval, you check in with the child and see if he needs any help or has any work left to do. If he completed his work, I recommend using the 80 percent guideline, which means that if at least 80 percent of the problems were answered accurately, the child is in good shape. We are building work ethic and confidence here, so micromanaging the child's homework to be perfect only creates more resistance and stress, and can even create perfectionistic behavior.

If the child has not achieved the 80 percent accuracy rate, then they will need to extend their homework window to work with you and get it to this level. A good tip is to build this homework window into a time of day before the child's free time. Many families allow a child to return home and have a snack before beginning their homework. The rest of the night is free. If your schedule is this cut and dried, then the child has motivation to work hard and be accurate because they won't want to cut into their free time.

This homework timeframe approach works well when it is consistently followed because it creates an expectation and pattern to which the child becomes accustomed. If they waste their time, they begin to lose their valuable free time because their homework window must now extend into their free time. If the child finishes his work quickly, he must continue to work on something quietly (e.g., reading an enjoyable book) until the window expires.

This approach deters the child from rushing and completing work carelessly and inaccurately just to get to do what they want to do. When it becomes part of their routine, they learn to expect and accept it, and you are helping your child develop lifelong study habits (or at least for the duration of their academic career) as well as time management skills that help prevent procrastination.

Families can determine if they want to have a homework timeframe on Friday evening, as parents may have plans then, but a babysitter can easily be instructed on this schedule (or the window can occur prior to a parent of family outing). Many children like to have their work out of the way and the entire weekend free. Homework could be saved until a homework timeframe on Sunday, if applicable. In this case, it may be preferable to do the work in the morning, depending on family events such as attending religious services. This serves two purposes: the child may do their best thinking earlier in the morning, and it frees up the rest of the day for relaxation or other activities and does not add to the stress often experienced by the Sunday night/Monday morning transition.

One final note about this approach, which applies to all of the behavioral methods in this book: when this plan begins to work for families, the consistency of adhering to it may begin to slip. Even if the child seems to be keeping up in school and following the plan well, be sure to stick to the schedule that you have established and check in at the end of the homework window. I see too many families have success with this for a few months, and when I see them for a follow-up appointment they tell me that the child is no longer turning in assignments or grades are slipping. When I do a compliance check, I find that the timeframe was not being used every day and the family needs to return to it.

Picking Up After Oneself

I encourage establishing a personal area (likely in a child's room) for each child in your family to store their personal possessions. If the child shares a room with a sibling, they should each have their own designated "off-limits" storage area for their personal things that others are not allowed to access without permission. If the personal area is the child's room that is not shared with a sibling, then siblings must ask or be invited to enter. Anyone other than the owner of the room (and the parents) who enters this space without permission or consent will have consequences.

If the child brings personal items out of their room and into the general area of the home and someone else decides to play with that item, these items become fair game and others can play with them on a first come, first served basis. If the items are left in a general living area of the home and not cleaned up at the end of the day, I recommend the parent complete the cleanup labor and put each item that was not picked up into a laundry basket or other "toy time-out bin" for at least 24 hours to signal to the child the importance of picking up after oneself. Do not say anything to the child until they ask where their favorite toy is. You then inform them it is in time out. This is a great way of teaching responsibility and executing a household rule without much interference. Just be sure that the child does not have access to the time-out toy area so that you control when the time out is over and the toys are returned. Note: children ages six and younger still need assistance while cleaning up large areas such as rooms and playrooms, and the toy time-out recommendation is most effective for children ages six and up.

Establish Household Rules

One of the most effective ways to minimize conflict from occurring in the home is to establish a set of rules in your household before problematic behavior occurs. These rules should be simple and clearly stated so that everyone understands them. All members of the family should follow the rules.

I tell families to limit themselves to three to five household rules. This way everyone can easily keep track of them and behave or respond to behaviors accordingly. Write them down and post them in a high-traffic area of the home, if necessary, as a reminder. I encourage rules emphasizing the values of safety, honesty, and respect. There may be subtexts under each heading. The main goal here is to keep rules easy to remember and be sure that you are practicing what you preach. Recall the emphasis about the power of antecedents with quirky kids. You will minimize arguments by spelling everything out in advance and referring to the stated rules when a situation arises. If necessary, you can have a biweekly or monthly family meeting to review the household rules and expectations as a refresher. Meetings are pretty boring for most of us, especially kids, so keep the rule review brief and then consider ending the meeting on a fun note such as movie/pizza night or a family game.

Discipline and the Extended Family

It can also be helpful to discuss parenting strategies with other family members, especially if they are actively involved with the child. Indeed, I encourage extended family members who have regular contact with a child to attend my counseling sessions with the child and his immediate family provided that the parents are comfortable with this. Educating all participants in the child's life (including teachers and classmates, as deemed appropriate) can be extremely helpful to the child's progress. This approach is especially useful if the child spends any time away from his parents and in the homes of those extended family members, for holiday visits or overnights. Whenever possible, having those family members be consistent in their approach with the child is critical.

This can be difficult for grandparents who want their grandchild to enjoy their visit and don't want to discipline him or her. However, if the child is misbehaving, then Grandma and Grandpa will not be able to fully enjoy the visit despite their unconditional love for the child. My suggestion is to address these behaviors immediately and in a firm, matter-of-fact manner so that the child understands that despite being in a different environment, the rules and expectations remain the same. Establishing a clear set of consequences for specific behaviors across environments is essential.

Depending on the severity of the behavioral issue, I may advise families to regulate the behavior in their home environment prior to allowing the child any extended visits with other family members. This restriction can be frustrating for extended family members who want to see the child, but the alternative is that they see the child misbehave in their home as well, which is potentially more frustrating for all involved. This approach also applies to taking the child out in public. The reality is that you will not be successful with public outings unless the child is in control of most of his behaviors and is well regulated. Thus, taking the child to a restaurant, for example, before he is able to sit through a meal at home for even five minutes will not be a productive exercise.

Instead, devote your time and efforts to rewarding the child for increasing amounts of time spent at the kitchen table during meals and once the child can sit successfully for 20 minutes, a restaurant experience may be indicated. You may need to start with a brief trip, such as ordering an appetizer only and then paying the check to begin to desensitize the child and allow him to gain familiarity with the experience. Proceed at a comfortable pace that builds on previous successes.

Demands, Structure, and Predictability

Life is full of changes. These may be small changes (chicken for dinner instead of steak) or big changes (moving to a different state). Quirky kids can experience adjustment-related difficulties in response to seemingly minor and temporary changes in routine like having a substitute teacher. During the school year, many parents acknowledge increased stress experienced by the child following long, extended breaks from school, such as returning to school after the holidays. The same can be true when transitions from school to home occur—as in the end of the school year. Although summer tends to be rewarding and relaxing, the anticipation itself can fuel anxiety about the unknown and the lack of structure.

I offer the following general suggestions to sustain happiness and sanity throughout summer and school breaks.

- Increase predictability at home. This involves scheduling the days, although flexibility should be allowed. For example, one rule may be "Awake by 10 A.M. because we have to go to camp." But there is no need to be overly scheduled for no apparent reason (e.g., "Be up by 9 A.M. because I said so"). The more children know what to expect, the less stress will occur when making transitions.
- Schedule a portion of each day, then allow the child to have input regarding the remainder of the day's activities. You may need to offer a list of suggestions for him to choose from, but you

should not be trying to win the contest for "entertainer of the year." It is not your responsibility to ensure that your child is having fun all the time!

- It may be useful to have a written or picture schedule for some children. This is especially helpful if, for example, the child is having resting time in the afternoon and comes to you to say, "I'm booooored!" You can calmly remind her that this is resting time, refer her to the schedule, and add "I know you will figure out something to do." Don't forget to engage the child in the task for a while if it is too difficult for the child to begin something independently.

- Children generally have fewer demands on them during breaks, which is why they often do better behaviorally. Parents need breaks, too! If you need breaks as a parent, then don't overschedule. Your kids will pick up on your stress and react accordingly.

- Remember to limit screen time. The recommendation for screen time (which includes television, computers, and video games) is one to two hours each day for children two years and older, as well as teens. Some children can effectively manage more, others cannot. Certainly, exceptions can be made for special treats like movie night, family videos, and so on. It is always a good idea to monitor the time being spent viewing screens because school will again be in session and the child will have to "detox" as they try to refocus on schoolwork. Maybe reading a fun book together in exchange for some of that screen time (e.g., library summer reading program for prizes) can help keep the brain cells fresh and sharp.

- Whenever possible, prepare the child in advance for extended breaks and changes in routine. It never hurts to discuss what will take place (as much as you can anticipate before the first family argument occurs), and how long the break will last.

There are certain times of the year when unwanted or inappropriate behaviors can intensify. This is especially obvious during the winter months, when kids have snow days. One would think that being off from school is relaxing for a child, and in many cases it is. However, if the child lives in a state like Michigan where it snows a lot in the winter, this becomes very disruptive to the rhythm and flow of the school year. Indeed, many children I counsel do well in school during the fall when they are able to get into a rhythm and the only interruptions are Thanksgiving and then the holiday break. Kids return to school after about two weeks off, and the weather might only allow a day or two of their school routine before another snow day. This is also difficult for parents because it is nearly impossible to prepare ahead of time for a snow day, especially given the difficulties of making an accurate weather prediction in the winter! Thus, although life is unpredictable and kids need to learn to adjust, it is our job as parents to consider increasing the structure of the day during these times.

During times of adjustment, then, it is essential to keep the demands that we place on children reasonable and realistic. Some kids can keep up with consistent demands throughout the school year, but for the child who is reacting strongly during transitional periods, we need to consider altering the demands. If the child is in school, it is recommended that workloads be kept low during transitional periods so that the child can regulate his stress and reintegrate. I am not saying that the child should get away with doing nothing, but we should give him space to rebuild confidence and ensure success. Perhaps we increase the amount of small breaks throughout each school day during these periods of time. We can increase the expectations and demands gradually over time as the adjustment period ends.

Take-home points:

- I ask parents to approach challenging situations effectively and consistently, but also with some humor when appropriate. This approach can serve two important purposes: (1) It allows parents to model the appropriate use of humor to further promote the child's social development; (2) It allows all involved to relax and alleviate stress, making problem solving easier while improving family relationships.

- If we want a child to be successful in real-world interactions, the only way to learn the necessary skills is to participate in real-world interactions. Online gaming is not a real-world interaction. As much as children enjoy these games and relieve stress while playing them, secondary to the dopamine release the occurs in their brains, they will eventually need more access to the game to continue to achieve the desired result, further blurring their fantasy and real lives and creating more social isolation and challenges.

- Many of the behavioral problems that I regularly treat are the by-product of boredom, frustration, and a child's inability to occupy himself productively without access to screens. I urge parents to remember the following when contemplating video game restrictions for a child: When the games are away, the child will play.

- The American Academy of Pediatrics guidelines recommend that parents limit a child's screen time (video games, computer, television) to one to two hours per day *at most*. This recommendation is for children ages two years and older, as well as teens. Children under the age of two should avoid any screen access due to the need to interact with people, which facilitates brain and language development.

- Tantrums get old very quickly if there is no audience available, and thus a child who is kicking, screaming, and throwing a fit is more likely to continue to engage in this behavior if someone is standing around talking to them and trying to get them to calm down.

- An escape plan procedure can be helpful for many quirky children. The anxiety a child experiences about a particular situation can result in behavioral escalation. If you can anticipate the social or sensory stress the child experiences and provide an acceptable out, you can often avoid the tantrum or meltdown. The escape plan involves determining an acceptable location where the child can retreat if they are overwhelmed.

- If your child has distractibility challenges, you want to "minimize the distance." First, the distance between where you are and the child is when you are giving him a direction needs to be short. The closer you are in proximity, the better. For some children, you need to go to them, get on their eye level to get their attention, give them the direction, and then stay with them as they follow through. Second, the distance in which a child must travel to accomplish a task needs to be kept as short as possible. If you live in a two-story house and the child needs to walk from the kitchen downstairs to their room upstairs, you are increasing the likelihood that he or she will become distracted by everything along that route, and decreasing the likelihood that they will successfully complete this task. The fewer steps, the greater the success.

- A parent's responsibility is to prepare the food and serve it. What the child chooses to eat from that point forward is just that—the child's choice. When the child refuses food so they can leave and play or because they don't like what you served, you can empathize with him when he complains about how hungry he is and remind him that eating what is served will fix this problem next time.

Conclusion

I know that raising any child in the 21st century is a formidable task. Given you just finished reading this book, there is a high likelihood that your child demonstrates at least some of the quirky characteristics you learned about in the STRESSED model. You are not alone, and neither is your child, although it may feel that way some days. Hang in there and don't be too proud or too nervous to ask for help. There are many developmental specialists out there who can help you.

Now that you have reached the final chapter of this book, you should have a clearer understanding of your child's unique developmental profile and some ideas about what you can to do to help. As stressful as social situations may become for your child, you need to expose him or her to as many different social contexts with as many different children as possible. Remain available to consult with the child and model appropriate interactions while you engage your child in these experiences. Once the child is demonstrating enough confidence and competence, you can remain available as an observer until the child can handle the social interactions alone. Ask the staff at your child's school to help you during the school day when you cannot be with your child. If necessary, seek out the guidance and treatment of a developmental specialist who can provide you with specific approaches for your child's profile. Finally, begin to help your child today by using the strategies outlined in this book.

Understand that a quirky child is most comfortable approaching activities and interests as a depth seeker. Participation in depth seeking activities and interests such as reading, building with

Legos, and video games results in a dopamine release in your child's brain that can be difficult to obtain by participating in any other activities, including school. While some depth seeking is acceptable for all children, you need to be sure that the quirky child is not spending too much time pursuing one area of interest or trying to discuss this topic with others at the expense of other methods of communication. You can help the quirky child engage in more breadth seeking by containment of the depth seeking (i.e., setting limits of how long the child can engage in these interests), as well as engagement with the child in a variety of different activities. To be successful, you must be with the child while beginning to explore any new activities so that he or she will participate in the activity long enough to determine whether it is something they would return to at a later time. Most often, quirky children want to quickly return to depth seeking interests, which provide them with comfort and familiarity. If it becomes too difficult to explore breadth seeking interests, you may need to consider elimination of the depth seeking activity, or at least a lengthy break (e.g., 3 months or more of no video game play).

When your child struggles to begin or end an activity, you may need to move close to him and help him make the necessary transitions to stop or start an activity. Telling the child to start or stop something (e.g., brush teeth, get ready for bed, stop playing a game) from a distance may be ineffective.

Use the A-B-C Model of behavior when you are attempting to understand what is motivating a child to behave in a certain manner and how you can best address the behavior. Remember that quirky kids respond best when you address what is causing the behavior in the first place, rather than punishing the behavior after it occurs. The obvious exception to this rule is when the child is aggressive or engaging in a dangerous manner. When this happens, consequences must be administered (e.g., Time Out). Aggression requires action on behalf of a parent. Otherwise you can try to ignore persistent behaviors or use the 1-2-3 Magic counting method (Phelan, 2010) to help the child know that they need to stop engaging in a persistent behavior.

Children as well as adults cannot logically solve problems when they are emotional. Thus, all involved in an emotional situation must calm down before attempting to resolve any conflict. Work with your family, friends, and professionals to build a support network both for you and your child. It really does take a village to raise a child. By helping others understand your child's experiences, you move away from blame and toward compassion and awareness. Take time to rest so that you can be present with your child when he or she needs you. Every commercial airline flight begins with the announcement, "If you are travelling with a child and we lose cabin pressure, put your mask on first before placing the mask onto the child." You are of no use to your child if you are exhausted or overwhelmed.

Many children who are having difficulties completing routine tasks such as activities of daily living or homework require an adult to scaffold the skill. This is often accomplished by doing the activity for the child while he or she watches, doing the activity with the child, and then eventually having the child do the activity while you supervise until you are confident that the child can independently experience success. You are not enabling a child to accomplish a task unless he or she is already capable of doing the task independently and you continue to provide help or complete the task for the child.

Monitor your child's social, emotional, and behavioral profile to determine if he is meeting criteria for any of the Four D's: Deviance, Distress, Dysfunction, or Danger. If this is the case, then a professional evaluation is warranted. When in doubt, check it out. If the Four D's criteria are not being met, then the child may be in the quirky category of development provided that she is experiencing any of the characteristics of the STRESSED model. Review the table at the end of the Introduction to review normative characteristics as well as the STRESSED model and the Four D's.

Don't be afraid to allow your child to struggle a little and learn from his or her experiences. Natural consequences are powerful teaching tools that result from opportunities without us as parents hovering. Allow your child time to generate solutions to commonly faced problems, and function as a coach and consultant more than someone who has all the answers. Children are more likely to use a solution in the future if they came up with it on their own.

Too often we give our children answers to remember
rather than problems to solve.
~Roger Lewin

Finally, and perhaps most importantly, build on your child's strengths and use these strengths as opportunities to promote confidence and self-esteem. It may feel like there is a lot to work on, but you can still have fun and use humor to help you get through your day.

I wish you and your child the best as you embark on this challenging, yet rewarding journey through life together. One of the most gratifying aspects of my work with children and families is hearing success stories. If you have a success story you would like to pass along, please visit *www.thequirkychild.com.* To all of the parents and adults who are a positive influence in the life of a child, I thank you for all that you do and I sincerely hope that the strategies outlined in this book bring you and your family much success.

Bibliography

American Psychiatric Association. (2013). *Diagnostic and Statistical Manual of Mental Disorders* (5th ed.). Arlington, VA: American Psychiatric Publishing.

Bellini, S., Peters, J. K., Benner, L., and Hopf, A. (2007). A meta-analysis of school-based social skills interventions for children with autism spectrum disorders. *Remedial and Special Education, 28*(3), 153–62.

Brown, S., & Vaughan, C. (2010). *Play: How it Shapes the Brain, Opens the Imagination, and Invigorates the Soul.* New York: Penguin.

Cline, F., & Fay, J. (2006). *Parenting with Love and Logic.* Carol Stream, IL: NavPress Publishing.

Dawson, P. & Guare, R. (2010). *Executive Skills in Children and Adolescents, Second Edition: A Practical Guide to Assessment and Intervention.* New York: Guilford Press.

Di Chiara, G. (1995). The role of dopamine in drug abuse viewed from the perspective of its role in motivation. *Drug and Alcohol Dependence 39*(2), 155.

Erickson, E. (1963). *Childhood and Society* (2nd ed.). New York: Norton.

Ferber, R. (2006). *Solve Your Child's Sleep Problems.* New York: Touchstone Publishing.

Gershoff, E. T. (2008). *Report on Physical Punishment in the United States: What Research Tells Us about its Effects on Children.* Columbus, OH: Center for Effective Discipline.

Goleman, D. (2005). *Emotional Intelligence: Why It Can Matter More Than IQ.* New York: Bantam Books.

Gottman, J. (1998). *Raising an Emotionally Intelligent Child: The Heart of Parenting.* New York: Simon and Schuster.

Matson, J. L., Matson, M. L., & Rivet, T. T. (2007). Social-skills treatments for children with autism spectrum disorders. *Behavior Modification, 31*(5), 682–707.

Mayer, J. D., Salovey, P., Caruso, D. R., & Sitarenios, G. (2001). Emotional intelligence as a standard intelligence. *Emotion*, 1, 232–242.

McNeil, C. B., & Hembree-Kigin, T. L. (2010). *Parent-Child Interaction Therapy (Issues in Clinical Child Psychology)*. New York: Springer.

Nelson, J. (2006). *Positive Discipline*. New York: Ballantine Books.

Perry, B. D. (2000). The neuroarcheology of childhood maltreatment: The neurodevelopmental costs of adverse childhood events. *Child Trauma Academy*. Retrieved January 2014 from http://www.childr trauma.org.

Perry, B. D. (2002). Childhood experience and the expression of genetic potential: What childhood neglect tells us about nature and nurture. *Brain and Mind*, 3, 79–100.

Perry, B. D. (2006). Applying principles of neurodevelopment to clinical work with maltreated and traumatized children: The neurosequential model of therapeutics. In N. B. Webb (Ed.), *Working with Traumatized Youth in Child Welfare* (pp. 27–52). New York: Guilford Press.

Phelan, T. (2010). *1-2-3 Magic* (3rd ed.). Glen Ellyn, IL: Parent Magic.

Piaget, J. (1952). *The Origins of Intelligence in Children*. Margaret Cook (Trans.). New York: International Universities Press.

Roberts, K. (2010) *Cyber Junkie: Escape the Gaming and Internet Trap*. Center City, MN: Hazelden.

Scannapieco, M. (2008). *Developmental Outcomes of Child Neglect*. Elmhurst, IL: American Professional Society on the Abuse of Children.

Shonkoff, J., and Phillips, D. (eds.). (2000). *From Neurons to Neighborhoods: The Science of Early Childhood Development*. Washington, DC: National Academy Press.

Snyder, S.H. (1986). *Drugs and the Brain*. Philadealphia: Freeman.

Stone, C. A. (1993). What is missing in the metaphor of scaffolding. In E.A. Foreman, N. Minick, & C.A. Stone (eds.), *Contexts for Learning: Sociocultural Dynamics in Children's Development*. New York: Oxford University Press.

Straus, M. A. (1994). *Beating the Devil out of Them: Corporal Punishment in American Families*. Lanham, MD: Lexington Books.

Vygotsky, L. S. (1978). *Mind in Society: The Development of Higher Psychological Processes*. Cambridge, MA: Harvard University Press.

White, S. W., Keonig, K., & Scahill, L. (2007). Social skills development in children with autism spectrum disorders: A review of the intervention research. *Journal of Autism and Developmental Disorders*, 37, 1858–1868.

Book References

Several books were referenced in the event that you want to explore additional strategies to address characteristics of the STRESSED model that your child may be exhibiting. They are provided below.

Dawson, P. & Guare, R. (2009). *Smart but Scattered: The Revolutionary "Executive Skills" Approach to Helping Kids Reach Their Potential*. New York: Guilford Press.

Dawson, P. & Guare, R. (2010). *Executive Skills in Children and Adolescents, Second Edition: A Practical Guide to Assessment and Intervention*. New York: Guilford Press.

Goleman, D. (2005). *Emotional Intelligence: Why It Can Matter More Than IQ*. New York: Bantam Books.

Gottman, J. (1998). *Raising an Emotionally Intelligent Child: The Heart of Parenting*. New York: Simon and Schuster.

Kranowitz, C. S., & Miller, L. (2006). *The Out-of-Sync Child: Recognizing and Coping with Sensory Processing Disorder*. New York: Penguin Group.

Nelson, J. (2006). *Positive Discipline*. New York: Ballantine Books.

Phelan, T. (2010). *1-2-3 Magic*. Glen Ellyn, IL: Parentmagic.

If you are in search of a thorough analysis of the importance of play, I highly recommend two books:

Brown, S., with Vaughan, C. (2009). *Play: How it Shapes the Brain, Opens the Imagination, and Invigorates the Soul*. New York: Penguin.

Gray, P. (2013). *Free to Learn: How Unleashing the Instinct to Play Will Make Our Children Happier, More Self-Reliant, and Better Students for Life*. New York: Basic Books.

Index